KU-590-616

Contents at a Glance

124507

005,756

SAMS Teach Yourself

MySQL™

eloni

in 24 Hours

SAMS   201 West 103rd St., Indianapolis, Indiana, 462

ST.HELENS COMMUNITY LIBRARIES

3 8055 00874 5903

Sams Teach Yourself MySQL™ in 24 Hours

Copyright © 2002 by Sams Publishing

All rights reserved. No part of this book shall be reproduced, stored in a retrieval system, or transmitted by any means, electronic, mechanical, photocopying, recording, or otherwise, without written permission from the publisher. No patent liability is assumed with respect to the use of the information contained herein. Although every precaution has been taken in the preparation of this book, the publisher and author assume no responsibility for errors or omissions. Nor is any liability assumed for damages resulting from the use of the information contained herein.

International Standard Book Number: 0-672-32349-4

Library of Congress Catalog Number: 2001096491

Printed in the United States of America

First Printing: April 2002

04 03 02   4   3   2

Trademarks

All terms mentioned in this book that are known to be trademarks or service marks have been appropriately capitalized. Sams Publishing cannot attest to the accuracy of this information. Use of a term in this book should not be regarded as affecting the validity of any trademark or service mark.

Warning and Disclaimer

Every effort has been made to make this book as complete and as accurate as possible, but no warranty or fitness is implied. The information provided is on an "as is" basis. The author and the publisher shall have neither liability nor responsibility to any person or entity with respect to any loss or damages arising from the information contained in this book.

MySQL is a trademark of MySQL AB in the United States and other countries.

ST. HELENS
COLLEGE

005.756 MEL

Oct 2009

124507

LIBRARY

ACQUISITIONS EDITORS
Jennifer Kost-Barker
Shelley Johnston

DEVELOPMENT EDITOR
Laura Bulcher

MANAGING EDITOR
Charlotte Clapp

PROJECT EDITOR
Michael Kopp
(Publication Services, Inc.)

COPY EDITOR
Jason Mortenson
(Publication Services, Inc.)

PRODUCTION EDITOR
Theodore Young, Jr.
(Publication Services, Inc.)

INDEXER
Richard Bronson
(Publication Services, Inc.)

PROOFREADER
Phil Hamer
(Publication Services, Inc.)

TECHNICAL EDITOR
John Ashenfelter

TEAM COORDINATOR
Amy Patton

INTERIOR DESIGNER
Gary Adair

COVER DESIGNER
Alan Clements

PAGE LAYOUT
Nina Betterly
Jennifer Faaborg
Michael Tarleton
Jessica Vonasch
(Publication Services, Inc.)

Contents

About the Author

JULIE MELONI is the technical director for i2i Interactive, a multimedia company located in Campbell, CA (that's just down the street from San Jose). She's been developing Web-based applications since the Web first saw the light of day and remembers the excitement surrounding the first GUI Web browser. She is the author of several books and articles on Web-based programming languages and database topics, and you can find translations of her work in several languages, including Chinese, Italian, Portuguese, and Polish.

Acknowledgments

Thanks to MySQL AB for creating such a great product, not only to use but also to write about!

Great thanks especially to Jennifer Kost-Barker and everyone at Sams who was involved with this book for their great ideas, assistance, and patience.

Enormous thanks to everyone at i2i Interactive for their never-ending support and encouragement.

Tell Us What You Think!

As the reader of this book, *you* are our most important critic and commentator. We value your opinion and want to know what we're doing right, what we could do better, what areas you'd like to see us publish in, and any other words of wisdom you're willing to pass our way.

You can e-mail or write me directly to let me know what you did or didn't like about this book—as well as what we can do to make our books stronger.

Please note that I cannot help you with technical problems related to the topic of this book, and that due to the high volume of mail I receive, I might not be able to reply to every message.

When you write, please be sure to include this book's title and author as well as your name and phone or fax number. I will carefully review your comments and share them with the author and editors who worked on the book.

E-mail: opensource@samspublishing.com

Mail: Mark Taber
Associate Publisher
Sams Publishing
201 West 103rd Street
Indianapolis, IN 46290 USA

Introduction

Welcome to *Sams Teach Yourself MySQL in 24 Hours*! This book will give you a quick and painless introduction to the world of MySQL, and you'll be developing databases in no time flat.

Through a series of 24 easy lessons, you'll learn the concepts necessary for working with a relational database system, then move into the specifics of using the MySQL client and server applications. Additionally, these lessons will introduce basic SQL—Structured Query Language; the language used to communicate with databases—as well as MySQL's built-in functions for working with numbers, strings, and dates.

These lessons also cover working with transactions (available in MySQL 4.0), basic server administration, and how to connect to MySQL using different programming languages. All in all, these 24 lessons provide good, fundamental knowledge of MySQL and prepare you for more advanced database design.

Who Should Read This Book?

This book is geared toward individuals who have no previous knowledge of MySQL or who have basic knowledge of databases in general and a desire to learn more about this particular database system. If you have used other database systems, such as Oracle or Microsoft SQL Server, you will find the relational concepts are quite similar, and you should have little problem learning "the MySQL way" of database programming.

Knowledge of SQL or additional programming languages is not required, but any programming or application development experience will help you to understand the activities better.

How This Book Is Organized

This book is divided into several parts, each corresponding to a particular topic. The lessons within each part were designed to be followed one right after the other, with each lesson building on the information found in the previous lesson.

If you find that you are comfortable with some of the topics, you can skip ahead to the next lesson. However, in some instances, the lessons will have you create specific tables or perform specific actions that may have consequences in the next lesson, so be aware that you may have to skim through a skipped lesson so that your development environment remains consistent with the book.

In this book, you'll discover

- Part I introduces MySQL and the concept of relational database systems. In these lessons, you'll learn basic database terminology, as well as what a relational database system does and how it differs from something like a spreadsheet or from data stored in a text file. The most important lesson in Part I takes you through database normalization techniques and stresses the importance of good database design.

- Part II introduces you to the command line environment for working with MySQL, as well as to the various graphical user interfaces (GUIs) that are available for MySQL. Also in these lessons, you'll learn to secure your environment and add new users and permissions to your database server.

- Part III goes through the process of planning and designing a relational database application. From the thought process to the actual table and relationship creation, these lessons all focus on a sample application that will be used in subsequent lessons.

- Part IV focuses on working with the tables in the sample application and introduces you to the SQL commands used to insert, select, modify, and delete data in your tables. Also, lessons in this section will teach you how to delete entire databases and tables and also how to modify the structure of existing tables.

- Part V details the intrinsic functions in MySQL, which help you to perform all sorts of actions with strings, numbers, and date and time data.

- Part VI focuses on transactions, which are available with specific table types in MySQL 3.23 and MySQL 4.0, as well as in the NuSphere release of MySQL. The transactional concept is explained, as well as how and when to implement transactions in your database-driven application.

- Part VII provides lessons for more advanced administration of the database server, including optimization and tuning, and backup and restore procedures.

- Part VIII contains lessons for interfacing with MySQL using Perl and PHP, two of the more common languages for use in dynamic Web site development.

- The appendices provide additional reference information.

At the end of each lesson, there are a few quiz questions that will test your recollection of what you've learned in that lesson. Additional activities provide another way to apply the information learned in the lesson and guide you toward using this newfound knowledge in the next lesson.

Conventions Used in This Book

This book uses different typefaces to differentiate between code and plain English and also to help you identify important concepts. Throughout the lessons, code, commands, and text you type or see on-screen will appear in a `computer typeface`. Additionally, icons will represent special blocks of information:

A Note presents interesting pieces of information related to the current topic.

A Tip offers advice or teaches an easier method for performing a task.

NEW TERM A New Term provides a clear definition of a new or essential term.

PART I

Introduction to MySQL and Relational Databases

Hour

HOUR 1

Introducing MySQL

Welcome to the first hour of *Sams Teach Yourself MySQL in 24 Hours*. This hour lays the groundwork for the relational database concepts you'll learn throughout this book. If you've used any type of relational database before, these concepts will not be new to you. However, there are some slight differences between MySQL and other systems, which will be explained as we go along. You see, MySQL was originally developed for use in Web applications, where the primary requirements for a database system are speed, scalability, and ease of administration. In achieving these lofty goals, some standard relational database features were left out. These features, including transaction support, useful foreign keys, and sub-selects within queries, are all part of the grand development plan of MySQL 4.0 and 4.1.

> Transaction-capable table types are slowly but surely making their way into versions of MySQL and are covered in this book.

If this is your first foray into databases, please pay close attention and get out your highlighters. But first, a word of advice—do not try to make the concepts more difficult than they are. Understanding the basics of relational database systems is not rocket science, it just uses a different part of your brain—the part used for abstract thinking.

In this hour, you will learn the following:

- What a relational database system is and how it can be used
- What SQL is
- What MySQL, the open source software product, is
- Some of the main features of MySQL
- How MySQL is used everyday

What Is a Relational Database?

Entire books have been written on this topic, but there's no need to overcomplicate the answer. In short, a relational database holds together a bunch of tables made up of columns and rows, and these tables relate to each other based on values in a particular column.

Human thought consists of shortcuts and associations, and this is mimicked by a relational database. In order to understand something complex or difficult, you usually break it down into small, related chunks and try to wrap your brain around each little piece. If you can understand the individual parts and visualize the relationships, then understanding the whole should be easier. A relational database is nothing more than a container for those small pieces and relationships.

A Practical Example of a Relational Database

In the real world of application development, one of the more common tasks developers perform is building a catalog for an online store—consider the store an application that is made up of smaller bits of data.

For example, say you're creating a catalog of sporting goods. Think about what makes up a good catalog. You might come up with a list similar to the following:

- The item ID
- The name of the item
- The color of the item
- The size of the item
- The price of the item
- A description of the item

You could enter all this information into one big table. If you went this route, you'd immediately run into questions like the following:

- How do you enter an item that has multiple colors and sizes?
- How do you represent items that are available in multiple sizes as well as multiple colors?
- What happens when a blue, extra-large sweatshirt is a different price than a red, small sweatshirt?

These questions are just the tip of the iceberg. Without a relational design, you would spend more time answering "what if" questions than you would developing the application or making money with your storefront!

Instead of one large nightmare of a list, you could create several small, related tables:

- Master table—Each row contains a unique item ID, item name and general item description.
- Colors table—Create one row for each color available for each item ID; a sweatshirt that comes in five colors would have five rows.
- Sizes table—Create one row for each size available for each item ID; a sweatshirt that comes in three sizes would have three rows.
- Price table—Create one row for each combination of size and color for each item; a sweatshirt that comes in five colors with three sizes per color would have 15 distinct entries.

These tables are related through the use of a key value—the item ID. In Figure 1.1, you can see these relationships.

Figure 1.1

Relationships between tables.

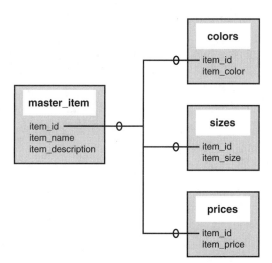

By breaking up your long list of repetitive data into smaller, logical structures, you've achieved what's called *normalization*. This example is by no means as complex as it would be in actual development, but you'll learn more about the different levels of normalization in Hour 3, "Learning the Database Design Process."

"SQL" is an abbreviation for "Structured Query Language," the language used to communicate with relational database systems. You can either pronounce "SQL" as separate letters ("ess cue ell") or as one word ("see-kwell"), and no one will laugh at you. Every command you send to MySQL will be written in a form of SQL, so this book is actually a partial primer to the language.

SQL isn't one of those new-fangled Internet concepts; it's been around since the early 1970s when it was created at an IBM research center. SQL was first introduced as part of a commercial database system in 1979 by Oracle, and then in 1986, the American National Standards Institute (ANSI) adopted SQL and it became an industry standard. The current version of SQL is commonly referred to as ANSI SQL.

Having a standard language promotes the portability of the applications that you develop. If you have to switch database systems midway through the development process, you won't have to re-write the entire application, change the logic, or learn an entirely new query language. Although each database system has its own set of deviations from the standard, the basics are present in all of the popular systems, and your task would be less than monumental.

What Is MySQL?

MySQL (pronounced "my ess cue ell") is the most widely used Open Source database, with several million users ranging from single users powering their own personal Web sites to large corporations powering high-traffic Web sites. An example of the latter is Yahoo! Finance, which uses MySQL to process hundreds of queries per second, or millions upon millions of queries per day.

You know what a relational database is, and in order to understand exactly what MySQL does, just tack on another couple of words; MySQL is a *relational database management system* (RDBMS).

In addition to storing all of your databases, tables, columns, and rows (and their data), MySQL manages them as one entity. Users are assigned access levels and permissions, all managed by the MySQL RDBMS. MySQL also logs the actions of these users and manages the responses to *queries*.

New Term *Queries* are commands, written in SQL, that you send to your RDBMS to create databases and tables, add and modify records, delete records, or extract information to be used in your application.

Application developers use MySQL because it is very fast and not nearly as complex and confusing as more robust systems, such as Oracle. It's also tens of thousands of dollars cheaper than Oracle because the open source version of MySQL is free in most cases.

> MySQL AB owns the copyright to the MySQL server source and licenses it for use in commercial applications that use MySQL. MySQL AB also sells support and consulting services to MySQL users and maintains the very thorough online manual for MySQL, which is found at `http://www.mysql.com/doc/`.

Main Features of MySQL

Developers turn to MySQL for several key reasons.

- Speed
- Portability
- Ability to interface with any programming language
- Price

MySQL is a multithreaded server, meaning that each time a connection is made, a new server process is started. Connections to MySQL do not share processes, so when one process ends unexpectedly or overloads the server by using an inordinate amount of memory, just that single process is shut down, and the entire server does not come crashing to a halt. This feature also increases the overall speed of MySQL.

The ability for MySQL to interface with virtually every programming language—PHP, Perl, C/C++, Java, Python, and Tcl—makes it a popular choice among developers. Also, portability between operating systems is a breeze; if you have to switch operating systems or languages mid-stream, use the `mysqldump` program to get your data out, and `mysqlimport` to get your data back into the system. These utilities will be explained throughout various lessons.

Another selling point of MySQL is that it's free, in most cases. You'll learn more about the different licensing requirements of MySQL later in this hour.

MySQL Distributions

You can use MySQL on any UNIX-like operating system, as well as on Windows 95/98/NT/2000/XP. That pretty much covers the vast majority of the operating systems in use! If you need to download MySQL, the MySQL Web site should be your first stop—http://www.mysql.com/. Windows users will almost always fall into this category, and the downloadable Windows version of MySQL has a wizard-based installation program.

If you are using MySQL as part of a Web-hosting package through an Internet Service Provider, you don't have to worry about downloading and installing the application. You'll just need to work with your ISP to get your username and password.

If you have a Linux workstation or server, MySQL is likely included on your OS distribution CDs as an installation option. In this case, you should check the MySQL Web site to compare the version numbers and download a newer version if yours is woefully out of date.

The open source distribution of MySQL is not the only version of MySQL available to you. There are commercial versions of MySQL, as well as distributions of MySQL bundled with application server software. Some companies that offer these options are AbriaSoft (http://www.abriasoft.com/) and NuSphere (http://www.nusphere.com/), which you can read about in Appendix A, "Installing MySQL."

MySQL Licensing and Support

If you're using the open source MySQL from MySQL AB, it's likely that you don't need to purchase a license and instead can use MySQL freely for whatever you do. The following instances do require a license:

- Using MySQL as an embedded server in an application that is not licensed under the GNU Public License
- Developing a commercial application that will work only with MySQL and shipping MySQL as part of the application
- Distributing MySQL and not providing the source code of MySQL, as defined in the GNU Public License

Using MySQL in a commercial context—such as for the backend to your online sporting goods store—does not require a license. It is encouraged, but not required, that you give a little of that profit back to the MySQL developers by purchasing a support contract or making a donation to the cause.

MySQL AB provides several levels of support contracts, ranging from e-mail to telephone support. Free support can be found through the MySQL mailing list, which is extremely active and very helpful. Many MySQL developers, as well as those recognized as experts in the field, subscribe to the mailing list and answer users' questions, ranging from basic installation to complex SQL queries.

Communicating with MySQL

There are several methods for communicating with MySQL for the purpose of issuing SQL commands and retrieving results. MySQL has a command-line interface for issuing commands, which you'll learn about in Hour 4, "Using the MySQL Client." Some ISPs also provide a Web-based interface to MySQL, or you can download and install additional client software if you don't like the Web-based interface provided by your ISP. MySQL AB maintains a list of clients at http://www.mysql.com/downloads/.

As with most freeware or shareware, the usability and design of these products range from useless to perfectly fine. The Web-based interfaces provided by most ISPs are usually quite good, with a rich feature set—everything that the MySQL command line interface does but with colors added to the display. But when it comes to the number of GUI clients, especially for Windows users, caveat emptor.

Another method of communicating with MySQL is through your programming language of choice. For example, if you are creating a Web-based application using PHP to communicate with MySQL, you will use special functions in PHP to connect to MySQL and issue queries. The next few sections provide brief descriptions of how different programming languages communicate queries to the MySQL server.

No matter what language or method you use to communicate with MySQL, you will ultimately be issuing commands in the SQL language, following this sequence:

1. Connect
2. Query
3. Retrieve result

PHP

The PHP scripting language has a whole host of functions for you to use with MySQL. These functions begin with the mysql_* prefix, and can be found in the MySQL section of the PHP manual at http://www.php.net/manual/en/ref.mysql.php.

Perl

Communicating with MySQL through Perl requires the use of the MySQL database driver (DBD::mysql) with the generic Perl database interface (DBI). Through DBD::mysql you can connect to the server and issue queries using the built-in methods of DBI, or you can use MySQL-specific functions.

Java

You can use JDBC drivers for MySQL to connect through Java applications, applets and Java Server Pages. Currently, there are two supported JDBC drivers:

- The mm driver—visit `http://mmmysql.sourceforge.net/` for more details
- The Reisin driver—visit `http://www.caucho.com/projects/jdbc-mysql/index.xtp` for more details

ODBC

MySQL AB developed a program called MyODBC, which you can use to connect ODBC-based applications to MySQL. MyODBC works on Windows95/98/NT and most Unix platforms and can be found at `http://www.mysql.com/downloads/api-myodbc.html`.

Additional Languages

In addition to the more popular programming interfaces listed above, you can also use MySQL with the C++, Python, and Tcl languages and many others. Each language has its own set of functions and methods for interfacing with MySQL, and if you'd like to learn more, you can find information in the MySQL APIs section of the MySQL manual at `http://www.mysql.com/doc/`.

Summary

MySQL is a popular open source relational database management system, known for its speed, functionality, portability, and cost (or lack thereof!). MySQL performs well for low-traffic and high-traffic sites and is used for content-only as well as e-commerce Web sites.

A relational database management system is made up of databases, tables, columns, and rows of data. These tables are tied together using keys. Using small, related tables instead of large sets of repetitive data helps you to streamline your application and maintain the integrity of your data.

Communication with the MySQL RDBMS can occur through a client interface or a programming interface. Many popular programming languages have built-in functions specifically for the purpose of communicating with MySQL. When you communicate with MySQL, you issue commands in a language called SQL, which is an industry standard.

In the next hour, you'll learn about the parts of the relational database system in detail: tables, fields, records, keys, and more!

Q&A

Q Where's the catch? You're telling me that I can build a multi-million dollar e-commerce site with free software?

A Absolutely. MySQL has the speed and the functionality to perform well in high-traffic e-commerce environments. Licensing is free, even for commercial use, as long as you are not distributing the database as part of an off-the-shelf product.

Q What features are found in other ANSI SQL-compliant relational database systems, but not in MySQL?

A Some advanced database functions, such as transactions, commit/rollback, stored procedures, and sub-selects, are not present in the current version of the open source MySQL. Many of these features will appear in the next major release of MySQL (version 4.0), which you'll learn more about in Hour 18, "Transactions Overview." For other features that are lacking, there are workarounds, which you'll start learning about throughout the lessons in this book.

Workshop

The Workshop is designed to help you anticipate possible questions, review what you've learned, and begin learning how to put your knowledge into practice.

Quiz

1. In a relational database system, you have sets of tables that are related to each other. What ties these tables together?

2. What are the three generic interface methods for communicating with MySQL?

3. If you use MySQL in a simple Web-based application that puts a million dollars in your pocket, are you obligated to purchase a license?

Answers

1. Keys are used to form the relationships between tables.

2. The MySQL client, third-party clients including Web-based interfaces, and any of the numerous available programming languages.

3. No, but you might think about purchasing a support contract from MySQL AB as a way of saying, "thanks for a great, free product!"

Activities

1. Explain the concept of relational databases to a friend. Feel free to use your hands a lot or draw boxes and lines on paper or a whiteboard. Explaining the concept to others will help you to understand it better.

2. Think about creating a set of database tables for an online address book. Using your basic knowledge of database normalization, think about how many small, logical chunks you should create.

Hour **2**

Understanding Database Terminology

In this hour, you'll learn about the elements that make up what we call a "database." As you learned in the previous hour, a relational database, such as MySQL, is just a home for tables, fields, and records. You'll learn more about each of these single items, so you'll have a better understanding of the database as a whole.

In particular, in this hour you will learn the following:

- What a table is and what it contains
- How field types are important
- What a record is and what it contains
- Different types of keys and how they are used
- What an index is and how it is used

Basic Elements Explained

It's important to understand the basic structural elements of a database; otherwise, you'll be behind the eight ball before you know it. Learning the details now will save you a lot of troubleshooting time later on! These basic structural elements are tables, fields, records, keys, and indexes.

Understanding Tables

A table is the largest of the elements in a database. In the order of creation, a table is the second in line, after creating the database itself. Figure 2.1 shows how a table is part of a database.

FIGURE 2.1

A table is part of a database.

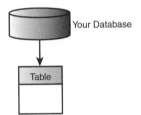

Your Database

Table

Most people start out thinking of tables as large, flat objects where items are stored—not unlike your kitchen table. This may be particularly true if you are used to storing your data in Microsoft Excel or other spreadsheet programs. However, a database table is not a single, flat file that lives on your filesystem. When you work with a database, you're not opening a file and inserting data then closing the file until you need it again. Instead, you use an interface to the database and issue queries that manipulate your tables and the information they store. You'll begin to create your own tables in Hour 7, "Creating Your Database Tables—Part I."

When a table is created in a MySQL database, three separate files are created on your filesystem. These files contain the definition of the table, the data itself, and the indexes used in the table. However, you will never work directly with the files that make up your tables.

There are several types of tables you can use in MySQL, which you'll learn more about in Hour 18, "Transactions Overview." Until then, you'll work with MyISAM tables, which are the default type used by MySQL.

Once tables are created, you can delete them (known as *dropping*, in database parlance) and alter their structures using queries. Because a table is a container for data, when you drop a table, you're deleting all the data in it. Similarly, when you alter a table, alterations affect the data inside it. For example, if you are changing a field from one that is 255 characters long to one that is 100 characters long, any data in that field that is longer than 100 characters will be chopped off and gone forever.

Understanding Fields

Fields give structure to a table and provide a place to store data. Using the spreadsheet analogy, a field is much like a column. You can have up to 3,398 fields in each MySQL database table, but if you do, you might want to take a look at redesigning, or normalizing, your database! You'll learn more about the different levels of normalization in Hour 3, "Learning the Database Design Process." Figure 2.2 shows an example of a table with six fields, named A through F.

FIGURE 2.2
Six fields within a table.

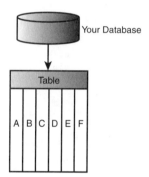

You will create your fields at the same time that you create your tables. In fact, defining your fields is the most important part of the table creation command, which you'll start using in Hour 7, "Creating Your Database Tables—Part I." When you define the fields you want to use in your tables, you need two things: the type and the length.

The type of your field is directly related to the type of data you want to store in that field. Properly defining your fields is crucial for creating an efficient database system. Think of it as being like putting presents in boxes. If you want to give someone a ring, you will probably put the ring in a small box. The person will likely already know that the present is a ring just by looking at the size and shape of the box, and she can open the box and quickly get to the goods because the box is just the right size for the ring.

So, if you want to store a 4-digit number, such as 4289, in your table, it's best to define that field as a SMALLINT (meaning small integer), which is meant to hold numbers from 0 to 65535. An example of an incorrect definition would be to use the TEXT type, which is meant for data up to 65535 characters in length. Your 4-digit number (4289) would use only 4 of the 65535 characters reserved for that field, which would be an inefficient use of space!

Other examples of common field definitions are

- DATE—For dates of numerous formats
- DECIMAL—For decimal numbers
- VARCHAR—For strings between 1 and 255 characters

You'll learn each of the many MySQL data types in Hour 7.

Understanding Records

So what is the relationship between fields and records? A record is an entry in your table. Again using the spreadsheet analogy, a record is like a row of data, with an entry in each column (field). Figure 2.3 shows five records in the table, labeled Row 1 through Row 5.

FIGURE 2.3

Showing records within a table.

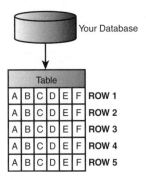

Records can be complete—all fields are filled in with accurate data—or incomplete. "Incomplete" may or may not mean "empty." Depending on how you defined the fields in your table, you can add default values for empty fields within a record.

For example, your real-world address book may have a place to write the person's name, street address, city, state, zip code, phone number, and e-mail address. If your MySQL database table has all of those fields plus an additional field for country, you can do one of two things: leave the field blank or use a default value.

If you assign a default value of "US" to the field called country, when you submit the query that adds one of your address book records, MySQL will automatically replace the empty field with "US", thus completing your record. If you will eventually perform conditional selections of data, you want to ensure that all of the possible data is available to you.

For example, suppose you leave the country field of your address book blank and don't use a default value. In time, you start entering addresses using the country field. One day, you decide to select all the records containing addresses in the United States, and you naturally assume that matching "US" in the country field is the way to go. If your country field is blank because you inserted the data without using specific default values, your result set will be missing a lot of records.

Having complete records, whether with actual values or default values, is important to maintaining the accuracy of your data.

Understanding Keys

Keys can be very powerful elements of your MySQL tables and records. As you create well-designed databases for use in applications, you will use keys to tie your tables together. Fields are defined as keys within the table creation query.

MySQL currently supports two types of keys: unique and primary. When you define a field as unique, you're telling MySQL that no matter what you try, you should never be able to insert the exact same data in that field for more than one row/record. For example, if you are creating a catalog for an online store, you will have several items to sell. Each unique catalog item should have an item number, and each item number should be unique.

When you create your table, you define the item number field to be a unique key. If you enter ABC001 as the item number for a Super Heavyweight Sweatshirt, then you can't enter a record into your table that has ABC001 as the item number for the Slinky Black Bikini.

A primary key is similar to a unique key in that both types of keys must contain unique values, but a primary key acts as the main link between two or more tables. There can be only one primary key per table, but you can have several unique keys.

The most common use of a primary key is an automatically incrementing ID field in a table. For example, suppose you have one table called orders that contains basic customer order information: date of order, shipping information, and so on. In another table, called items_ordered, you have all the items that make up the order: order ID, item ID, and quantity. The primary key for the orders table would be the ID. This ID would then be used in the items_ordered table to tie one or more line items to that particular order.

In Figure 2.4, you see the orders and items_ordered tables, with common fields shown for these types of tables. The line drawn from the id field in the orders table to the order_id field in the items_ordered table shows the relationship between these two tables.

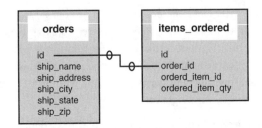

FIGURE 2.4

This diagram shows the primary key relationship between two tables.

You'll learn about keys in detail in Hour 8, "Creating Your Database Tables—Part II," but keep in mind the importance of keys.

Understanding Indexes

Database indexes are functionally similar to the index in the back of a book—indexes help you find things quickly. When you define a field in a table as a primary key, MySQL automatically adds that information to an index. You can also manually add indexes to your table, in order to index fields other than the primary key field or to index fields that provide indexes, which are combinations of one or more fields.

When you select records that have been indexed by the database, the query will execute more quickly and therefore return a result more quickly than if the table has no indexes. Conversely, when you add a record to a table that must index a value, the query is a bit slower than if an index is not required. Therefore, you have to decide when it is best to add more indexes and when it is best just to leave well enough alone.

In most cases, you can count on adding indexes to tables that are more "read" than "write"; in other words, tables whose primary function is to hold data for display rather than to store data for occasional use. An example of a good table to index would be the table containing the items in an online store catalog. You may start out with a hundred items in your table and perhaps add a few new items each week or month. But users will be browsing your catalog hundreds of times per hour, so you would want to use an index on that table. An indexed catalog of items will quickly return the results to the user, while also producing less strain on the server—a win-win situation.

The general rule of thumb for creating additional indexes is to create an index that mimics common select queries. For example, if your application calls for a query that selects all items that are blue (a color) and large (a size), you would add an index that is a combination of the two fields, color and size. An index on the item ID would not speed up the query, but this multi-column index sure would.

Summary

A table is the largest of the elements in a database, and it is made up of three files on the filesystem: one for structure, one for data, and one for indexes. The structure comes through elements called fields, which have specific types.

The type of a field should match the data you wish to insert in each record. This makes the database more efficient. Records are sets of values that go into each field.

Some fields are called keys and are either primary keys or unique keys. Sometimes these keys are used to relate fields to data in their tables during the process of database normalization, while at other times they exist only to guard against entering duplicate information into a table.

Primary keys are automatically indexed, and you can use the resulting index to produce faster searches. You can also add your own indexes to further customize your application and decrease server load on highly accessed tables.

In the next hour, you'll learn how to visualize and normalize a set of database tables before going off and creating tables on your own.

Q&A

Q If a relational database isn't like a spreadsheet, why does it look the same when I draw a table on a piece of paper?

A Tables and spreadsheets look the same in 2-dimensional drawings because they do contain the same concepts of fields and rows. However, a database is better displayed as of a set of those 2-dimensional drawings stacked on top of each other, sitting next to each other, or in some other related manner.

Q If there's a limit of 3398 fields in a table, is there also a limit to the number of records I can store?

A MySQL does not limit the number of records you can store in your table, but you will be limited by the amount of space on your disk drive, since data for a table is stored in the data file. Some MySQL tables contain millions and millions of records without problems.

Workshop

The Workshop is designed to help you anticipate possible questions, review what you've learned, and begin learning how to put your knowledge into practice.

Quiz

1. Name two types of keys supported by MySQL.

2. Do indexes speed up or slow down a query for selecting data?

3. If you were creating a table to hold customer order information, would the last name of the customer be a good use of a unique key?

Answers

1. Primary keys and unique keys.

2. Indexes speed up queries that retrieve data but slow down queries when adding records.

3. No, unless you wanted only the first person with a last name of "Smith" to be able to order something from your store!

Activity

Suppose you are developing a database for an online bookstore. Think of all the ways you would want to search through the records and how you could use an index to speed up the query.

Hour **3**

Learning the Database Design Process

In this hour, you'll learn the thought processes behind designing a relational database. This will be the last theory-focused hour; you'll soon be ready to jump headlong into creating MySQL databases for use in your own applications.

Topics covered in this hour are

- Some advantages to good database design
- Three types of table relationships
- How to normalize your database
- How to implement a good database design process

The Importance of Good Database Design

Good database design is crucial for a high performance application, just like an aerodynamic body is important to a racecar. If the racecar doesn't have smooth lines, it will produce drag and go slower. The same holds true for databases. If a database doesn't have optimized relationships—normalization—it won't be able to perform as efficiently as possible.

Beyond performance is the issue of maintenance. Your database should be easy to maintain. This includes storing a limited amount (if any) of repetitive data. If you have a lot of repetitive data and one instance of that data undergoes a change (such as a name change), that change has to be made for all occurrences of the data. To eliminate duplication and enhance your ability to maintain the data, you would create a table of possible values and use a key to refer to the value. That way, if the value changes names, the change occurs only once—in the master table. The reference remains the same throughout other tables.

For example, suppose you are responsible for maintaining a database of students and the classes in which they're enrolled. If thirty-five of these students are in the same class, called "Advanced Math," this class name would appear thirty-five times in the table. Now, if the instructor decides to change the name of the class to "Mathematics IV," you must change thirty-five records to reflect the new name of the class. If the database were designed so that class names appeared in one table and just the class ID number was stored with the student record, you would only have to change one record—not thirty-five—in order to update the name change.

The benefits of a well-planned and designed database are numerous, and it stands to reason that the more work you do up front, the less you'll have to do later. A really bad time for a database redesign is after the public launch of the application using it—although it does happen, and the results are costly.

So, before you even start coding your application, spend a lot of time designing your database. Throughout the rest of this hour, you'll learn more about relationships and normalization, two important pieces to the design puzzle.

Types of Table Relationships

In Hour 2, you learned that keys are used to tie tables together. These relationships come in several forms:

- One-to-one relationships
- One-to-many relationships
- Many-to-many relationships

For example, suppose you have a master employees table for employees, containing their Social Security number, name, and the department in which they work. You also have a separate table containing the list of all available departments, made up of a Department ID and a name. In the employees table, the Department ID field will match an ID found in the departments table. As you've learned by now, this is a type of relationship, which you can see in Figure 3.1. The "PK" next to the field name stands for *primary key*, which you'll learn more about during this lesson.

FIGURE 3.1

The employees *and* departments *tables are related through the* DeptID.

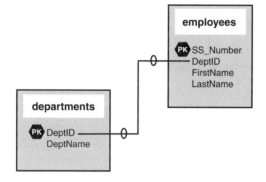

The next few sections will take a closer look at each of the relationship types.

One-to-One Relationships

In a one-to-one relationship, a key will appear only once in a related table. The example of the employees and departments tables is not a one-to-one relationship, as many employees will undoubtedly belong to the same department. An example of a one-to-one relationship is if each employee is assigned one computer within a company. Figure 3.2 shows the one-to-one relationship of employees to computers.

FIGURE 3.2

One computer is assigned to each employee.

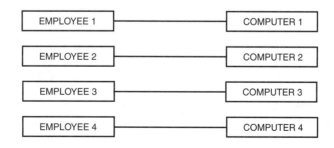

The employees and computers tables in your database would look something like Figure 3.3, which represents a one-to-one relationship.

FIGURE 3.3
One-to-one relation-
ship in the data model.

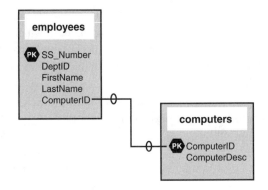

One-to-Many Relationships

In a one-to-many relationship, keys from one table will appear multiple times in a related table. The example shown in Figure 3.1, indicating a connection between employees and departments, is an example of a one-to-many relationship. A real-world example would be an organizational chart of the department, shown in Figure 3.4.

FIGURE 3.4

One department con-
tains many employees.

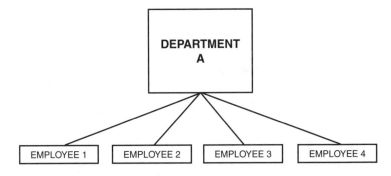

The one-to-many relationship is the most common type of relationship. Another practical example is the use of a state abbreviation in an address database; each state has a unique identifier (CA for California, PA for Pennsylvania, and so on) and each address in the United States has a state associated with it.

If you have eight friends in California and five in Pennsylvania, you will use only two distinct abbreviations in your table. One abbreviation represents a one-to-eight relationship (CA), and the other represents a one-to-five (PA) relationship.

Many-to-Many Relationships

The many-to-many relationship often causes problems in practical examples of normalized databases, so much so that it is common to simply break many-to-many relationships into a series of one-to-many relationships. In a many-to-many relationship, the key value of one table can appear many times in a related table. So far, it sounds like a one-to-many relationship, but here's the curveball: the opposite is also true, meaning that the primary key from that second table can also appear many times in the first table.

Think of it this way, using the example of students and classes. A student has an ID and a name. A class has an ID and a name. A student will usually take more than one class at a time, and a class will always contain more than one student, as you can see in Figure 3.5.

FIGURE 3.5

Students take classes, classes contain students.

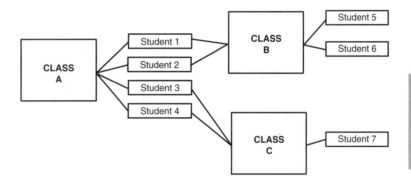

As you can see, this sort of relationship doesn't present an easy method for relating tables. Your tables could look like Figure 3.6, seemingly unrelated.

FIGURE 3.6

The students *table and the* classes *table, unrelated.*

In order to make the theoretical many-to-many relationship, you would create an intermediate table, one that sits between the two tables and essentially maps them together. You might build one similar to that in Figure 3.7.

FIGURE 3.7

The table students_classes_map *acts as an intermediary.*

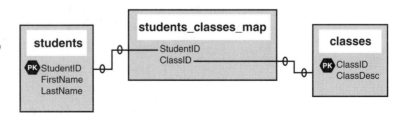

If you take the information in Figure 3.5 and put it into the intermediate table, you would have something like Figure 3.8.

FIGURE **3.8**

The table
students_classes_map
populated with data.

STUDENTID	CLASSID
STUDENT 1	CLASS A
STUDENT 2	CLASS A
STUDENT 3	CLASS A
STUDENT 4	CLASS A
STUDENT 5	CLASS B
STUDENT 6	CLASS B
STUDENT 7	CLASS C
STUDENT 1	CLASS B
STUDENT 2	CLASS B
STUDENT 3	CLASS C
STUDENT 4	CLASS C

As you can see, many students and many classes happily co-exist within the students_classes_map table.

With this introduction to the types of relationships, learning about normalization should be a snap!

Understanding Normalization

Normalization is simply a set of rules that will ultimately make your life easier when you're wearing your database administrator hat. It's the art of organizing your database in such a way that your tables are related where appropriate and flexible for future growth.

The sets of rules used in normalization are called *normal forms*. If your database design follows the first set of rules, it's considered in the *first normal form*. If the first three sets of rules of normalization are followed, your database is said to be in the *third normal form*.

Throughout this hour, you'll learn about each rule in the first, second, and third normal forms and hopefully will follow them as you create your own applications. You'll be using an example set of tables for a students and courses database and taking it to the third normal form.

Problems with the Flat Table

Before launching into the first normal form, you have to start with something that needs to be fixed. In the case of a database, it's the *flat table*. A flat table is like a spreadsheet—many, many columns. There are no relationships between multiple tables; all the data you could possibly want is right there in that flat table. This scenario is inefficient and consumes more physical space on your hard drive than a normalized database.

In your students and courses database, assume you have the following fields in your flat table:

- StudentName—The name of the student.
- CourseID1—The ID of the first course taken by the student.
- CourseDescription1—The description of the first course taken by the student.
- CourseIntructor1—The instructor of the first course taken by the student.
- CourseID2—The ID of the second course taken by the student.
- CourseDescription2—The description of the second course taken by the student.
- CourseInstructor2—The instructor of the second course taken by the student.
- Repeat CourseID, CourseDescription, and CourseInstructor columns many more times to account for all the classes a student can take during their academic career.

With what you've learned so far, you should be able to identify the first problem area: CourseID, CourseDescription, and CourseInstructor columns are repeated groups.

Eliminating redundancy is the first step in normalization, so next you'll take this flat table to first normal form. If your table remained in its flat format, you could have a lot of unclaimed space, and a lot of space being used unnecessarily—not an efficient table design!

First Normal Form

The rules for the first normal form include

- Eliminate repeating information.
- Create separate tables for related data.

If you think about the flat table design, with many repeated sets of fields for the student and courses database, you can identify two distinct topics: students and courses. Taking your student and courses database to the first normal form would mean that you create two tables: one for students and one for courses, shown in Figure 3.9.

FIGURE **3.9**
Breaking the flat table into two tables.

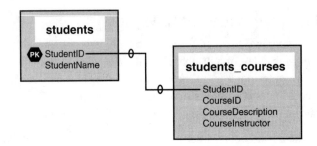

Your two tables now represent a one-to-many relationship of one student to many courses. Students can take as many courses as they wish and are not limited to the number of CourseID/CourseDescription/CourseInstructor groupings that existed in the flat table.

The next step is to put the tables into second normal form.

Second Normal Form

The rule for the second normal form is

- No non-key attributes depend on a portion of the primary key.

In plain English, this means that if fields in your table are not entirely related to a primary key, you have more work to do. In the students and courses example, it means breaking out the courses into their own table, and modifying the students_courses table.

CourseID, CourseDesc, and CourseInstructor can become a table called courses with a primary key of CourseID. The students_courses table should then just contain two fields: StudentID and CourseID. You can see this new design in Figure 3.10.

FIGURE **3.10**
Taking your tables to second normal form.

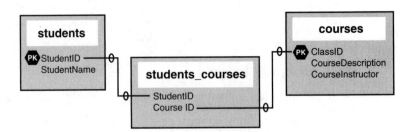

This structure should look familiar to you as a many-to-many relationship using an intermediary mapping table. The third normal form is the last form we'll look at, and you'll find it's just as simple to understand as the first two.

Third Normal Form

The rule for the third normal form is

- No attributes depend on other non-key attributes.

This rule simply means that you need to look at your tables and see if more fields exist that can be broken down further and that aren't dependent on a key. Think about removing repeated data and you'll find your answer—instructors. Inevitably, an instructor will teach more than one class. However, `CourseInstructor` is not a key of any sort. So, if you break out this information and create a separate table purely for the sake of efficiency and maintenance (as shown in Figure 3.11), that's the third normal form.

FIGURE 3.11

Taking your tables to third normal form.

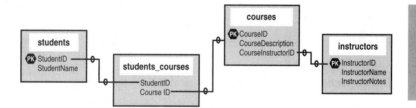

3

Third normal form is usually adequate for removing redundancy and allowing for flexibility and growth. The next section will give you some pointers for the thought process of database design and where it fits in the overall design process of your application.

Following the Design Process

The greatest problem in application design is a lack of forethought. As it applies to database-driven applications, the design process must include a thorough evaluation of your database—what it should hold, how data relates to each other, and most importantly, is it scalable?

The general steps in the design process are

- Define the objective.
- Design the data structures (tables, fields).
- Discern relationships.
- Define and implement business rules.
- Create the application.

Creating the application is the last step—not the first! Many developers take an idea for an application, build it, then go back and try to make a set of database tables fit into it. This approach is completely backwards, inefficient, and will cost a lot of time and money.

Before starting any application design process, sit down and talk it out. If you can't describe your application—including the objectives, audience, and target market—then you're not ready to build it, let alone model the database.

Once you can describe the actions and nuances of your application to other people and have it make sense to them, you can start thinking about the tables you want to create. Start with big flat tables because, once you write them down, your newfound normalization skills will take over. You will be able to find your redundancies and visualize your relationships.

The next step is to do the normalization. Go from flat table, to first normal form, and so on, up to the third normal form if possible. Use paper, pencils, Post-it Notes, or whatever helps you to visualize the tables and relationships. There's no shame in data modeling on Post-it Notes until you're ready to create the tables themselves. Plus, they're a lot cheaper than buying software to do it for you, which range from one hundred to several thousands of dollars!

After you have a preliminary data model, look at it from the application's point of view. Or look at it from the point of view of the person using the application you're building. This is the point where you define business rules and see if your data model will break. An example of a business rule for an online registration application is, "Each user must have one e-mail address, and it must not belong to any other user." If `EmailAddress` weren't a unique field in your data model, then your model would be broken based on the business rule.

After your business rules have been applied to your data model, only then can application programming begin. You can rest assured that your data model is solid and you will not be programming yourself into a brick wall. The latter event is all too common.

Summary

Proper database design is the only way your application will be efficient, flexible, and easy to manage and maintain. An important aspect of database design is to use relationships between tables instead of throwing all your data into one long flat file. Types of relationships include one-to-one, one-to-many, and many-to-many.

Using relationships to properly organize your data is called normalization. There are many levels of normalization, but the primary levels are the first, second, and third normal forms. Each level has a rule or two that must be followed. Following all of the rules will help ensure that your database is well organized and flexible.

To take an idea from inception through to fruition, you should follow a design process. This process essentially says "think before you act." Discuss rules, requirements, and objectives, and then create the final version of your normalized tables.

In the next hour, you'll get underway with using MySQL through any number of interfaces.

Q&A

Q Are there only three normal forms?

A No, there are more than three normal forms. Additional forms are the Boyce-Codd Normal Form, Fourth Normal Form, Fifth Normal Form/Join-Projection Normal Form. These forms are not often followed because the benefits of doing so are outweighed by the cost in man-hours and database efficiency.

Workshop

The Workshop is designed to help you anticipate possible questions, review what you've learned, and begin learning how to put your knowledge into practice.

Quiz

1. Name the three types of data relationships.
2. Because many-to-many relationships are difficult to represent in an efficient database design, what should you do?

Answers

1. One-to-one, one-to-many, many-to-many.
2. Create a series of one-to-many relationships using intermediary mapping tables.

Activity

Explain each of the three normal forms to a person who works with spreadsheets and flat tables. Think of it as evangelizing.

PART II

Setting Up Your Environment

Hour

Hour 4

Using the MySQL Client

In this hour, you'll learn how to use many of the MySQL client applications that are bundled with the MySQL distribution. These applications are used to administer your database server and to issue SQL commands to manipulate your table and data.

Topics covered in this hour are

- Using the MySQL monitor
- Using the MySQL administration tools
- Working with other application interfaces to MySQL

 This hour assumes MySQL is installed and running on a machine accessible to you. If this is not the case, please refer to Appendix A, "Installing MySQL."

Working with the MySQL Command-Line Interface

Included in the MySQL distribution is the standard MySQL command line interface client, commonly referred to as the MySQL monitor. The MySQL monitor allows you to connect to your MySQL server, then issue queries and see results.

All examples throughout the remainder of this book are based on using the MySQL monitor as the interface to your MySQL server. If you're not used to command line interfaces, you may find yourself out of your element. Using a command line interface is not difficult, and you will find you have a better understanding of the tasks you're performing if you're not simply pressing a button and having another application do the work for you.

Starting the MySQL Monitor in Windows

The MySQL monitor is a command-line application, and for most Windows users, the command-line is a foreign concept. If you follow these basic instructions, you shouldn't get lost.

The out-of-the-box installation of MySQL provides a default user without a password, which you can use to connect to and administer your MySQL server before creating "real" users. You'll learn about creating users and granting permissions in Hour 5, "Securing MySQL."

To start the MySQL monitor, first go to your Start menu and select Run. This will launch the Run dialog box, and in the box you should type **dosprmpt** (Windows 95/98) or **cmd** (Windows NT/2000). Figure 4.1 shows the Run dialog box.

FIGURE 4.1

Type **dosprmpt** *in the Run dialog box to launch the Windows command line interface. From here, you can start the MySQL monitor.*

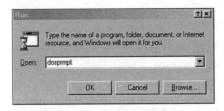

Press Enter on your keyboard, or click the OK button in the dialog box in order to execute the command and open a window to the command-line interface. Once the window opens, you should have a prompt such as

```
C:\Windows\Desktop>
```

At this point, you need to change your directory to the `bin` directory within the MySQL installation directory. By default, this location is `C:\mysql\bin`. To change directories in DOS, the command is `cd`. So, to change to the particular directory you need, type

```
cd C:\mysql\bin
```

Your window should now look something like Figure 4.2.

FIGURE 4.2

Changed directories to the MySQL bin *directory.*

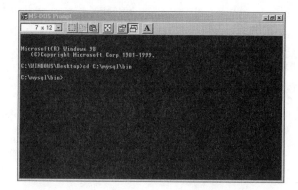

Now that you are in the MySQL `bin` directory, type **mysql** and press Enter to start the MySQL monitor. Your window should now look something like Figure 4.3.

4

FIGURE 4.3

The MySQL monitor has been started.

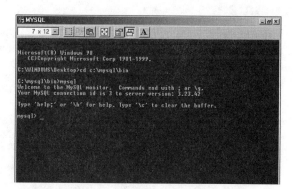

Unless you also have a Linux/UNIX box running MySQL, you can skip the next topic and move on to "Issuing Commands."

Starting the MySQL Monitor on Linux/UNIX

As a Linux/UNIX user, you should be familiar with the command line. However, if you are struggling with the command line, a primer is a good investment, and both *Sams Teach Yourself Linux in 10 Minutes* and *Sams Teach Yourself UNIX in 10 Minutes* would fit the bill.

If you are accessing the command line at your Internet Service Provider, you should have been given a specific username and password to use to connect to MySQL. But, if you are the administrator of the server (or if it's your own workstation), the out-of-the-box installation of MySQL provides a default user without a password, which you can use to connect to and administer your MySQL server before creating "real" users. You'll learn about creating users and granting permissions in Hour 5.

To start the MySQL monitor using the Linux/UNIX command line, change directories to the MySQL installation directory. This is usually /usr/local/bin/mysql/bin or /usr/bin/mysql/bin, or another location given to you by your Internet Service Provider. Once in the bin directory, simply type ./mysql to start the MySQL monitor.

```
#prompt> ./mysql
Welcome to the MySQL monitor.  Commands end with ; or \g.
Your MySQL connection id is 3264 to server version: 3.23.42

Type 'help;' or '\h' for help. Type '\c' to clear the buffer.


mysql>
```

With the MySQL monitor started and the command-line prompt waiting for your next move, you can begin issuing commands.

Issuing Commands

Once you have logged into the MySQL monitor, its operation is platform independent, as you can see in the examples that follow. Figure 4.4 shows a command on the Windows platform.

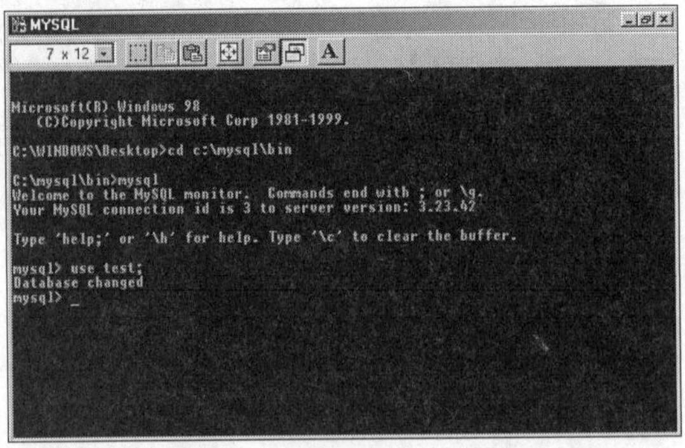

FIGURE 4.4

Issuing a MySQL command with the MySQL monitor on Windows.

Issuing the same command with the MySQL monitor on Linux/UNIX produces the same results:

```
#prompt> mysql
Welcome to the MySQL monitor.  Commands end with ; or \g.
Your MySQL connection id is 3264 to server version: 3.23.42

Type 'help;' or '\h' for help. Type '\c' to clear the buffer.

mysql> use test;
Database changed.
mysql>
```

Throughout the remainder of this book, the Linux/UNIX version of the MySQL monitor will be used in examples; Windows users, do not despair—it's the same functionality.

All commands will follow the `mysql>` prompt, as shown in the previous examples. Each command you issue through the MySQL monitor will be an SQL statement, as you learned in Hour 1, "Introducing MySQL." You will learn more about specific SQL commands as the book progresses, but the most important tidbit of info is that all commands end with a semicolon (`;`).

Additionally, in an SQL statement, you can enclose your strings in single quotes (`'string'`) or double quotes (`"string"`). If either character should happen to be part of the string itself, you must *escape* it.

NEW TERM *Escape* Putting a backslash (`\`) behind a character is called escaping the character, which allows it to be used literally within your code or command.

> For users of other database systems, such as Oracle, be aware that MySQL does not support the double-character escape method within SQL statements.

This is an important concept to understand, as it will save a lot of headaches should you find queries failing throughout your application—looking for unescaped quotation marks will be your first troubleshooting step.

For example, if you were trying insert the name O'Connor using single quotes, you will have a problem: `'O'Connor'` would end the string at `'O'`, and `Connor'` would be some extra bit of data that doesn't belong anywhere. You have two choices: enclose the string in double quotes (`"O'Connor"`) or escape the single quote so that it is used literally (`'O\'Connor'`).

If your string is

```
O'Connor said "Boo"
```

then you have to escape something, no matter which of the following you choose:

```
'O\'Connor said "Boo"'
```

or

```
"O'Connor said \"Boo\""
```

The use of single quotes around strings is the SQL standard, but it doesn't make a bit of difference to MySQL. For consistency's sake, pick one method—either single or double quotes—and stick with it.

Working with the MySQL Administration Tools

In addition to the MySQL monitor, the MySQL distribution contains numerous administrative applications. These programs are all found in the MySQL `bin` directory and are command line applications just like the MySQL monitor.

You might never have to or want to use any of these programs, but two in particular are quite useful: `mysqladmin` and `mysqldump`. The next few sections describe these two applications specifically, but for more information and for descriptions of the other programs in the distribution, refer to the MySQL manual topic "MySQL Client-Side Scripts and Utilities" at `http://www.mysql.com/doc/C/l/Client-Side_Scripts.html`.

Using `mysqladmin`

The `mysqladmin` application is used to perform administrative operations on your MySQL server, such as creating or dropping databases and viewing the current status of the server.

You can get a complete list of `mysqladmin` commands and options by typing the following at your prompt:

```
#prompt> mysqladmin --help
```

The command syntax is not complicated; to create a database using `mysqladmin`, the command syntax is

```
#prompt> mysqladmin create [databasename]
```

So, to create a database called `test_DB`, the command is

#prompt> mysqladmin create test_DB

To drop a database named `test_DB`, use

#prompt> mysqladmin drop test_DB

Other `mysqladmin` commands follow the same pattern and may or may not return a message upon completion of the command. Checking the status of the server is an example of a `mysqladmin` command with a response. Issue the following command to receive a status response like the one shown below:

#prompt> mysqladmin status
```
Uptime: 2016685  Threads: 1  Questions: 154543  Slow queries: 1   Opens: 255
Flush tables: 2  Open tables: 64 Queries per second avg: 0.077
```

If you are using MySQL through your Internet Service Provider, you may have limited access to the `mysqladmin` function. If you are the administrator of your own server, or you have installed MySQL on your own machine for testing purposes, all of the `mysqladmin` commands should be available to you.

Using `mysqldump`

The `mysqldump` application is extremely useful for creating backup copies of your table structures. The output file created by `mysqldump` contains not only the commands to create the tables, but also to populate the tables, if they already contain data.

Suppose you have a table called `fruit` in your `test_DB` database, with a field called `fruit_name` that contains several records. Dump the database using `mysqldump` and the database name, as follows:

#prompt> mysqldump test_DB
```
# MySQL dump 8.16
#
# Host: localhost    Database: test_DB
#--------------------------------------------------------
# Server version       3.23.42

#
# Table structure for table 'fruit'
#

CREATE TABLE fruit (
  id int(11) NOT NULL auto_increment,
  fruit_name varchar(50) NOT NULL default '',
  PRIMARY KEY  (id)
) TYPE=MyISAM;
```

4

```
#
# Dumping data for table 'fruit'
#

INSERT INTO fruit VALUES (1,'apple');
INSERT INTO fruit VALUES (2,'banana');
INSERT INTO fruit VALUES (3,'pear');
```

You can see the table creation syntax (CREATE TABLE...) as well as the data insertion syntax (INSERT INTO...).

Dumping contents to the screen doesn't help you if you want to use these SQL statements elsewhere. You can fix this by sending the output to a file. The following command performs the same dump of data but to a file called mydump.sql instead of to the screen:

```
#prompt> mysqldump test_DB > mydump.sql
```

Do not confuse the term "dump" with "drop." Dropping is deleting, whereas dumping is what you want to do before you delete to back up your table structures and data for posterity's sake.

You can get a complete list of mysqldump commands and options by typing the following at your prompt:

```
#prompt> mysqldump --help
```

Other Interfaces to MySQL

If the command line interface to MySQL is too confusing or unwieldy, or if your Internet Service Provider does not grant access to it, there are other options. Many Internet Service Providers have installed a Web-based interface called phpMyAdmin, which allows you to perform all sorts of queries as well as retrieve results. Additionally, Windows users might want to install a free application called MySQL-Front if the MySQLManager application (included with the Windows distribution) is not to your liking.

The next sections take a look at these applications, but to learn more about them you will be directed to their own informational Web sites.

phpMyAdmin

The phpMyAdmin application requires not only the MySQL server, but also PHP and a Web server to be installed. This application is commonly found in a virtual hosting environment through an Internet Service Provider, as it allows the user complete access to only their own database. Figure 4.5 shows a table creation example using phpMyAdmin.

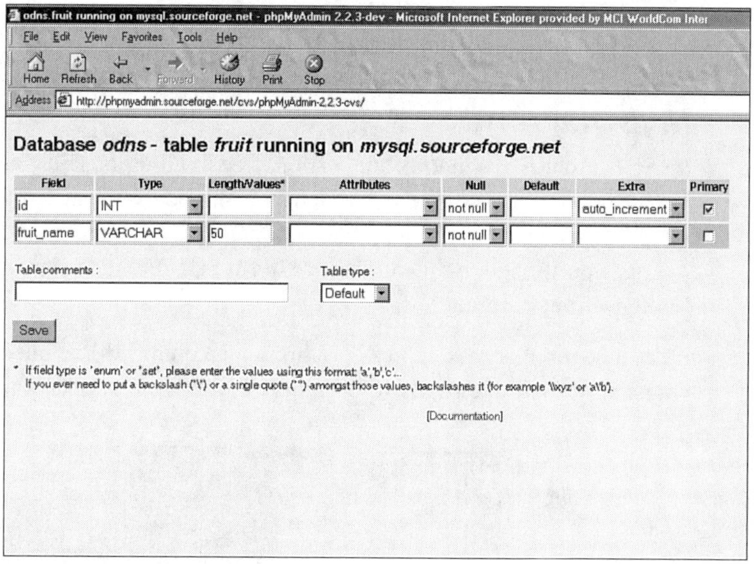

FIGURE 4.5

Creating a table using phpMyAdmin.

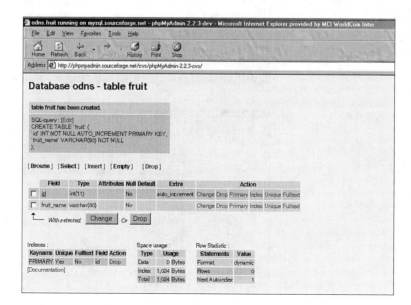

You can use the form-based creation as shown in Figure 4.5, or you can type the queries directly. Either way, when a successful query is issued, the application will tell you if your query was successful or if an error occurred. A sample response is shown in Figure 4.6.

FIGURE 4.6

After creating the table, perform additional queries or administration tasks.

For more information on phpMyAdmin, check with your Internet Service Provider or at
`http://sourceforge.net/projects/phpmyadmin/`.

MySQL-Front

MySQL-Front is a Windows application, free to all users, that can be downloaded from
`http://www.mysqlfront.de/`. Once installed, you can create tables and insert and select
records—just about everything you can imagine. If you are used to using Microsoft
Access, you'll find a lot of similarities in MySQL-Front. Figures 4.7 and 4.8 show
MySQL-Front in action.

If the thought of accessing MySQL through a command-line interface scares you, or if
you simply don't like it, MySQL-Front is a wonderful application for Windows users.

FIGURE 4.7

Creating a table using MySQL-Front.

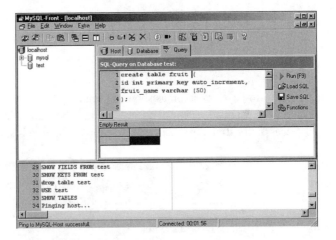

FIGURE 4.8

Viewing table properties using MySQL-Front.

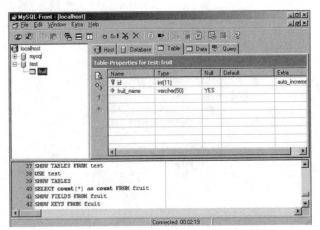

MySQLManager

MySQLManager is a Windows application that is distributed by MySQL AB as part of the official MySQL 4.0 product. This application is another graphical interface to MySQL, allowing you to bypass the stale command-line interface and instead issue queries in a nice, clean window. Figures 4.9 and 4.10 show the process of issuing queries and seeing results using MySQLManager.

FIGURE 4.9

Issuing a query within MySQLManager.

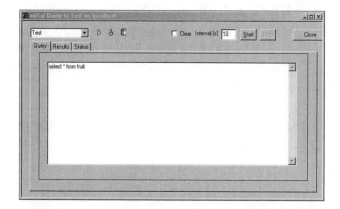

FIGURE 4.10

Seeing query results in MySQLManger.

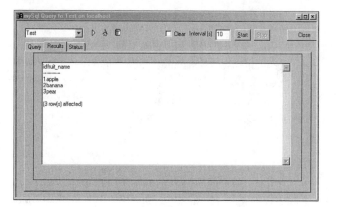

4

Summary

Working directly with MySQL is often done using the MySQL monitor, a command line tool that allows you to issue queries and retrieve results. Whether you're using MySQL on Windows or on Linux/UNIX, after you start the MySQL monitor the commands are the same. These commands are written in SQL and end with a semicolon. In some commands, you will have to escape special characters, such as single or double quotes, in order for the command to be successful.

Along with the MySQL monitor, the MySQL distribution contains several administrative tools to help you with tasks like creating databases, seeing the server status, or dumping data for use in backups. These helper applications are also based on the command line but follow a simple syntax.

In addition to the command line interface to MySQL, there are Web-based interfaces, such as phpMyAdmin, and Windows applications, such as MySQL-Front and MySQLManager, to help you perform your tasks.

In the next hour, you'll learn about securing MySQL, including how to add users and grant permissions.

Q&A

Q Are there more than two additional client interfaces to MySQL?

A There are many user-contributed client interfaces to MySQL, and you can find a list at `http://www.mysql.com/downloads/contrib.html`. These applications range from free to commercial, and the usefulness and design qualities of each also are broad. You can check out each application and pick one that you like the best or stick with the command line interface for all of your tasks.

Workshop

The Workshop is designed to help you anticipate possible questions, review what you've learned, and begin learning how to put your knowledge into practice.

Quiz

1. What is the command to create a database called MyDB using `mysqladmin`?
2. What is the command to dump the contents of a database called MyDB to a file called `backup.sql`?
3. What three pieces of technology are required to use phpMyAdmin?

Answers

1. `mysqladmin MyDB`

2. `mysqldump MyDB > backup.sql`

3. MySQL, a Web server, and the PHP scripting language

Activity

View the list of available commands and options in `mysqladmin` and try each of them except "shutdown."

4

Hour 5

Securing MySQL

A vulnerable database server puts your data at risk, and if you're storing sensitive information, you'll see the lawsuits coming from a mile away. In this hour, you'll learn basic security measures, including how the MySQL privilege system is used.

Topics covered in this hour are

- Starting MySQL with security in mind
- The MySQL user privilege system
- Adding, updating, and deleting MySQL users

Basic Security Guidelines

It doesn't matter if you administer your own server or use a system provided by your Internet Service Provider—every developer needs to understand basic security guidelines. If you are accessing MySQL through your Internet Service Provider, there are several aspects of server security that you, as a non-root user, should not be able to modify or circumvent. Unfortunately, many Internet Service Providers pay no mind to security guidelines, leaving their clients exposed—and for the most part, unaware of it.

Starting MySQL

Securing MySQL begins with the server startup procedure. If you are not the administrator of the server, you won't be able to change this, but you can check it out and report vulnerabilities to your Internet Service Provider.

If your MySQL installation is on Linux/UNIX, your primary concern should be the owner of the MySQL daemon—it should not be "root." Running the daemon as a non-root user, such as "mysql," "database," or any other user besides "root," will limit the ability of malicious individuals from gaining access to the server and overwriting files.

You can verify the owner of the process using the ps (process status) command on your Linux/UNIX system. The following output shows MySQL running as a non-root user:

```
#prompt> ps auxw | grep mysqld
mysql 153  0.0  0.6 12068 2624 ? S   Nov16  0:00 /usr/local/bin/mysql/bin/mysqld
--defaults-extra-file=/usr/local/bin/mysql/data/my.cnf
--basedir=/usr/local/bin/mysql --datadir=/usr/local/bin/mysql/data
--user=mysql --pid-file=/usr/local/bin/mysql/data/mike.pid --skip-locking
```

The following output shows MySQL running as a root user:

```
#prompt> ps auxw | grep mysqld
root 21107  0.0  1.1 11176  1444  ? S  Nov 27 0:00 /usr/local/mysql/bin/mysqld
--basedir=/usr/local/mysql --datadir=/usr/local/mysql/data --skip-locking
```

If you see that MySQL is running as root on your system, immediately contact your Internet Service Provider and complain. If you are the server administrator, you should start the MySQL process as a non-root user or specify the user name in the startup command line:

```
mysqld --user=non_root_user_name
```

For example, if you want to run MySQL as user mysql, use

```
mysqld --user=mysql
```

Securing Your MySQL Connection

Connecting to the MySQL monitor or other MySQL applications can occur several different ways, each of which has their own security risks. If your MySQL installation is on your own workstation, you have less to worry about than users who have to go across a network connection to reach their server.

If MySQL is installed on your own workstation, your biggest security concern is leaving your workstation unattended with your MySQL monitor or MySQL GUI administration tool up and running. In this type of situation, anyone can walk over and delete data, insert bogus data, or shut down the server. Utilize a screen saver or lock screen mechanism with a password if you must leave your workstation unattended in a public area.

If MySQL is installed on a server outside of your network, the security of the connection should be of some concern. As with any transmission of data over the Internet, it can be intercepted. If the transmission is unencrypted, the person who intercepted it could piece it together and use the information. Suppose the unencrypted transmission is your MySQL login information—a rogue individual now has access to your database, masquerading as you.

One way to prevent this from happening is to connect to MySQL through a secure connection. Instead of using telnet to reach the remote machine, use SSH instead. SSH looks and acts like telnet, but all transmissions to and from the remote machine are encrypted. Similarly, if you use a Web-based administration interface, such as phpMyAdmin (as you should recall from Hour 4, "Using the MySQL Client") or another tool used by your Internet Service Provider, access that tool over a secure HTTP connection.

In the next section, you'll learn how the MySQL privilege system works, which will help secure your database even further.

Introducing the MySQL Privilege System

The MySQL privilege system is always "on." From the time you try to connect and for each subsequent action, MySQL checks the following three things:

- Where you are accessing from (your host)
- Who you say you are (your username and password)
- What you're allowed to do (your command privileges)

All of this information is stored in the database called mysql, which is automatically created when MySQL is installed. There are several tables in the mysql database:

- columns_priv—Defines user privileges for specific fields within a table.
- db—Defines the permissions for all databases on the server.
- func—Defines user-created functions.
- host—Defines the acceptable hosts that can connect to a specific database.
- tables_priv—Defines user privileges for specific tables within a database.
- user—Defines the command privileges for a specific user.

5

These tables will become more important to you later in this hour as you add a few sample users to MySQL. For now, just remember that these tables exist and must have relevant data in them in order for users to complete actions.

The Two-Step Authentication Process

As you've learned, MySQL checks three things during the authentication process. These actions are performed in two steps:

1. MySQL looks at the host you are connecting from and the username and password pair that you are using. If your host is allowed to connect, your password is correct for your username, and the username matches one assigned to the host, then MySQL moves to the second step.

2. For whichever command you are attempting to use (SELECT, UPDATE, DELETE, INSERT, and so forth), MySQL checks that you have the ability to perform that action for that database, table, and field.

If Step 1 fails, you'll see an error about it and won't be able to continue along to Step 2. For example, suppose you are connecting to MySQL with a username of joe and a password of abc123 and you want to access a database called myDB. If any of those connection variables are incorrect for any of the following reasons, you will receive an error message:

- Your password is incorrect.
- Username joe doesn't exist.
- User joe can't connect from localhost.
- User joe can connect from localhost but cannot use the myDB database.

You may see the following:

```
#prompt> /usr/local/bin/mysql/bin/mysql -h localhost -u joe -pabc123 test
Error 1045: Access denied for user: 'joe@localhost' (Using password: YES)
```

If user joe with a password of abc123 is allowed to connect from localhost to the myDB database, then in Step 2 of the process, MySQL will check the actions that joe can perform. For our purposes here, suppose that joe is allowed to select data but not allowed to insert data. The sequence of events and errors would look like the following:

```
#prompt> /usr/local/bin/mysql/bin/mysql -h localhost -u joe -pabc123 test
Reading table information for completion of table and column names
You can turn off this feature to get a quicker startup with -A

Welcome to the MySQL monitor.  Commands end with ; or \g.
Your MySQL connection id is 3439 to server version: 3.23.42
```

```
Type 'help;' or '\h' for help. Type '\c' to clear the buffer.

mysql> select * from test_table;
+----+------------+
| id | test_field |
+----+------------+
+----+------------+
|  1 | blah       |
|  2 | blah blah  |
+----+------------+
2 rows in set (0.0 sec)
mysql> insert into test_table values ('', 'my text');
Error 1044: Access denied for user: 'joe@localhost' (Using password: YES)
```

Action-based permissions are common in applications with several levels of administration. For example, if you have created an application containing personal financial data, you might grant only SELECT privileges to entry-level staff members, but INSERT and DELETE privileges would be granted to executive-level staff with security clearances.

Working with User Privileges

In most cases when you are accessing MySQL through an Internet Service Provider, you will have only one user and one database available to you. By default, that one user would have access to all tables in that database and be allowed to perform all commands. In this case, the responsibility is on you as the developer to create a secure application through your programming.

If you are the administrator of your own server or have the ability to add as many databases and users as you want, as well as modify the access privileges of your users, these next few sections will take you through the process.

Adding Users

Administering your server through a third-party application may afford you a simple method for adding users, following a wizard-like process or a graphical interface. Adding users through the MySQL monitor is not difficult, however, especially if you understand the security checkpoints used by MySQL, which you just learned.

The simplest method for adding new users is the GRANT command. By connecting to MySQL as the root user, you can issue one command to set up a new user. The other method is to issue INSERT statements into all of the relevant tables in the mysql database, which requires you to know all of the fields in the tables used to store permissions. This method works just as well but is more complicated than the simple GRANT command.

The simple syntax of the GRANT command is

```
GRANT privileges
ON databasename.tablename
TO username@host
IDENTIFIED BY "password";
```

The privileges you can grant are

- ALL—Gives the user all of the following privileges.
- ALTER—User can alter (modify) tables, columns, and indexes.
- CREATE—User can create databases and tables.
- DELETE—User can delete records from tables.
- DROP—User can drop (delete) tables and databases.
- FILE—User can read and write files; this is used to import data or to dump data.
- INDEX—User can add or delete indexes.
- INSERT—User can add records to tables.
- PROCESS—User can view and stop system processes; only trusted users should be able to do this.
- REFERENCES—Not currently used by MySQL, but a column for references privileges exists in the user table.
- RELOAD—User can issue FLUSH statements; only trusted users should be able to do this.
- SELECT—User can select records from tables.
- SHUTDOWN—User can shutdown the MySQL server; only trusted users should be able to do this.
- UPDATE—User can update (modify) records in tables.
- USAGE—User can connect to MySQL but has no privileges.

Thus, if you want to create a user called john with a password of 99hjc, with SELECT and INSERT privileges on all tables in the database called myDB, and this user can connect from any host, use

```
GRANT SELECT, INSERT
ON myDB.*
TO john@"%"
IDENTIFIED BY "99hjc";
```

Note the use of two wildcards: * and %. These wildcards are used to replace values; in this example, * replaces the entire list of tables, and % replaces a list of all hosts in the known world—a very long list indeed.

Here's another example of adding a user using the GRANT command, this time to add a user called jane with a password of 45sdg11, with ALL privileges on a table called employees in the database called myCompany. This new user can connect only from a specific host:

```
GRANT ALL
ON myCompany.employees
TO jane@janescomputer.company.com
IDENTIFIED BY "45sdg11";
```

If you know that janescomputer.company.com has an IP address of 63.124.45.2, you can substitute that in the hostname portion of the command, as follows:

```
GRANT ALL
ON myCompany.employees
TO jane@'63.124.45.2'
IDENTIFIED BY "45sdg11";
```

One note about adding users: always use a password and make sure that password is a good one! MySQL does allow you to create users without a password, but that leaves the door wide open should someone with bad intentions guess the name of one of your users with full privileges granted to them!

If you use the GRANT command to add users, the changes will immediately take effect. To make absolutely sure of this, you can issue the FLUSH PRIVILEGES command in the MySQL monitor to reload the privilege tables.

Removing Privileges

Removing privileges is as simple as adding them; instead of a GRANT command, you use REVOKE. The REVOKE command syntax is

```
REVOKE privileges
ON databasename.tablename
FROM username@hostname;
```

As with granting permissions, you can also revoke permissions by issuing DELETE commands to remove records from tables in the mysql database. Again, this requires you to have familiarity with the fields and tables, and it's just much easier and safer to use REVOKE.

To revoke the ability for user john to INSERT items in the myCompany database, you would issue the following REVOKE statement:

```
REVOKE INSERT
ON myDB.*
FROM john@"%";
```

5

Changes made to the privilege tables take effect immediately. If you use REVOKE, you can issue the FLUSH PRIVILEGES command in the MySQL monitor to be absolutely sure.

Summary

Security is always a priority, and there are several steps you can take to run a safe and secure installation of MySQL. Even if you are not the administrator of the server, you should be able to recognize breaches and raise a ruckus with the server admin!

Primarily, MySQL should not run as the root user. Additionally, named users within MySQL should always have a password, and their access privileges should be well defined.

MySQL uses the privilege tables in a two-step process for each request that is made. MySQL needs to know who you are and where you are connecting from, and each of those pieces of information must match an entry in its privilege tables. Also, that user must be granted specific permission to perform the type of request being made.

Adding user privileges occurs through the GRANT command, which uses a simple syntax to add entries to the user table in the mysql database. The REVOKE command, equally as simple, is used to remove those privileges.

Q&A

Q How do I completely remove a user? The REVOKE command just eliminates the privileges.

A To completely remove a user from the privilege table, you have to issue a specific DELETE command from the user table in the mysql database. You'll learn more about the DELETE command in Hour 12, "Modifying and Deleting Data," including the specific statement that will remove a user.

Q What if I tell my Internet Service Provider to stop running MySQL as root, and they won't?

A Switch providers. Seriously, if your Internet Service Provider doesn't recognize the risks of running something as important as your database as the root user, and they don't listen to your request, find another provider. There are providers with plans as low as $9.95/month that don't run important processes as root!

Workshop

The Workshop is designed to help you anticipate possible questions, review what you've learned, and begin learning how to put your knowledge into practice.

Quiz

1. True or False: Telnet is a perfectly acceptable method to securely connect to MySQL from a remote host.

2. Which three pieces of information does MySQL check each time a request is made?

3. What would be the command to grant SELECT, INSERT, and UPDATE privileges to a user named bill on localhost to all tables on the BillDB database? Also, what piece of information is missing from this statement that is recommended for security purposes?

Answers

1. False. The keyword is "secure," and telnet does not encrypt data between hosts. Instead, use SSH to connect to your server.

2. Who you are, where you are accessing from, and what actions you're allowed to perform.

3. The command is
   ```
   GRANT SELECT, INSERT, UPDATE
   ON BillDB.*
   TO bill@localhost;
   ```

   The important missing piece is a password for the user!

Activities

1. Think of situations where you might want to restrict command access at the table level. For example, you wouldn't want the intern-level administrator to have shutdown privileges for the corporate database.

2. If you have administrative privileges to MySQL, issue several GRANT commands to create dummy users. It doesn't matter if the tables and databases you name are actually present.

3. Use REVOKE to remove some of the privileges of the users created in Activity 1.

5

PART III

Learning to Plan for Your Database-Driven Applications

Hour

HOUR 6

Planning and Creating Your Database

In this hour, you'll begin working on your first functional database. Over the next several hours, you'll create an "address book" system, but you'll take it several steps further to include multiple contact methods, personal notes, and so forth. As you've learned in previous hours, this hour of planning is the most important stage in the table creation process.

In this hour, you will

- Define the tables used in your database
- Determine table relationships
- Issue the database creation command
- Add two users for your database

Determine Your Goals

In Hour 3, "Learning the Database Design Process," several examples were used to explain the design and normalization process. Now you'll apply those principles to an address book and use this database over the next several hours to learn the ins and outs of SQL commands.

The goals of this address book database are to be extendable and useful in real life. In fact, you could call this a contact management system instead of an address book, if you wanted to get all crazy and impress your friends.

Think about the basic contact information you want to include:

- Name
- Address
- Telephone number
- Fax number
- E-mail address
- Job function
- Company
- Personal notes

Sounds basic enough, but then think about the multiplicity factor—how many people do you know who have only one telephone number or one e-mail address? These are just examples, but, in the list above, I would venture to guess that only name, job function, and company would be single entries, as even personal notes can occur at different times and thus require different entries. So, your database has to support multiple entries for all but a few items, which brings us to the subject of normalization.

Conceptualize the Tables

In this section, you'll bring the conceptual tables to Third Normal Form. To get there, you have to follow the rules for First Normal Form—to eliminate repeating information and to create separate tables for related data.

Separate from your table, list the single entity tables—items you know do not require multiple entries. Those are

- Name
- Job function
- Company

For each of these tables, think about what needs to go into them, as in Table 6.1.

TABLE 6.1 Requirements for Single-Entry Tables

Table	Requirements
Name	An ID, first name, and last name
Job Function	An ID and the job function
Company	An ID and the company name

If "ID" wasn't on the tip of your tongue, remember that fields like ID fields are used to establish relationships between tables.

Next, think about the tables that can hold multiple entries, similar to those in Table 6.2.

TABLE 6.2 Requirements for Multiple-Entry Tables

Table	Requirements
Address	An ID, street address, city, state, zip code, home/work/other indicator
Telephone Number	An ID, country code, number, home/work/other indicator
Fax Number	An ID, country code, number, home/work/other indicator
E-Mail Address	An ID, e-mail address, home/work/other indicator
Personal Notes	An ID, date added, notes

Each of the tables also has an ID field, which will be used to create relationships as the normalization process continues.

In the table for personal notes, a "date added" field is indicated. It would make sense to note the date added for every record in every table, as well as the date the record was modified.

These dates will help you maintain the data stored in your database; for example, you could choose to delete any records not modified within a given period of time. Since there is no automatic date stamping of records, the only dates associated with records are the ones added by the administrator.

6

Table 6.3 shows the updated requirements for the tables.

TABLE 6.3   Updated Requirements for Tables

Table	Requirements
Name	An ID, date added, date modified, first name, last name
Job Function	An ID, date added, date modified, job function
Company	An ID, date added, date modified, company name
Address	An ID, date added, date modified, street address, city, state, zip-code, home/work/other indicator
Telephone Number	An ID, date added, date modified, country code, number, home/work/other indicator
Fax Number	An ID, date added, date modified, country code, number, home/work/other indicator
E-Mail Address	An ID, date added, date modified, e-mail address, home/work/other indicator
Personal Notes	An ID, date added, date modified, notes

By breaking the information into several small tables, as shown in Figure 6.1, you've taken a step toward normalization.

Next, you'll determine the relationships between your tables and reach Second Normal Form.

Determining Relationships

So far, you've determined each table has at least one ID field. This is perfect for creating the relationships that will normalize your database.

When splitting up the data, one table was kept as the "master" table—the one holding the name information. All of the other tables will be related to the person who appears in that main table.

Table 6.4 shows the updated requirements for the tables, with "related name ID" listed where the relationship is required.

FIGURE 6.1

Your information is organized into several small tables.

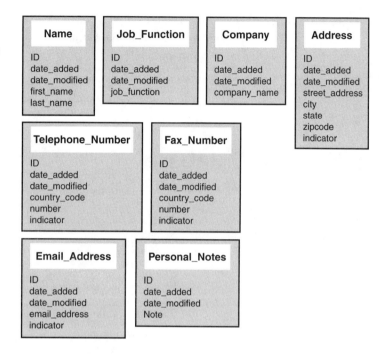

6

TABLE 6.4 Table Requirements Showing Relationships

Table	Requirements
Name	An ID, date added, date modified, first name, last name
Job Function	An ID, name ID, date added, date modified, job function
Company	An ID, date added, date modified, company name
Address	An ID, name ID, date added, date modified, street address, city, state, zipcode, home/work/other indicator
Telephone Number	An ID, name ID, date added, date modified, country code, number, home/work/other indicator
Fax Number	An ID, name ID, date added, date modified, country code, number, home/work/other indicator
E-mail Address	An ID, name ID, date added, date modified, e-mail address, home/work/other indicator
Personal Notes	An ID, name ID, date added, date modified, notes

Additional relationships and other nuances of these tables will be introduced during table creation time. For the most part, these conceptual tables are in the Second Normal Form, where the rule is "No non-key attributes depend on a portion of the primary key."

In the next two hours, you'll define the SQL statements for your tables and issue the commands to create them, but for now move on to the next section and create the database and a few users.

Creating the Database

In Hour 4, "Using the MySQL Client," you learned how to use `mysqladmin` to create a database. Time to put that knowledge to work! If your Internet Service Provider does not allow you to create additional databases, you will have to add the example tables to your master database, and you can skip this section.

 In the examples throughout this section, substitute your own information where dummy data is used for hostname, username, and password. This dummy data is italicized in the examples.

Pick a name for your contact management database (`contactDB` is a good name) and issue the creation command:

```
#prompt> mysqladmin -u username -ppassword create contactDB
```

If there was an error during the database creation, you'll get a nice message about it. In the following example, an attempt was made to connect without a username and password:

```
#prompt> /usr/local/bin/mysql/bin/mysqladmin  create contactDB
/usr/local/bin/mysql/bin/mysqladmin: connect to server at 'localhost' failed
error: 'Access denied for user: 'julie@localhost' (Using password: NO)'
```

If the creation was successful, you'll simply be returned to the command prompt.

```
#prompt>
```

Now that you have your database, you assign privileges to it and can create users.

Define the User Privileges

Let's assume you won't be the only person using your contact management system, but you will be the only person making updates to it. For security reasons, you should create two separate users, as you learned in Hour 5, "Securing MySQL."

If your Internet Service Provider does not allow you to create additional users, these next commands will not work for you.

Even if you have a master or root user with all access to all databases on your server, create one superuser (called `supercontact`) who has access only to this database.

First, connect to the MySQL monitor as the root user, or another user with permissions to create additional users:

```
#prompt> /usr/local/bin/mysql/bin/mysql -h localhost -u root --pyourpass
```

At the MySQL monitor prompt, type the following to switch to the `mysql` database.

```
mysql> use mysql
Database changed
```

Now you can issue the GRANT command to add the user and privileges.

```
mysql> GRANT ALL ON contactDB.* TO supercontact@'yourhost' IDENTIFIED BY
"somepass";
Query OK, 0 rows affected (0.01 sec)
```

When MySQL returns `Query OK`, you know the command was successful. Next, add a user who has only SELECT abilities for your database.

```
mysql> GRANT SELECT ON contactDB.* TO simpleuser@'yourhost' IDENTIFIED BY
"somepass";
Query OK, 0 rows affected (0.00 sec)
```

Congratulations—you're now officially a database administrator. In the next hour, you'll begin to define the SQL statements for your fourteen database tables.

Summary

The planning stage is perhaps the most important of all stages when creating a database-driven application. By taking the time to think about your tables and requirements, it's easier to normalize your data structures.

In this contact management database, you need tables for name, address, telephone and fax numbers, e-mail address(es), job function, and company and personal notes. Additionally, you need tables to map the secondary tables to the master (name) table.

Because security should always be a concern, creating two different users is a good idea. One user has access to all commands, whereas another user can only SELECT data and not INSERT, UPDATE, or DELETE it.

6

Q&A

Q Do I have to use `mysqladmin` to create the database?

A No, you can also issue a full SQL statement to create a database within the MySQL monitor:

```
CREATE DATABASE database_name;
```

Workshop

The Workshop is designed to help you anticipate possible questions, review what you've learned, and begin learning how to put your knowledge into practice.

Quiz

1. How will ID fields be used in the example tables?

2. Why is the use of date fields in a table important to a database administrator?

3. With the privileges assigned to the user called "simpleuser," can this user update the e-mail address of an entry in your contact management system?

Answers

1. IDs will be used as identifiers in each table and as relationship indicators in some tables.

2. There is no other mechanism for telling when a record is added or changed, unless a date-related field has been defined in the table. The creation and modification dates are important when cleaning up old data or viewing entries that were added during a specific timeframe.

3. No. The user called `simpleuser` can only `SELECT` data and cannot perform any administrative functions such as adding, modifying, or deleting data.

Activity

Think about the use of the address table and how it should be extended for international use. This includes people who have international addresses for both, or just one type of address (that is, home, work, other).

HOUR 7

Creating Your Database Tables—Part I

In the previous hour, you thought long and hard about the tables to include in your super-sized address book, or contact management system. In this hour, you will determine the preliminary table creation statements, which will be finalized in the next hour.

In this hour, you will

- Learn the common types of fields you can define in your MySQL tables
- Learn the table creation syntax
- Define the preliminary statements to create your tables

Learning the MySQL Data Types

As you learned in Hour 2, "Understanding Database Terminology," properly defining your fields is important to the overall optimization of your database.

You should use only the type and size of field you really need to use. These types of fields (or columns) are also referred to as *data types,* because it's the type of data you will be storing in those fields.

MySQL uses many different data types, which are broken into three categories: numeric, date and time, and string types. These next sections will briefly define the more common data types. Pay close attention because defining the data type is more important than any other part of the table creation process.

Numeric Data Types

MySQL uses all of the standard ANSI SQL numeric data types, so if you're coming to MySQL from a different database system, these definitions will look familiar to you. The list that follows shows the common numeric data types and their descriptions.

> The terms *signed* and *unsigned* will be used in the list of numeric data types. If you remember your basic algebra, you'll recall that a signed integer is a positive or negative integer, whereas an unsigned integer is a non-negative integer.

- TINYINT—A very small integer that can be signed or unsigned. If signed, the allowable range is from –128 to 127. If unsigned, the allowable range is from 0 to 255.
- SMALLINT—A small integer that can be signed or unsigned. If signed, the allowable range is from –32768 to 32767. If unsigned, the allowable range is from 0 to 65535.
- MEDIUMINT—A medium-sized integer that can be signed or unsigned. If signed, the allowable range is from –8388608 to 8388607. If unsigned, the allowable range is from 0 to 16777215.
- INT—A normal-sized integer that can be signed or unsigned. If signed, the allowable range is from –2147483648 to 2147483647. If unsigned, the allowable range is from 0 to 4294967295.

> INT and INTEGER are synonymous. If it helps you to remember the data type by using INTEGER instead of INT, go for it.

- BIGINT—A large integer that can be signed or unsigned. If signed, the allowable range is from –2147483648 to 2147483647. If unsigned, the allowable range is from 0 to 18446744073709551615.

- FLOAT(M,D)—A floating point number that cannot be unsigned. You can define the display length (M) and the number of decimals (D). This is not required and will default to 10,2, where 2 is the number of decimals. Decimal precision can go to 24 places for a FLOAT.

- DOUBLE(M,D)—A double precision floating point number that cannot be unsigned. You can define the display length (M) and the number of decimals (D). This is not required and will default to 16,4, where 4 is the number of decimals. Decimal precision can go to 53 places for a DOUBLE. REAL is a synonym for DOUBLE.

- DECIMAL(M,D)—An unpacked floating point number that cannot be unsigned. In unpacked decimals, each decimal corresponds to one byte. Defining the display length (M) and the number of decimals (D) is required. NUMERIC is a synonym for DECIMAL.

Of all the MySQL numeric data types, you will likely use INT most often. You can run into problems if you define your fields to be smaller than you actually need; for example, if you define an ID field as an unsigned TINYINT, you won't be able to successfully insert that 256th record if ID is a primary key (and thus required).

Date and Time Types

MySQL has several data types available for storing dates and times, and these data types are flexible in their input. In other words, you can enter dates that are not really days, such as February 30—February has only 28 or 29 days, never 30. Also, you can store dates with missing information. If you know that someone was born sometime in November of 1980, you can use 1980-11-00, where "00" would have been for the day, if you knew it.

The flexibility of MySQL's date and time types also means that the responsibility for date checking falls on the application developer. MySQL checks only two elements for validity: that the month is between 0 and 12 and the day is between 0 and 31. MySQL does not automatically verify that the 30th day of the second month (February 30th) is a valid date.

The MySQL date and time data types are

- DATE—A date in YYYY-MM-DD format, between 1000-01-01 and 9999-12-31. For example, December 30th, 1973 would be stored as 1973-12-30.

7

- DATETIME—A date and time combination in YYYY-MM-DD HH:MM:SS format, between 1000-01-01 00:00:00 and 9999-12-31 23:59:59. For example, 3:30 in the afternoon on December 30th, 1973 would be stored as 1973-12-30 15:30:00.

- TIMESTAMP—A timestamp between midnight, January 1, 1970 and sometime in 2037. You can define multiple lengths to the TIMESTAMP field, which directly correlates to what is stored in it. The default length for TIMESTAMP is 14, which stores YYYYMMDDHHMMSS. This looks like the DATETIME format above, only without the hyphens between numbers; 3:30 in the afternoon on December 30th, 1973 would be stored as 19731230153000. Other definitions of TIMESTAMP are 12 (YYMMDDHHMMSS), 8 (YYYYMMDD), and 6 (YYMMDD).

- TIME—Stores the time in HH:MM:SS format.

- YEAR—Stores a year in 2 digit or 4 digit format. If the length is specified as 2, then YEAR can be 1970 to 2069 (70 to 69). If the length is specified as 4, YEAR can be 1901 to 2155. The default length is 4.

You will likely use DATETIME or DATE more often than any other date- or time-related data type.

String Types

Although numeric and date types are fun, most data you'll store will be in string format. This list describes the common string data types in MySQL.

- CHAR—A fixed-length string between 1 and 255 characters in length, right-padded with spaces to the specified length when stored. Defining a length is not required, but the default is 1.

- VARCHAR—A variable-length string between 1 and 255 characters in length. You must define a length when creating a VARCHAR field.

- BLOB or TEXT—A field with a maximum length of 65535 characters. BLOBs are "Binary Large Objects" and are used to store large amounts of binary data, such as images or other types of files. Fields defined as TEXT also hold large amounts of data; the difference between the two is that sorts and comparisons on stored data are case sensitive on BLOBs and case insensitive in TEXT fields. You do not specify a length with BLOB or TEXT.

- TINYBLOB or TINYTEXT—A BLOB or TEXT column with a maximum length of 255 characters. You do not specify a length with TINYBLOB or TINYTEXT.

- MEDIUMBLOB or MEDIUMTEXT—A BLOB or TEXT column with a maximum length of 16777215 characters. You do not specify a length with MEDIUMBLOB or MEDIUMTEXT.

- LONGBLOB or LONGTEXT—A BLOB or TEXT column with a maximum length of 4294967295 characters. You do not specify a length with LONGBLOB or LONGTEXT.

- ENUM—An enumeration, which is a fancy term for "list." When defining an ENUM, you are creating a list of items from which the value must be selected (or it can be NULL). For example, if you wanted your field to contain either "A" or "B" or "C", you would define your ENUM as ENUM ('A', 'B', 'C') and only those values (or NULL) could ever populate that field. ENUMs can have 65535 different values.

You will probably use VARCHAR and TEXT fields more often than other field types, and ENUMs are useful as well.

Learning the Table Creation Syntax

Creating tables requires three important bits of information:

- Name of the table
- Names of fields
- Definitions for each field

Okay, that's more than three bits of information if you add up all the fields in all the tables, but you get the idea—you name the table and fields, define the fields, and add keys and indexes. Keys and indexes will be covered in the next hour. The goal of this hour is to create the structure of the basic tables in your contact management database.

The generic table creation syntax is

```
CREATE TABLE table_name (column_name column_type);
```

This is an oversimplification of the table creation syntax, but you'll take this slow so as to understand all the pieces of the puzzle. If you make a mistake during table creation, the ALTER table command gives you the opportunity to redefine fields, drop fields, and perform other actions on the structure of your table. You'll learn about ALTER in Hour 14, "Modifying Table Structure."

Naming Your Fields

Field names are important for data administration. They should be as concise as possible and relevant to the function they serve and data they hold. If your database is normalized, you'll probably have a mess of little tables, and you'll want your field names to make sense in order to preserve your own sanity. For example, ten different fields called ID will drive you crazy, but if you append a descriptor to the name, like name_ID, you can keep a handle on things. Try not to duplicate your field names, if you can help it.

7

> The field names used below are meant as examples and at times do not fall
> into the "concise as possible" category. Please feel free to change the field
> names when you create your own tables, but remember that the example
> SQL statements will use the example names.

Table 7.1 shows example table and field names to use in your contact management
database.

TABLE 7.1 Table and Field Names

Table Name	Field Names
master_name	name_id, name_dateadded, name_datemodified, firstname, lastname
job_function	job_id, name_id, job_dateadded, job_datemodified, jobfunction
company	company_id, company_dateadded, company_datemodified, companyname
address	add_id, name_id, add_dateadded, add_datemodified, streetaddress, city, state, zipcode, add_type
telephone	tel_id, name_id, tel_dateadded, tel_datemodified, tel_countrycode, tel_number, tel_type
fax	fax_id, name_id, fax_dateadded, fax_datemodified, fax_countrycode, fax_number, fax_type
email	email_id, name_id, email_dateadded, email_datemodified, email, email_type
personal_notes	notes_id, name_id, notes_dateadded, notes_datemodified, note

Your list is beginning to look pretty technical. Take it one step further in the next section
and define the field types within preliminary table creation statements.

Preliminary Table Creation Statements

These statements are "preliminary" because you will finalize them in the next hour when
you add keys and index definitions. For now, focus on the definitions of the fields named
in Table 7.1. All of the CREATE TABLE statements can be written on single lines (or multiple lines with word wrap), but the statements have line breaks after each field definition
for clarity. Do not send these commands to MySQL quite yet, since you'll be modifying
them in the next hour.

You can issue your statements through the MySQL monitor using as many line breaks as you want. All MySQL cares about are the opening and closing theses around the field definitions, commas between each definition, and a semicolon at the end.

As a rule of thumb, use a DATETIME definition for all date-related fields in your tables—each of the date added/date modified fields in the first seven tables. Also, use SMALLINT UNSIGNED for all ID fields. If you have more than 65535 rows in any of the first seven tables, you can ALTER the table to change the fields to INT.

The master_name table has two fields besides the ID and date-related fields. There's a high probability that you will never meet a person with a first or last name longer than 75 characters, so you can use VARCHAR (75) for those fields.

```
CREATE TABLE master_name (
name_id SMALLINT UNSIGNED,
name_dateadded DATETIME,
name_datemodified DATETIME,
firstname VARCHAR (75),
lastname VARCHAR (75)
);
```

The job_function table has one field besides the ID, relationship ID, and date-related fields—jobfunction. Most job functions will be short, like "teacher" or "editor," but you may have someone in your database with a job like "Senior Management Analyst for Organizational Effectiveness," which is considerably longer than "plumber." Use VARCHAR (100) just to be sure you can accommodate your pretentious friends.

```
CREATE TABLE job_function (
job_id SMALLINT UNSIGNED,
name_id SMALLINT UNSIGNED,
job_dateadded DATETIME,
job_datemodified DATETIME,
jobfunction VARCHAR (100)
);
```

The company table can be defined just like the job_function table, except the relationship ID will not be present:

```
CREATE TABLE company (
company_id SMALLINT UNSIGNED,
company_dateadded DATETIME,
company_datemodified DATETIME,
companyname VARCHAR (100)
);
```

7

The address table has some interesting items besides the standard ID, relationship ID, and date-related fields. Assuming this is a US-address only table, you have to consider the street address, city name, state, and ZIP code. You know that ZIP codes are at least 5 characters long and no greater than 10 characters. Storing state abbreviations instead of full names will reduce the amount of storage space you need. Also, there is an add_type field used to store one of three values: home, work, other. You can use ENUM for the add_type field.

```
CREATE TABLE address (
add_id SMALLINT UNSIGNED,
name_id SMALLINT UNSIGNED,
add_dateadded DATETIME,
add_datemodified DATETIME,
streetaddress VARCHAR (255),
city VARCHAR (50),
state CHAR (2),
zipcode VARCHAR (10),
add_type ENUM ('home', 'work', 'other')
);
```

The telephone, fax, and email tables are all variations on the same theme:

```
CREATE TABLE telephone (
tel_id SMALLINT UNSIGNED,
name_id SMALLINT UNSIGNED,
tel_dateadded DATETIME,
tel_datemodified DATETIME,
tel_countrycode CHAR (3),
tel_number VARCHAR (25),
tel_type ENUM ('home', 'work', 'other')
);

CREATE TABLE fax (
fax_id SMALLINT UNSIGNED,
name_id SMALLINT UNSIGNED,
fax_dateadded DATETIME,
fax_datemodified DATETIME,
fax_countrycode CHAR (3),
fax_number VARCHAR (25),
fax_type ENUM ('home', 'work', 'other')
);

CREATE TABLE email (
email_id SMALLINT UNSIGNED,
name_id SMALLINT UNSIGNED,
email_dateadded DATETIME,
email_datemodified DATETIME,
email VARCHAR (150),
email_type ENUM ('home', 'work', 'other')
);
```

The `personal_notes` table contains a field you can use `TEXT` to define—`note`. Since you don't know exactly how long your notes would be, and it's likely they'll be longer than 255 characters, using a `TEXT` definition is a safe bet.

```
CREATE TABLE personal_notes (
notes_id SMALLINT UNSIGNED,
name_id SMALLINT UNSIGNED,
notes_dateadded DATETIME,
notes_datemodified DATETIME,
note TEXT
);
```

With all of this initial groundwork behind you, the next hour should be a breeze as you finish up your table statements by defining keys and adding indexes, and as you tweak your relationships just a little more.

Summary

The table creation command requires three important pieces of information—the table name, the field name, and the field definitions. Field definitions are important, as a well-designed table will help speed along your database.

MySQL has three different categories of data types: numeric, date and time, and string. There are many different types within each category, but common definitions include `INT`, `DATETIME`, `VARCHAR`, `TEXT`, and `ENUM`.

Each of the basic tables for the contact management database has been preliminarily designed, but the `CREATE TABLE` commands have not yet been issued. The next hour will add keys and indexes to the definitions before actually creating the tables.

Q&A

Q What characters can I use to name my tables and fields, and what is the character limit?

A The maximum length of database, table, or field names is 64 characters. Any character that you can use in a directory or file name, you can use in database and table names—except / and .. These limitations are in place because MySQL creates directories and files in your file system, which correspond to database and table names. There are no character limitations (besides length) in field names.

Q Are there any reserved words, or words that I cannot use to name my fields?

A Yes. MySQL has approximately 170 reserved words. You can find a list in Appendix C, "Reserved Words."

7

Workshop

The Workshop is designed to help you anticipate possible questions, review what you've learned, and begin learning how to put your knowledge into practice.

Quiz

1. The integer 56678685 could be which data type(s)?

2. Think of another way you could define the state field in the address table.

3. How would you define a field that could contain the following strings: apple, pear, banana, cherry?

Answers

1. MEDIUMINT, INT, or BIGINT.

2. You could create the state field as an ENUM containing 51 state abbreviations (50 states plus the District of Columbia).

3. ENUM ('apple', 'pear', 'banana', 'cherry')

Activities

1. Create a preliminary table creation statement for an address table that will hold international addresses.

2. Think ahead to the many ways you will be selecting data from your tables. This will help you to determine indexes in the next hour.

HOUR 8

Creating Your Database Tables—Part II

In the previous hour, you built your table creation statements by defining your fields and their appropriate data types. In this hour, you will finalize your table structure by adding keys and indexes, then issue the creation statements.

In this hour, you will

- Define specific keys within your tables
- Add indexes to your tables
- Create your tables

Identifying Keys in Your Tables

As you learned in Hour 2, "Understanding Database Terminology," there are two types of keys used by MySQL: primary and unique. By default, a primary key is also unique, meaning each value in a primary key column appears only once in that column.

You can do many wonderful things with key fields, including making them automatically increment if it's an integer field. In the next few sections, you'll determine which fields in your tables are primary or unique keys.

Primary Keys

A primary key should exist in all tables, if for no other reason than to facilitate relationships. For example, the name_id field of the master_name table in your contact management database appears in several other tables to tie several other bits of information to the master name record.

 Primary keys should always be numeric for flexibility and speed.

You can add primary keys two ways within the CREATE TABLE statement. In addition to adding PRIMARY KEY to the statement, you'll also add NOT NULL. If a column is a primary key, it cannot contain null values.

The first method for adding a primary key looks like this:

```
CREATE TABLE table_name (column_name column_type PRIMARY KEY NOT NULL);
```

You can also add the key definition after all of the fields have been defined, but NOT NULL still has to appear in the field definition:

```
CREATE TABLE table_name (
column_name column_type NOT NULL,
column_name2 column_type,
PRIMARY KEY (column_name)
);
```

Using primary keys poses an interesting question: how do you keep the values not null? One answer is the DEFAULT clause. Using DEFAULT in the column definition allows you to use a default value if someone is trying to shove a NULL into your table. For example:

```
CREATE TABLE table_name (
column_name column_type PRIMARY KEY NOT NULL DEFAULT '0'
);
```

Finally, we come to my personal favorite, the use of AUTO_INCREMENT on integer fields. It works just like it sounds—if the field using AUTO_INCREMENT is blank or 0 when inserting data, MySQL will fill the field with the next highest integer for that field.

The syntax for using AUTO_INCREMENT is

```
CREATE TABLE table_name (
column_name column_type PRIMARY KEY NOT NULL DEFAULT '0' AUTO_INCREMENT
);
```

You will find something as simple as AUTO_INCREMENT to be of great help in your application development. Without AUTO_INCREMENT, you would have to perform an additional query before adding a record to manually obtain the current highest value in the field.

Unique Keys

Adding unique keys is similar to adding primary keys. One difference is that fields defined as unique keys can contain null values. The term "primary" implies "1"—there can be only one primary key, but you can define many other unique keys in your table if warranted.

```
CREATE TABLE table_name (
column_name column_type PRIMARY KEY NOT NULL DEFAULT '0' AUTO_INCREMENT,
column_name2 column_type UNIQUE
);
```

You may find yourself never defining a unique key in your tables if they already contain a primary key. Don't be alarmed by this—as you'll soon learn, keys are great, but overusing them does more harm than good.

Adding Indexes to Your Tables

In Hour 2, you learned that a database index is quite similar to the index in the back of a book—it helps you to find things faster. If you have a table with a primary key, that column is indexed automatically. Other indexes may be defined during the table creation statement:

```
CREATE TABLE table_name (
column_name column_type PRIMARY KEY NOT NULL DEFAULT '0' AUTO_INCREMENT,
column_name2 column_type UNIQUE,
column_name3 column_type,
INDEX idx_col3 (column_name3)
);
```

In this example, the index is named idx_col3 and contains information from the column_name3 field. You can also index multiple columns by adding them to the field list. For example, to index column_name2 and column_name3 in the same index (called idx_cols), use

```
...
INDEX idx_cols (column_name2, column_name3)
...
```

Another method for adding an index is the CREATE INDEX statement. If you have created your table, you can issue the following command to add an index after the fact:

```
CREATE INDEX idx_cols ON table_name (column_name2, column_name3);
```

Just like keys, indexes can be either useful or a drag on performance. The next section will explain when to use indexes for best performance.

When to Use, or Not to Use, Keys and Indexes

Any time you add new information to a field that is indexed (including primary key fields), the index must be updated. MySQL does this for you automatically, but indexing does take up system resources. If your application is the centerpiece for a large corporation, and thus receives heavy amounts of traffic, you will have to pay close attention and use indexes only when absolutely necessary; for example, when your tables are predominantly used for reading large amounts of data.

Some rules of thumb for using keys and indexes include the following:

- If you are adding or updating information more than you are selecting information from a given table, don't use indexes on that table. For example, if you are storing customer purchase information that is used only for archiving, an index is unnecessary. But, if you are storing personal profile information for a personalized Web-based application, an index is of great help.

- Even in read-heavy tables, don't index fields that would return a large number of similar results when searched. For example, in a table holding personal profile information, don't index a "state" field. If you have 3000 profiles stored and one-third are from California, an index won't do much good. This is akin to indexing the word "the" in a bound book—why do it?

- Don't index small tables. If you can select all records in all rows in a table in under a second or two, your table is small enough that it doesn't really need an index. If you find your table growing by leaps and bounds, you can always add an index later on.

- If you're going to search by it, index it. In other words, if your application will contain specific queries to return specific results—for example, "show all the people I know named X"—index the field you're searching by. In this example, it would be the field holding first names.

- Don't overdo adding unique keys. There is a limit to the number of keys in a MySQL table (16), but a normalized database shouldn't have much call for that many keys anyway!

These are just a few tips on using keys and indexes. You'll learn more on your own by creating different types of applications in different environments. You'll find that the only hard and fast rules that exist are ones of your own creation. Everything else is simply a guideline.

Finalizing Your Table Creation Statements

This section will take you through the thought process of adding keys and indexes to your table creation statements. A few global changes and notes:

- All SMALLINT ID fields will be auto-incrementing primary keys if they are not used as relationships between tables.
- You may find that you won't use other unique fields, but you will create additional indexes.
- Add default values for date-related fields.

The first table is the master_name table. In addition to the name_id field becoming an auto-incrementing primary key, there are two fields ripe for indexing: firstname and lastname. You may want to retrieve records ordered by lastname or search for all contacts with a particular first or last name. Thus, you should use separate indexes for each of the two fields.

```
CREATE TABLE master_name (
name_id SMALLINT UNSIGNED NOT NULL PRIMARY KEY AUTO_INCREMENT,
name_dateadded DATETIME DEFAULT '0000-00-00 00:00:00',
name_datemodified DATETIME DEFAULT '0000-00-00 00:00:00',
firstname VARCHAR (75),
lastname VARCHAR (75),
INDEX idx_fn (firstname),
INDEX idx_ln (lastname)
);
```

The job_function table has one field besides the ID and date-related fields— jobfunction. If you envision searching by job function, add an index to that field.

```
CREATE TABLE job_function (
job_id SMALLINT UNSIGNED NOT NULL PRIMARY KEY AUTO_INCREMENT,
name_id SMALLINT UNSIGNED NOT NULL DEFAULT '0',
job_dateadded DATETIME DEFAULT '0000-00-00 00:00:00',
job_datemodified DATETIME DEFAULT '0000-00-00 00:00:00',
jobfunction VARCHAR (100),
INDEX idx_job (jobfunction)
);
```

The same rules apply for the company table as for the job_function table; if you think you'll be searching by company name, index the companyname field.

```
CREATE TABLE company (
company_id SMALLINT UNSIGNED NOT NULL PRIMARY KEY AUTO_INCREMENT,
company_dateadded DATETIME DEFAULT '0000-00-00 00:00:00',
company_datemodified DATETIME DEFAULT '0000-00-00 00:00:00',
companyname VARCHAR (100),
INDEX idx_co (companyname)
);
```

The company table is meant to hold distinct company names, which leads to the question of relating the company to the person working there. Many people will work at the same company, and there may be the occasion where a person works for more than one company. For example, a consultant may split time between companies. For this situation, create a table that maps the potential many-to-many relationship between the master_name and company tables:

```
CREATE TABLE name_company_map (
name_id SMALLINT UNSIGNED NOT NULL,
company_id SMALLINT UNSIGNED NOT NULL
);
```

The address table gets into that sticky situation of when an index is useful or not; if all of your contacts are in one state, why index the state field? Same question applies to the city and zipcode fields. That leaves streetaddress as a searchable field, but if you're searching for people on a particular street, you probably already know whom they are, unless you're really bored and just like performing queries. So, there are no indexes for this table.

```
CREATE TABLE address (
add_id SMALLINT UNSIGNED NOT NULL PRIMARY KEY AUTO_INCREMENT,
name_id SMALLINT UNSIGNED NOT NULL DEFAULT '0',
add_dateadded DATETIME DEFAULT '0000-00-00 00:00:00',
add_datemodified DATETIME DEFAULT '0000-00-00 00:00:00',
streetaddress VARCHAR (255),
city VARCHAR (50),
state CHAR (2),
zipcode VARCHAR (10),
add_type ENUM ('home', 'work', 'other')
);
```

The telephone, fax, and email tables are all variations on the same theme, none of which should use an index. If you find yourself performing a lot of number or email lookups, you can add indexes later.

You may be tempted to add a unique key to the email field in the email table, but consider the situation where family members share e-mail addresses. If you have already added Joe Smith and his e-mail address, yet he shares the e-mail address with Jane Smith, then you've dug yourself into a hole—if Jane's and Joe's e-mail address is the same but the email field is unique, only one of them gets the data. That's not fair to the other person, so email cannot be unique.

```
CREATE TABLE telephone (
tel_id SMALLINT UNSIGNED NOT NULL PRIMARY KEY AUTO_INCREMENT,
name_id SMALLINT UNSIGNED NOT NULL DEFAULT '0',
tel_dateadded DATETIME DEFAULT '0000-00-00 00:00:00',
tel_datemodified DATETIME DEFAULT '0000-00-00 00:00:00',
```

```
tel_countrycode CHAR (3),
tel_number VARCHAR (25),
tel_type ENUM ('home', 'work', 'other')
);

CREATE TABLE fax (
fax_id SMALLINT UNSIGNED NOT NULL PRIMARY KEY AUTO_INCREMENT,
name_id SMALLINT UNSIGNED NOT NULL DEFAULT '0',
fax_dateadded DATETIME DEFAULT '0000-00-00 00:00:00',
fax_datemodified DATETIME DEFAULT '0000-00-00 00:00:00',
fax_countrycode CHAR (3),
fax_number VARCHAR (25),
fax_type ENUM ('home', 'work', 'other')
);

CREATE TABLE email (
email_id SMALLINT UNSIGNED NOT NULL PRIMARY KEY AUTO_INCREMENT,
name_id SMALLINT UNSIGNED NOT NULL DEFAULT '0',
email_dateadded DATETIME DEFAULT '0000-00-00 00:00:00',
email_datemodified DATETIME DEFAULT '0000-00-00 00:00:00',
email VARCHAR (150),
email_type ENUM ('home', 'work', 'other')
);
```

The personal_notes table can go without an index as well:

```
CREATE TABLE personal_notes (
notes_id SMALLINT UNSIGNED NOT NULL PRIMARY KEY AUTO_INCREMENT,
name_id SMALLINT UNSIGNED NOT NULL DEFAULT '0',
notes_dateadded DATETIME DEFAULT '0000-00-00 00:00:00',
notes_datemodified DATETIME DEFAULT '0000-00-00 00:00:00',
note TEXT
);
```

Now that you have your table creation statements complete, the next section will show you two ways to issue the commands.

Issuing Your Table Creation Statements

There are two common methods for issuing the table creation statements:

1. Start the MySQL monitor, issue the commands, and see the results of the query.

2. Put all of your statements into a text file and simply tell MySQL where to go pick it up and use it.

So that you learn both methods, you'll issue a few table creation commands within the MySQL monitor and a few using the external file method.

Creating Tables in the MySQL Monitor

To add tables to the contactDB database, you must log in as the supercontact user. This user was granted all privileges, whereas the simpleuser user was granted only SELECT privileges.

```
prompt#> /usr/local/bin/mysql/bin/mysql -u supercontact -psomepass
Welcome to the MySQL monitor.  Commands end with ; or \g.
Your MySQL connection id is 10138 to server version: 3.23.42-log

Type 'help;' or '\h' for help. Type '\c' to clear the buffer.

mysql>
```

At the prompt, switch to the contactDB database:

```
mysql> use contactDB;
Database changed
```

Now you're ready to issue the creation commands. Three important rules for table creation statements:

1. Enclose your field and index definitions with parentheses.

2. Separate column definitions with a comma.

3. End the statement with a semicolon.

Failure to follow these rules will result in errors, and you'll have to weed through your statement, fix the error, and then issue it again.

In the "Finalizing Your Table Creation Statements" section earlier in this hour, you did just that. If you type the statements exactly as written, you won't receive any errors. Instead, you'll see a pleasant Query OK response:

```
mysql> CREATE TABLE master_name (
    -> name_id SMALLINT UNSIGNED NOT NULL PRIMARY KEY AUTO_INCREMENT,
    -> name_dateadded DATETIME DEFAULT '0000-00-00 00:00:00',
    -> name_datemodified DATETIME DEFAULT '0000-00-00 00:00:00',
    -> firstname VARCHAR (75),
    -> lastname VARCHAR (75),
    -> INDEX idx_fn (firstname),
    -> INDEX idx_ln (lastname)
    -> );
Query OK, 0 rows affected (0.00 sec)
```

You can type the queries all on one line if you want, or use multiple lines as in the example above. When you press Enter in the MySQL monitor, it means nothing; queries aren't executed until the magical semicolon is used.

Here's an example of what you'll see if you drop a comma:

```
mysql> CREATE TABLE master_name (
    -> name_id SMALLINT UNSIGNED NOT NULL PRIMARY KEY AUTO_INCREMENT,
    -> name_dateadded DATETIME DEFAULT '0000-00-00 00:00:00',
    -> name_datemodified DATETIME DEFAULT '0000-00-00 00:00:00',
    -> firstname VARCHAR (75),
    -> lastname VARCHAR (75),
    -> INDEX idx_fn (firstname)
    -> INDEX idx_ln (lastname)
    -> );
ERROR 1064: You have an error in your SQL syntax near
'INDEX idx_ln (lastname)' at line 8
```

This is a helpful error message, as it gives you a starting place to look for an error (near the INDEX creation clause).

Go ahead and issue the statements for the master_name, job_function, company, and name_company_map tables. When you are finished, you can see that they're all really in there, using the SHOW TABLES command:

```
mysql> show tables;
+--------------------+
| Tables_in_contactDB |
+--------------------+
| company            |
| job_function       |
| master_name        |
| name_company_map   |
+--------------------+
4 rows in set (0.00 sec)
```

This is very impressive and is not painful at all. In the next section, you'll add the rest of the tables.

Using SQL Commands from External Files

Some database architects prefer to create their table structures in external files and then import these scripts into MySQL. Also, people who use data modeling tools also have the option to create their table structures graphically, then export scripts to re-create what they're seeing in their software. I've always felt the hands-on approach gives you a better understanding of what you're actually creating, but everybody is different.

If you create your scripts in text files or have a piece of software export scripts for you, you still have to send those commands to MySQL. To see how this works, follow these steps:

1. Create a text file on your server called tables.sql.

2. At the top, type

   USE contactDB;

3. After the USE statement, type the table creation statements for the address, telephone, fax, email, and personal_notes tables and save the file.

4. Issue the following command at the prompt, replacing the path to the tables.sql file with your own:

```
/usr/local/bin/mysql/bin/mysql -u supercontact -psomepass <
/path/to/tables.sql
```

Unless you receive an error message, the import procedure was successful. You can log in to the MySQL monitor and issue a SHOW TABLES statement to make sure. You should see the following tables in your database:

```
mysql> show tables;
+--------------------+
| Tables_in_contactDB |
+--------------------+
| address            |
| company            |
| email              |
| fax                |
| job_function       |
| master_name        |
| name_company_map   |
| personal_notes     |
| telephone          |
+--------------------+
9 rows in set (0.00 sec)
```

Summary

MySQL uses two types of keys, primary and unique, for relationships and data integrity. There is an internal limit of 16 keys per table, but well-designed tables may need only a few, if that many. In fact, you may create an entire application using only primary keys with no unique keys at all.

Primary keys cannot contain null values, but unique keys can. When defining fields, you can specify default values or even have MySQL automatically increment integers for you. Complete field definitions lead to better optimization.

Indexes can, at times, adversely affect database performance, but can also increase the speed of queries. The advantages of appropriate indexes far outweigh any performance issues. There are specific times and places for indexes, and not all tables in all applications require indexes beyond the automatically indexed primary keys. In general, create an index when a table is used mostly for selecting and not updating, and index only appropriate fields.

After defining fields and indexes, you can finally create your tables. Of course, you can always go back and add indexes later on if you find your application needs them.

When creating a table, you can type the commands directly into the MySQL monitor, or you can place all of your commands in an external file and simply tell MySQL to go grab it and execute the commands. Both methods achieve the same results, although the first method is more hands-on.

Q&A

Q **I've used foreign keys before, and you didn't talk about them. What gives?**

A Currently, MySQL does not support explicit foreign keys. Foreign keys are planned for MySQL version 4.1.

Q **Without explicit foreign keys, you have to do your own referential integrity checks, correct?**

A Correct. As you'll learn in the upcoming hours, you'll have to perform extra queries to verify that entries actually exist before modifying and deleting them. You could also go on blind faith, but that would leave a lot of straggly data in your tables.

Q **Can you indicate a starting number for AUTO_INCREMENT fields?**

A Not directly. However, since AUTO_INCREMENT will use the next highest number, you can insert the first row manually and specify a starting number. AUTO_INCREMENT will use it as a base and continue upward.

Workshop

The Workshop is designed to help you anticipate possible questions, review what you've learned, and begin learning how to put your knowledge into practice.

Quiz

1. Why shouldn't you add an index to a field that will return many similar results?
2. Can primary keys be null?
3. How many keys are allowed in one table?

Answers

1. Adding or using indexes adds overhead, and in this case it would be unnecessary. You should use an index when you're searching for a needle in a haystack—not for hay.
2. Nope. A NULL primary key wouldn't do you much good when creating relationships.
3. 16

Activities

1. If you disagree with not adding indexes to some of the tables in the `contactDB` database, use the `CREATE INDEX` command to add your own.

2. Use the `DESCRIBE` command to verify the table structure of the tables in the `contactDB` database. The syntax is

   `DESCRIBE table_name;`

   where `table_name` is replaced with the name of the table you want to describe.

PART IV

Working with Your Tables

Hour

Hour 9

Populating Your Database Tables

By now, you have a well-planned, normalized database—and no data! By the end of this hour, you will have plenty of data to work with and will have learned several methods for populating your tables.

In this hour, you will learn

- How to use the INSERT command
- How to prepare data from other sources for import to MySQL
- How to use mysqlimport and LOAD DATA INFILE to import data from other sources

Using the INSERT Command

The SQL command for adding new records to a table is called INSERT. The syntax for adding records using INSERT is quite simple, but it also leaves room for mistakes and parsing errors, as does any command.

The basic syntax of INSERT is

```
INSERT INTO table_name (column list) VALUES (column values);
```

Within the parenthetical list of values, you must enclose strings within quotation marks. The SQL standard is single quotes, but MySQL allows the usage of either single or double quotes. Remember to escape the type of quotation mark used if it's within the string itself.

| Integers do not require quotation marks around them. |

In Hour 4, "Using the MySQL Client," the following example string was used to show when escaping is necessary:

```
O'Connor said "Boo"
```

If you enclose your strings in double quotes, the INSERT statement would look like this:

```
INSERT INTO table_name (column1) VALUES ("O'Connor said \"Boo\"");
```

If you enclose your strings in single quotes instead, the INSERT statement would look like this:

```
INSERT INTO table_name (column1) VALUES ('O\'Connor said "Boo"');
```

A Closer Look at INSERT

Besides the table name, there are two main parts of the INSERT statement—the column list and the value list. Only the value list is actually required, but if you omit the column list, you must specifically name each column in your values list in order.

Using the `master_name` table in the `connectDB` database as an example, you have five fields: `name_id`, `name_dateadded`, `name_datemodified`, `firstname`, and `lastname`. To insert a complete record, you could use either of these statements:

1. A statement with all columns named:

```
INSERT INTO master_name
(name_id, name_dateadded, name_datemodified, firstname, lastname)
VALUES
('1','2001-10-29 13:11:00','2001-10-29 13:11:00', 'John', 'Smith');
```

2. A statement that uses all columns but does not explicitly name them:

```
INSERT INTO master_name
VALUES ('2','2001-10-29 13:11:00','2001-10-29 13:11:00', 'Jane', 'Smith');
```

Now for some more interesting versions of INSERT. Because `name_id` is an auto-incrementing integer, you don't have to put it in your values list. However, if there's a value you specifically don't want to list (such as `name_id`), you then must list the remaining columns in use. For example, the following statement, which does not list the columns and also does not give a value for `name_id`, will produce an error:

```
mysql> INSERT INTO master_name
    -> VALUES
    -> ('2001-10-29 13:11:00','2001-10-29 13:11:00', 'Jimbo', 'Jones');
ERROR 1136: Column count doesn't match value count at row 1
```

Because you didn't list any columns, MySQL expects all of them to be in the value list, causing an error on the previous statement.

If the goal was to let MySQL do the work for you by auto-incrementing the `name_id` field, you could use either of these statements:

1. A statement with all columns named except `name_id`:

```
INSERT INTO master_name
(name_dateadded, name_datemodified, firstname, lastname)
VALUES
('2001-10-29 13:11:00','2001-10-29 13:11:00', 'Jimbo', 'Jones');
```

2. A statement that uses all columns but does not explicitly name them and indicates a null entry for `name_id`:

```
INSERT INTO master_name
VALUES ('','2001-10-29 13:11:00','2001-10-29 13:11:00', 'Andy', 'Smith');
```

Decisions, decisions! You'll work out on your own which version you prefer to use. It makes no different to MySQL, but as with everything that is a preference, be consistent in your application development. Consistent structures will be easier for you to debug later, since you'll know what to expect.

Using Function Results in INSERT Statements

As if using auto-incrementing fields wasn't cool enough, you can also use built-in MySQL functions to replace those long date and time values automatically. You'll learn more about MySQL's built-in date and time functions in Hour 17, "Using MySQL Date and Time Functions," but this one is so useful that it just had to make an appearance here.

This useful function is called NOW(), and you can use it wherever you might be inserting the current date and/or time. So, instead of using 2001-10-29 13:11:00 as the value of the name_dateadded and name_datemodified fields, just use NOW(). For example, try this statement:

```
INSERT INTO master_name VALUES ('',NOW(),NOW(), 'Chris', 'Jones');
```

MySQL is doing the work for you in three of the five fields: name_id contains an auto-incremented integer, and name_dateadded and name_datemodified are populated with the actual date and time.

> Do not enclose functions like NOW() inside quotation marks. If you do, MySQL will think they're strings.

Importing Data from Other Databases

It's not uncommon to switch from flat file data storage, or another commercial database system, to MySQL. If you've already populated these other files or databases with a ton of information, re-entering it all into MySQL is simply unacceptable. There are a few options for importing data into MySQL that won't take an eternity to complete, lucky for you!

Remember, data is just data—it's the container that's different. You can easily take data from one system to another with a little massaging of the format. One method is to obtain the schema of the old database. If your tables include data, the schema will include the insert statements to populate the tables. In Hour 4, you saw mysqldump output a schema to a text file, and in Hour 8, "Creating Your Database Tables—Part II," you learned how to use MySQL to run queries from an external file. If you put those two tasks together, you have one method for transferring your database from another system to MySQL.

Not all databases will dump a schema, but if they do, look closely at the data types, methods of escaping characters, and table creation statements, and change them to match those used in MySQL.

Other options for getting pre-existing data into MySQL include using the mysqlimport client application and the LOAD DATA INFILE command within the MySQL monitor. Neither of these options uses schemas or INSERT statements but instead work with raw data such as comma-delimited or tab-delimited rows of text.

However, transferring data from a single flat file to a database structure with multiple tables requires you to do some work with the data before importing it. In the next two sections, you'll use both mysqlimport and LOAD DATA INFILE to get flat file data into MySQL, first going through and preparing the data for import.

Preparing Data for Import

Both mysqlimport and the LOAD DATA INFILE command use delimited fields, with data surrounded by quotation marks no matter if it's a string or an integer. Also, each row is ended with a specific character—a semicolon, line break, or some other character of your choice. The field delimiter is also up to you—it can be a comma, a tab, or some other character.

Even when you're importing data, if your data includes a double quote within double quotation marks, or a single quote within single quotation marks, you have to escape that character.

When choosing delimiters, either between fields or at the end of rows, try to pick something that you're sure doesn't appear within your data. For example, commas can pop up in your data, and although it shouldn't matter to the import utility since it's within the quotation marks surrounding the data, better safe than sorry. If the import utility abruptly stops at a comma within a field, your row will be split and your import will be skewed. I often use a character like the pipe (|) or sometimes three colons in a row (:::).

Using Data from a Flat File

If your contact management database has multiple tables and you're importing data from one flat file, something has to give. In this case, it's the flat file.

During import, the relationships won't be touched—instead, default values will be used and you'll have to go back and manually update the relationships once all the data is in its proper tables. During the importing of data, all you should be concerned with is getting it into MySQL—you can work with it once it's in there.

If you keep all of your contact information in a single file, it's probably structured in a way that makes sense to you and not necessarily to a database. It could look like Figure 9.1, with separate chunks for each address, or it could look like Figure 9.2, with entries on single lines. It may not look like either figure, and that makes no difference because no matter what it looks like, it's not going to go into MySQL like that.

FIGURE 9.1

Example address book using a text file.

FIGURE 9.2

Another version of flat file address book entries.

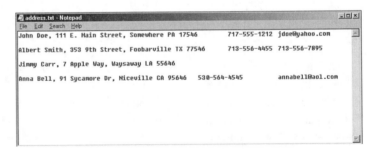

Think about the tables in contactDB, and you'll realize that separate tables exist for all of the information in your flat files—master_name, address, telephone, fax, and email. This means you'll first have to break apart your flat files into five separate flat files. Use the table names for the file names, for example master_name.txt.

In the `master_name.txt` file, you would have

```
John Doe
Albert Smith
Jimmy Carr
Anna Bell
```

One problem—the `master_name` table has five fields: `name_id`, `name_dateadded`, `name_datemodified`, `firstname`, and `lastname`. You can leave each of the fields blank, but you have to separate the fields in the import file so MySQL knows to enter the default values. A structured import file for the `master_name` table could look like this, using `:::` as the field separator:

```
:::::::::"John":::"Doe"
:::::::::"Albert":::"Smith"
:::::::::"Jimmy":::"Carr"
:::::::::"Anna":::"Bell"
```

Now you can create four more text files, one for the `address`, `telephone`, `fax`, and `email` tables, respectively. The `address` table has eight fields, including the `name_id` field that will be 0 for now:

```
:::::::::::::"111 E. Main Street":::"Somewhere":::"PA":::"17546"
:::::::::::::"353 9th Street":::"Foobarville":::"TX":::"77546"
:::::::::::::"7 Apple Way":::"Waysaway":::"LA":::"55646"
:::::::::::::"91 Sycamore Dr":::"Niceville":::"CA":::"95646"
```

The `telephone` table has seven fields, two of which are not represented in the flat file—`tel_countrycode` and `tel_type`. Since it's your data, you can fill in the blanks. The examples below show a country code of 1 and an indication that it's a home telephone number. Also, note that only three of the four contacts in your flat file have telephone numbers. This makes no difference, as you'll map the data to their appropriate person after you get all the data into MySQL.

```
:::::::::::::"1":::"717-555-1212":::"home"
:::::::::::::"1":::"713-556-4455":::"home"
:::::::::::::"1":::"530-564-4545":::"home"
```

The `fax` table is structured like the `telephone` table in that it has one entry:

```
:::::::::::::"1":::"713-556-7896":::"work"
```

The `email` table is the last table you need to worry about, and it will have two entries:

```
::::::::::::::"jdoe@yahoo.com":::"home"
::::::::::::::"annabell@aol.com":::"home"
```

These five files are now ready for importing, using either `mysqlimport` or the `LOAD DATA INFILE` command.

Using Data from Microsoft Access

If you have stored your data in a Microsoft Access database, you can easily export data to text files. In fact, the Microsoft Access export process even allows you to select the field separators.

For example, Figure 9.3 shows how it might look if your data is in a single table.

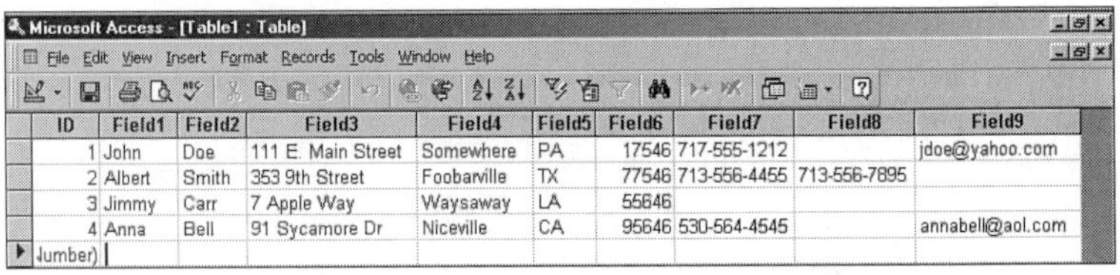

FIGURE 9.3

Single table in Microsoft Access.

If you use the Export Text Wizard in Microsoft Access, you will see a dialog box for selecting the delimiter, as shown in Figure 9.4.

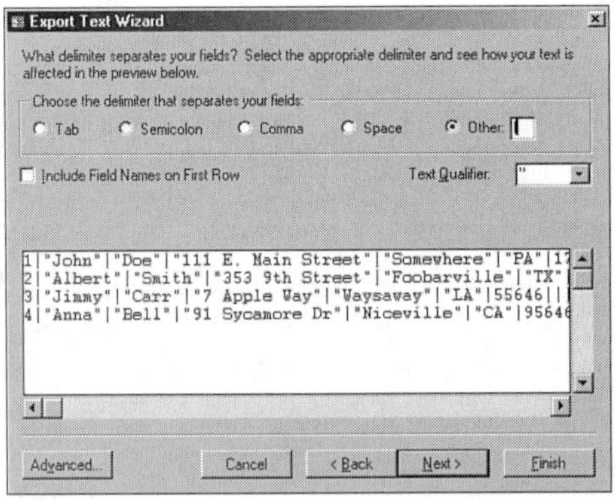

FIGURE 9.4

Using the Export Text Wizard to select | as the delimiter.

The resulting text file will look like Figure 9.5, with a | between fields and double quotes around fields.

FIGURE 9.5

Pipe-delimited text file.

The file shown in Figure 9.5 contains the Microsoft Access ID numbers. If your MySQL tables are empty, importing the ID field won't be an issue. But if your table already contains data, those records have their own IDs and the insertion of the new records will fail; an ID is a primary key and cannot be repeated.

Since you're moving from one table to many tables in this example, you still have to break the information apart into separate text files for each table. You can do this manually, as with the manipulations you did with the flat text files in the previous section, or you can create Microsoft Access queries and save the results as text files.

If you choose the latter route, go to the Queries tab of the Database dialog box and press the New button, as shown in Figure 9.6.

FIGURE 9.6

Select New from the Queries dialog box to create a new query in Microsoft Access, which can be run at any time to produce data results.

Since you'll be selecting all data from specific fields, the Simple Query Wizard would be the best choice. To create the query that will export all address information, select fields 3 through 7, as shown in Figure 9.7.

FIGURE 9.7

Choosing fields for a query.

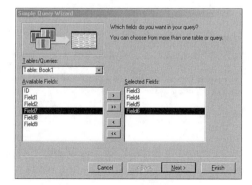

The Simple Query Wizard will take you through a few more steps, including the naming of the query. When you press Finish, you will see the query results, like in Figure 9.8.

FIGURE 9.8

Address Query results.

If you switch back to the Queries tab of the Database dialog box, you can now quickly export the results of that query by right-clicking and selecting "Save As/Export" from the pop-up menu. Figure 9.9 shows how:

FIGURE 9.9

*Selecting
Save As/Export
from the pop-up
menu to export the
results of your query
to a text file.*

This action will take you through the same Export Text Wizard as before, but this time it will export only the results of the query—the street address, city, state, and zip code. Figure 9.10 shows the contents of the exported Address Query.txt file using the | field delimiter.

FIGURE 9.10

*Results of the
Address Query,
saved as a text file.*

This file is now ready for importing through the use of either mysqlimport or the LOAD DATA INFILE command.

Using `mysqlimport`

The `mysqlimport` utility must be run from the command-line. If you do not have command-line access to MySQL, you can use the `LOAD DATA INFILE` command described in the next section to achieve the same results.

Running the `mysqlimport` utility looks like this:

```
#prompt> mysqlimport [options] database textfile
```

The options are numerous, and you can see a complete list by typing

```
#prompt> mysqlimport --help
```

The options you'll use most are shown in Table 9.1.

TABLE 9.1 Common `mysqlimport` Options

Option	Action Performed
-L	Use a local file.
--fields-enclosed-by	Specify the character that encloses your data, such as double quotes.
--fields-escaped-by	If you have to escape characters in your strings, this option tells how they're escaped. Usually, characters are escaped with the backslash (\).
--fields-terminated-by	Specify the character used to separate fields, such as the pipe or a colon.
--lines-terminated-by	Specify the method for ending the entry for a record. The default is a newline character, so unless you use a specific string to indicate the end of a line, you don't have to use this option.

A practical example of `mysqlimport` would be to add the records from the `master_name.txt` flat file to the `master_name` table.

> The `mysqlimport` utility uses the filename to determine which table will get the data, disregarding the file extension. Files named `master_name.txt`, `master_name`, or `master_name.blah` would all import data into the table called `master_name`.

You must also specify the host, username, and password, just like when you use the MySQL monitor. The command and response to import the master_name.txt file would look like this:

```
#prompt> mysqlimport -L -h localhost -u supercontact -psomepass
--fields-terminated-by=::: --fields-enclosed-by=\" contactDB master_name.txt
```

You should see a response like the following, indicating success:

```
contactDB.master_name: Records: 4  Deleted: 0  Skipped: 0  Warnings: 0
```

Using the LOAD DATA INFILE Command

The LOAD DATA INFILE command is similar to the command-line options of the mysqlimport utility, only LOAD DATA INFILE is issued from within the MySQL monitor.

The basic syntax of the command is

```
LOAD DATA [LOCAL] INFILE 'file_name.txt'
INTO TABLE table_name
FIELDS TERMINATED BY 'somechar'
ENCLOSED BY 'somechar'
ESCAPED BY 'somechar'
LINES TERMINATED BY 'somechar';
```

To import the master_name.txt file using LOAD DATA INFILE, the complete SQL statement would be

```
mysql> LOAD DATA LOCAL INFILE '/path/to/master_name.txt'
    -> INTO TABLE master_name
    -> FIELDS TERMINATED BY ':::'
    -> ENCLOSED BY '"';
```

The result you're looking for is

```
Query OK, 4 rows affected (0.00 sec)
Records: 4  Deleted: 0  Skipped: 0  Warnings: 0
```

This result indicates a successful import of four records into the master_name table.

Summary

You can populate your database tables several different ways, including using INSERT commands and external files. The INSERT command is an SQL statement that names the table and columns you wish to populate and then defines the values. When placing values in the INSERT statement, strings must be enclosed with single or double quotes.

MySQL will help you out by automatically inserting values into blank fields if you provided default values when you created the table. You can also use MySQL functions to provide values when you issue the SQL statement, such as using NOW() to insert the current date and time.

If you have data stored in other databases, you may not have to retype it to get it into MySQL. If your old database will perform a dump of the table schema and data insertion statements, you can run those commands directly from an external file. If all you have are flat files to work with, a little elbow grease will get them ready for import.

If you are moving from a flat file system to a relational system, you will have to create individual files for each new table before performing the insertion. Files can be imported using the mysqlimport utility, or the LOAD DATA INFILE command within the MySQL monitor. Each of these methods require your data to be delimited by commas, colons, pipes, or other characters. Also, the values of the fields must be enclosed with a character such as single or double quotes, and that character must be escaped if it appears in the string.

Q&A

Q Will MySQL issue meaningful error messages if the command fails when importing data using mysqlimport or LOAD DATA INFILE?

A Yes. You can expect warnings similar to those issued from the MySQL monitor if a query is malformed or if the user privileges don't allow the action.

Q Can you specify which columns you want to import using mysqlimport and LOAD DATA INFILE, as you can with the INSERT statement?

A Yes for both. For mysqlimport, the option is

```
mysqlimport -c=column1, column2, column3
```

At the end of the LOAD DATA INFILE statement, specify the list of columns in a parenthetical statement:

```
LOAD DATA INFILE … (column1, column2, column3)
```

Workshop

The Workshop is designed to help you anticipate possible questions, review what you've learned, and begin learning how to put your knowledge into practice.

Quiz

1. In the following INSERT statement, what needs to be escaped?

```
INSERT INTO master_name ('', NOW(), NOW(), 'Patrick', 'O'Brien');
```

2. Assuming address.txt looks like this:

```
""|""|""|""|"111 E. Main Street"|"Somewhere"|"PA"|17546
""|""|""|""|"353 9th Street"|"Foobarville"|"TX"|77546
""|""|""|""|"7 Apple Way"|"Waysaway"|"LA"|55646
""|""|""|""|"91 Sycamore Dr"|"Niceville"|"CA"|95646
```

Why will the following command fail?

```
LOAD DATA LOCAL INFILE 'address.txt'
INTO TABLE address
FIELDS TERMINATED BY ','
ENCLOSED BY '"';
```

Answers

1. The single quote in O'Brien must be escaped.

2. The LOAD DATA INFILE command says that fields are terminated with a comma, but the text file uses a pipe (|). Plus there are no quotes around the zipcode, and the field is defined as a VARCHAR field.

Activities

1. Use INSERT statements to add records to the master_name personal_notes, job_function, and company tables. The company table is a little different than the others, as it contains distinct company names—if Joe and John work for the same company, only enter the company once in the table. You will perform the mapping in the next hour.

2. Use mysqlimport to import data into the address and telephone tables. If you do not have command line access, skip this activity.

3. Use LOAD DATA INFILE to import data into the remaining tables (fax and email).

Hour **10**

Selecting Data from Your Tables

You've finally populated your tables with some data; now it's time to learn how to get it back out! The SQL command for retrieving data is SELECT, and in this hour you'll learn how to use it to select everything in your table or just specific pieces of information from that table.

In this hour, you will learn

- The SELECT command syntax
- How to order and limit your results
- How to use basic functions in SELECT expressions
- How to use the WHERE clause

Using the SELECT Command

SELECT is the SQL command used to retrieve records. This command syntax can be totally simplistic or very complicated. As you become more comfortable with database programming, you will learn to enhance your SELECT statements, ultimately making your database do as much work as possible and not overworking your programming language of choice.

The most basic SELECT syntax looks like this:

```
SELECT expressions_and_columns FROM table_name
[WHERE some_condition_is_true]
[ORDER BY some_column [ASC | DESC]]
[LIMIT offset, rows]
```

Start with the first line:

```
SELECT expressions_and_columns FROM table_name
```

One handy expression is the * symbol, which stands for "everything". So, to select "everything" (all rows, all columns) from the master_name table, your SQL statement would be

```
SELECT * FROM master_name;
```

Depending on how much data you inserted into the master_name table during the previous hour, your results will vary, but it may look something like this:

```
mysql> SELECT * FROM master_name;
+---------+---------------------+---------------------+-----------+----------+
| name_id | name_dateadded      | name_datemodified   | firstname | lastname |
+---------+---------------------+---------------------+-----------+----------+
|       1 | 2001-10-29 13:11:00 | 2001-10-29 13:11:00 | John      | Smith    |
|       2 | 2001-10-29 13:11:00 | 2001-10-29 13:11:00 | Jane      | Smith    |
|       3 | 2001-10-29 13:11:00 | 2001-10-29 13:11:00 | Jimbo     | Jones    |
|       4 | 2001-10-29 13:11:00 | 2001-10-29 13:11:00 | Andy      | Smith    |
|       7 | 2001-10-29 14:16:21 | 2001-10-29 14:16:21 | Chris     | Jones    |
|      45 | 0000-00-00 00:00:00 | 0000-00-00 00:00:00 | Anna      | Bell     |
|      44 | 0000-00-00 00:00:00 | 0000-00-00 00:00:00 | Jimmy     | Carr     |
|      43 | 0000-00-00 00:00:00 | 0000-00-00 00:00:00 | Albert    | Smith    |
|      42 | 0000-00-00 00:00:00 | 0000-00-00 00:00:00 | John      | Doe      |
+---------+---------------------+---------------------+-----------+----------+
9 rows in set (0.00 sec)
```

As you can see, MySQL creates a lovely table as part of the result set, with the names of the columns along the first row. If you want to select only specific columns, replace the * with the names of the columns, separated by commas. The following statement selects just the name_id, firstname and lastname fields from the master_name table.

```
mysql> SELECT name_id, firstname, lastname FROM master_name;
+---------+-----------+----------+
| name_id | firstname | lastname |
+---------+-----------+----------+
|       1 | John      | Smith    |
|       2 | Jane      | Smith    |
|       3 | Jimbo     | Jones    |
|       4 | Andy      | Smith    |
|       7 | Chris     | Jones    |
|      45 | Anna      | Bell     |
|      44 | Jimmy     | Carr     |
|      43 | Albert    | Smith    |
|      42 | John      | Doe      |
+---------+-----------+----------+
9 rows in set (0.00 sec)
```

A useful expression used with SELECT is DISTINCT, which (not surprisingly) will return distinct occurrences in a result set. For example, the master_name table has more than one person with the last name of "Smith". If you wanted to select last names without repeating results, you would use DISTINCT:

```
mysql> SELECT DISTINCT lastname FROM master_name;
+----------+
| lastname |
+----------+
| Bell     |
| Carr     |
| Doe      |
| Jones    |
| Smith    |
+----------+
5 rows in set (0.00 sec)
```

Ordering SELECT Results

By default, results of SELECT queries are ordered as they appear in the table. If you want to order results a specific way, such as by date, ID, name, and so on, specify your requirements using the ORDER BY clause. In the following statement, results are ordered by lastname:

```
mysql> SELECT name_id, firstname, lastname FROM master_name ORDER BY lastname;
+---------+-----------+----------+
| name_id | firstname | lastname |
+---------+-----------+----------+
|      45 | Anna      | Bell     |
|      44 | Jimmy     | Carr     |
|      42 | John      | Doe      |
|       3 | Jimbo     | Jones    |
|       7 | Chris     | Jones    |
```

10

```
|       1 | John      | Smith    |
|       2 | Jane      | Smith    |
|       4 | Andy      | Smith    |
|      43 | Albert    | Smith    |
+---------+-----------+----------+
9 rows in set (0.00 sec)
```

> When selecting results from a table without specifying a sort order, the results may or may not be ordered by their key value. This occurs because MySQL reuses the space taken up by previously deleted rows. In other words, if you add records with ID values of 1 through 5, then delete the record with ID number 4, then add another record (ID number 6), the records may appear in the table in this order: 1, 2, 3, 6, 5.

The default sorting of ORDER BY results is ascending (ASC); strings sort from A to Z, integers start at 0, dates sort from oldest to newest. You can also specify a descending sort, using DESC:

```
mysql> SELECT name_id, firstname, lastname FROM master_name
    -> ORDER BY lastname DESC;
+---------+-----------+----------+
| name_id | firstname | lastname |
+---------+-----------+----------+
|       1 | John      | Smith    |
|       2 | Jane      | Smith    |
|       4 | Andy      | Smith    |
|      43 | Albert    | Smith    |
|       3 | Jimbo     | Jones    |
|       7 | Chris     | Jones    |
|      42 | John      | Doe      |
|      44 | Jimmy     | Carr     |
|      45 | Anna      | Bell     |
+---------+-----------+----------+
9 rows in set (0.00 sec)
```

You're not limited to sorting by just one field—you can specify as many fields as you want, separated by commas. The sorting priority is by list order, so if you use ORDER BY lastname, firstname, the results will be sorted by lastname, then by firstname:

```
mysql> SELECT name_id, firstname, lastname FROM master_name
    -> ORDER BY lastname, firstname;
+---------+-----------+----------+
| name_id | firstname | lastname |
+---------+-----------+----------+
|      45 | Anna      | Bell     |
|      44 | Jimmy     | Carr     |
|      42 | John      | Doe      |
|       7 | Chris     | Jones    |
```

```
|        3 | Jimbo      | Jones     |
|       43 | Albert     | Smith     |
|        4 | Andy       | Smith     |
|        2 | Jane       | Smith     |
|        1 | John       | Smith     |
+----------+------------+-----------+
9 rows in set (0.00 sec)
```

Limiting Your Results

You can use the LIMIT clause to return only a certain number of records in your SELECT query result. There are two requirements when using the LIMIT clause: offset and number of rows. The offset is the starting position, and the number of rows should be self-explanatory.

 For the most part, counting while programming always starts at 0, not 1. For example: 0, 1, 2, 3 instead of 1, 2, 3, 4.

An example would be to select only the first 5 records from master_name, ordered by lastname:

```
mysql> SELECT * FROM master_name ORDER BY lastname LIMIT 0, 5;
+----------+---------------------+---------------------+-----------+-----------+
| name_id  | name_dateadded      | name_datemodified   | firstname | lastname  |
+----------+---------------------+---------------------+-----------+-----------+
|       45 | 0000-00-00 00:00:00 | 0000-00-00 00:00:00 | Anna      | Bell      |
|       44 | 0000-00-00 00:00:00 | 0000-00-00 00:00:00 | Jimmy     | Carr      |
|       42 | 0000-00-00 00:00:00 | 0000-00-00 00:00:00 | John      | Doe       |
|        3 | 2001-10-29 13:11:00 | 2001-10-29 13:11:00 | Jimbo     | Jones     |
|        7 | 2001-10-29 14:16:21 | 2001-10-29 14:16:21 | Chris     | Jones     |
+----------+---------------------+---------------------+-----------+-----------+
5 rows in set (0.00 sec)
```

The LIMIT clause can be quite useful in an actual application. For example, you can use the LIMIT clause within a series of SELECT statements to essentially page through results in steps:

1. SELECT * FROM master_name ORDER BY lastname LIMIT 0, 5;

2. SELECT * FROM master_name ORDER BY lastname LIMIT 6, 5;

3. SELECT * FROM master_name ORDER BY lastname LIMIT 11, 5;

If you specify an offset and number of rows in your query and no results are found, you won't see an error—just an empty result set. For example, if the master_name table contains only 9 records, a query with a LIMIT offset of 11 will produce no results:

```
mysql> SELECT * FROM master_name ORDER BY lastname LIMIT 11, 5;
Empty set (0.00 sec)
```

In Web-based applications, when lists of data are displayed with links like "previous 10" and "next 10," it's a safe bet that a LIMIT clause is at work.

Using Some Aggregate Functions with SELECT

MySQL has many built-in functions that allow you to perform all sorts of operations on integers, strings, and dates. These functions will be explained in detail in later hours, but a few of the simpler functions described here should whet your appetite.

If you want to know how many records are in your table, you could just select all records and look for the response that says "5 rows in set," or however many there are. If you have a million rows, selecting all one million rows just to see how many there are is not the speediest way to find your answer. Instead, you can use the COUNT() function, which counts all non-NULL values in a given column. If you have a primary key defined in your table, you know that field can't be NULL. Knowing this, if you use COUNT() on the primary key, you can obtain a count of all the records in the table.

Using a test table containing almost 4000 rows of integer and string data, a select of all the rows took 0.03 seconds.

```
mysql> SELECT * FROM test_table;
+----+--------------+
| id | string_field |
+----+--------------+
|  1 | I Love MySQL |
|  2 | I Love MySQL |
|  3 | I Love MySQL |
|  4 | I Love MySQL |
|  5 | I Love MySQL |
...
| 3890 |              |
+------+--------------+
3890 rows in set (0.03 sec)
```

Using COUNT(), the query was faster:

```
mysql> SELECT COUNT(id) FROM test_table;
+-----------+
| count(id) |
+-----------+
|      3890 |
+-----------+
1 row in set (0.00 sec)
```

COUNT() returns only one row in the result set. This result is equal to the actual number of rows in the table, which is what your query was asking. The column header for the result set is COUNT(id), the expression used in the SELECT query.

You can use AS to produce your own column headers—not just when using functions but during any SELECT statement. For example, to name your column row_count, use:

```
mysql> SELECT COUNT(id) AS row_count FROM test_table;
+-----------+
| row_count |
+-----------+
|      3890 |
+-----------+
1 row in set (0.00 sec)
```

You can use COUNT() in conjunction with the DISTINCT expression you learned earlier. Instead of selecting the actual distinct last names from the master_name table, you can select the count of those names:

```
mysql> SELECT COUNT(DISTINCT lastname) AS lastname_count FROM master_name;
+----------------+
| lastname_count |
+----------------+
|              5 |
+----------------+
1 row in set (0.00 sec)
```

A few other basic functions are MIN() and MAX(), which are used to select the minimum and maximum values in a field.

For example, select the minimum and maximum values for name_id from the master_name table:

```
mysql> SELECT MIN(name_id) FROM master_name;
+--------------+
| MIN(name_id) |
+--------------+
|            1 |
+--------------+
1 row in set (0.00 sec)
```

```
mysql> SELECT MAX(name_id) FROM master_name;
+--------------+
| MAX(name_id) |
+--------------+
|           45 |
+--------------+
1 row in set (0.00 sec)
```

Using MAX(name_id) would not produce an accurate count of the number of records in the master_name table. Although the primary key auto-increments, records could have been deleted throughout the table's existence. In the current master_name table, there are only 9 records, but the value of MAX(name_id) is 45 because numerous dummy records have been added and deleted. Always use COUNT() and not MAX() to find the number of records in a table.

10

If the field is a date, `MIN()` will return the earliest date, while `MAX()` returns the latest date:

```
mysql> SELECT MIN(name_dateadded) FROM master_name;
+---------------------+
| MIN(name_dateadded) |
+---------------------+
| 0000-00-00 00:00:00 |
+---------------------+
1 row in set (0.00 sec)

mysql> SELECT MAX(name_dateadded) FROM master_name;
+---------------------+
| MAX(name_dateadded) |
+---------------------+
| 2001-10-29 14:16:21 |
+---------------------+
1 row in set (0.00 sec)
```

This is just a sampling of the numerous built-in MySQL functions, which range from obscure to "can't live without them," most of which you'll learn about in Hours 15, 16, and 17.

Using WHERE in Your Queries

You have learned numerous ways to retrieve particular columns from your tables, but not specific rows. This is when the WHERE clause comes into play. From the basic SELECT syntax, you see that WHERE is used to specify a particular condition:

```
SELECT expressions_and_columns FROM table_name
[WHERE some_condition_is_true]
```

An example would be to retrieve all the records for people with the last name of "Smith":

```
mysql> SELECT * FROM master_name WHERE lastname = 'Smith';
+---------+---------------------+---------------------+-----------+----------+
| name_id | name_dateadded      | name_datemodified   | firstname | lastname |
+---------+---------------------+---------------------+-----------+----------+
|       1 | 2001-10-29 13:11:00 | 2001-10-29 13:11:00 | John      | Smith    |
|       2 | 2001-10-29 13:11:00 | 2001-10-29 13:11:00 | Jane      | Smith    |
|       4 | 2001-10-29 13:11:00 | 2001-10-29 13:11:00 | Andy      | Smith    |
|      43 | 0000-00-00 00:00:00 | 0000-00-00 00:00:00 | Albert    | Smith    |
+---------+---------------------+---------------------+-----------+----------+
4 rows in set (0.00 sec)
```

Just like when you add records, if you use strings or dates in your WHERE clauses, you must surround them with quotation marks. Using single quotes or double quotes makes no difference, but the same rules for escaping characters apply here as well. For example, if you insert a record into the `master_name` table for Patrick O'Brien using single quotes:

```
mysql> INSERT INTO master_name VALUES ('', NOW(), NOW(), 'Patrick', 'O\'Brien');
```

When you select the record using `WHERE`, you have to escape the single quote character:

```
mysql> SELECT * FROM master_name WHERE lastname = 'O\'Brien';
+---------+---------------------+---------------------+-----------+----------+
| name_id | name_dateadded      | name_datemodified   | firstname | lastname |
+---------+---------------------+---------------------+-----------+----------+
|      46 | 2001-10-31 08:32:53 | 2001-10-31 08:32:53 | Patrick   | O'Brien  |
+---------+---------------------+---------------------+-----------+----------+
1 row in set (0.00 sec)
```

If you use an integer as part of your `WHERE` clause, quotation marks are not required:

```
mysql> SELECT firstname, lastname FROM master_name WHERE name_id = 1;
+-----------+----------+
| firstname | lastname |
+-----------+----------+
| John      | Smith    |
+-----------+----------+
1 row in set (0.00 sec)
```

Using Operators in WHERE Clauses

You've been using the equal sign (=) in your `WHERE` clauses to determine the truth of a condition—is one thing equal to another. There are many types of operators you can use, with comparison operators and logical operators being the most popular types.

Comparison operators should look familiar to you if you think about the first day of Algebra class.

TABLE 10.1 Basic Comparison Operators and Their Meanings

Operator	Meaning
=	Equal to
!=	Not equal to
<=	Less than or equal to
<	Less than
>=	Greater than or equal to
>	Greater than

When you use comparison operators on strings, the comparison is case insensitive. Look at the next two queries and their results as an example. If the comparison were case sensitive, the first query would return no results.

```
mysql> SELECT firstname, lastname FROM master_name WHERE lastname = 'SMITH';
+-----------+----------+
| firstname | lastname |
+-----------+----------+
| John      | Smith    |
| Jane      | Smith    |
| Andy      | Smith    |
| Albert    | Smith    |
+-----------+----------+
4 rows in set (0.00 sec)

mysql> SELECT firstname, lastname FROM master_name WHERE lastname = 'Smith';
+-----------+----------+
| firstname | lastname |
+-----------+----------+
| John      | Smith    |
| Jane      | Smith    |
| Andy      | Smith    |
| Albert    | Smith    |
+-----------+----------+
4 rows in set (0.01 sec)
```

There's also a handy operator called BETWEEN, which is useful with integer or data comparisons because it searches for results between a minimum and a maximum value. For example:

```
mysql> SELECT * FROM master_name WHERE name_id BETWEEN 1 AND 10;
+---------+---------------------+---------------------+-----------+----------+
| name_id | name_dateadded      | name_datemodified   | firstname | lastname |
+---------+---------------------+---------------------+-----------+----------+
|       1 | 2001-10-29 13:11:00 | 2001-10-29 13:11:00 | John      | Smith    |
|       2 | 2001-10-29 13:11:00 | 2001-10-29 13:11:00 | Jane      | Smith    |
|       3 | 2001-10-29 13:11:00 | 2001-10-29 13:11:00 | Jimbo     | Jones    |
|       4 | 2001-10-29 13:11:00 | 2001-10-29 13:11:00 | Andy      | Smith    |
|       7 | 2001-10-29 14:16:21 | 2001-10-29 14:16:21 | Chris     | Jones    |
+---------+---------------------+---------------------+-----------+----------+
5 rows in set (0.00 sec)
```

Other operators are logical operators, which allow you to use multiple comparisons within your WHERE clause. The basic logical operators are AND and OR. When using AND, all comparisons in the clause must be true in order to retrieve results, while using OR allows a minimum of one comparison to be true.

For example, if you want to find records in the master_name table for people named John Smith, use

```
mysql> SELECT * FROM master_name WHERE firstname = 'John'
    -> AND lastname = 'Smith';
```

```
+---------+---------------------+---------------------+-----------+----------+
| name_id | name_dateadded      | name_datemodified   | firstname | lastname |
+---------+---------------------+---------------------+-----------+----------+
|       1 | 2001-10-29 13:11:00 | 2001-10-29 13:11:00 | John      | Smith    |
+---------+---------------------+---------------------+-----------+----------+
1 row in set (0.00 sec)
```

If you want to find records for people with the last name of Smith or Jones, use

```
mysql> SELECT * FROM master_name WHERE lastname = 'Smith' OR lastname = 'Jones';
+---------+---------------------+---------------------+-----------+----------+
| name_id | name_dateadded      | name_datemodified   | firstname | lastname |
+---------+---------------------+---------------------+-----------+----------+
|       1 | 2001-10-29 13:11:00 | 2001-10-29 13:11:00 | John      | Smith    |
|       2 | 2001-10-29 13:11:00 | 2001-10-29 13:11:00 | Jane      | Smith    |
|       3 | 2001-10-29 13:11:00 | 2001-10-29 13:11:00 | Jimbo     | Jones    |
|       4 | 2001-10-29 13:11:00 | 2001-10-29 13:11:00 | Andy      | Smith    |
|       7 | 2001-10-29 14:16:21 | 2001-10-29 14:16:21 | Chris     | Jones    |
|      43 | 0000-00-00 00:00:00 | 0000-00-00 00:00:00 | Albert    | Smith    |
+---------+---------------------+---------------------+-----------+----------+
6 rows in set (0.00 sec)
```

In order to keep your statements tidy—and in the case of complex queries this will help clarify your logic—surround the conditions within parentheses. The above queries could be re-written as

```
SELECT * FROM master_name WHERE ((firstname = 'John') AND (lastname = 'Smith'));
SELECT * FROM master_name WHERE ((lastname = 'Smith') OR (lastname = 'Jones'));
```

String Comparison Using LIKE

You were introduced to matching strings within a WHERE clause by using = or !=, but there's another useful operator for string comparisons: LIKE. This operator uses two characters as wildcards in pattern matching.

- %—Matches multiple characters
- _—Matches exactly one character

If you want to find records in the master_name table where the first name of the person starts with the letter "A", use

```
mysql> SELECT name_id, firstname, lastname FROM master_name
    -> WHERE firstname LIKE 'A%';
+---------+-----------+----------+
| name_id | firstname | lastname |
+---------+-----------+----------+
|      43 | Albert    | Smith    |
|       4 | Andy      | Smith    |
|      45 | Anna      | Bell     |
+---------+-----------+----------+
3 rows in set (0.00 sec)
```

If you wanted to find only people named "Anna" or "Anne", use

```
mysql> SELECT name_id, firstname, lastname FROM master_name
    -> WHERE firstname LIKE 'Ann_';
+---------+-----------+----------+
| name_id | firstname | lastname |
+---------+-----------+----------+
|      45 | Anna      | Bell     |
+---------+-----------+----------+
1 row in set (0.00 sec)
```

In this case, the _ wildcard is replacing just the "e" or "a". Anyone in your table named "Annabelle" would not be selected.

Summary

The SELECT SQL command is used to retrieve records from specific tables. The * character allows you to easily select all fields for all records in a table, but you can also specify particular column names. If the result set is too long, the LIMIT clause provides a simple method for extracting slices of results if you indicate a starting position and the number of records to return.

To order the results, use the ORDER BY clause to select the columns to sort. Sorts can be performed on integers, dates, and strings, in either ascending or descending order. The default order is ascending. Without specifying an order, results are displayed in the order they appear in the table.

Using built-in functions like COUNT(), MIN(), and MAX(), you can gather more information about the tables and records besides the data in them. COUNT() will return the count of a column, and MIN() and MAX() return the minimum and maximum values for a column.

You can pick and choose which records you want to return using WHERE clauses to test for the validity of conditions. Comparison or logical operators are used in WHERE clauses, and sometimes both types are used for compound statements. Another type of operator is LIKE, used for string comparisons.

Q&A

Q If strings in WHERE clauses are case insensitive, what is and isn't case insensitive?

A SQL commands and names of fields are case insensitive. The following statements return the same results:

```
SELECT * FROM master_name WHERE NAME_ID = 1;
select * from master_name where name_id = 1;
```

Table names and database names are case insensitive on Windows but are case sensitive on Linux/UNIX. On Linux/UNIX, the following query fails because the table name is master_name and not MASTER_NAME:

```
mysql> select * from MASTER_NAME;
ERROR 1146: Table 'contactDB.MASTER_NAME' doesn't exist
```

Workshop

The Workshop is designed to help you anticipate possible questions, review what you've learned, and begin learning how to put your knowledge into practice.

Quiz

1. What would be the LIMIT clauses for selecting the first 25 records of a table? Then the next 25?

2. How would you formulate a string comparison using LIKE to match first names of "John" or "Joseph"?

3. What would be the query to select all records in the master_name table that were added before October 30, 2001. Also, order the records from newest to oldest and exclude any with the default date.

Answers

1. LIMIT 0, 25 and LIMIT 26, 25

2. LIKE 'Jo%'

3. SELECT * FROM master_name WHERE ((name_dateadded < '2001-10-30') and (name_dateadded != '0000-00-00 00:00:00')) ORDER BY name_dateadded DESC;

Activity

Select all the records in the master_name and company tables. Using your knowledge of the INSERT statement, populate the name_company_map table with the correct values.

For example, if John Doe works at NASA, select from the master_name table and the company table to find the IDs you need:

```
mysql> SELECT name_id, firstname, lastname FROM master_name;
+---------+-----------+----------+
| name_id | firstname | lastname |
+---------+-----------+----------+
|       1 | John      | Smith    |
|       2 | Jane      | Smith    |
|       3 | Jimbo     | Jones    |
|       4 | Andy      | Smith    |
|       7 | Chris     | Jones    |
|      46 | Patrick   | O'Brien  |
|      45 | Anna      | Bell     |
|      44 | Jimmy     | Carr     |
|      43 | Albert    | Smith    |
|      42 | John      | Doe      |
+---------+-----------+----------+
10 rows in set (0.00 sec)
```

John Doe's name_id is 42.

```
mysql> select company_id, companyname from company;
+------------+-----------------+
| company_id | companyname     |
+------------+-----------------+
|          1 | Sun Microsystems |
|          2 | Joe's Steakhouse |
|          3 | Sams Publishing  |
|          4 | NASA            |
+------------+-----------------+
4 rows in set (0.00 sec)
```

Joe works at NASA, and that company_id is 4.

To create the relationship, add the following into the name_company_map table:

INSERT INTO name_company_map (name_id, company_id) VALUES (42,4);

HOUR 11

Advanced Usage of SELECT Statements

You can get all crazy with SELECT statements, using them with INSERT statements, aggregating data, and even pulling together multiple tables with one statement.

In this hour, you will learn

- How to use the GROUP BY clause
- How to use SELECT within INSERT statements
- How to select from multiple tables, using JOIN

Using the GROUP BY Clause

The GROUP BY clause is part of a SELECT statement, which essentially lumps together elements of your result set. The GROUP BY clause usually works together with the HAVING or ORDER BY clauses to produce more meaningful results in SELECT statements, but these additional clauses are not required when using GROUP BY.

For example, suppose you use MySQL to track accesses by registered users to particular areas of a Web site. For argument's sake, this table is called user_access, and it has columns called id, username, access_date, and accessed_area. Each time a registered user hits an area of the Web site that is tracked, their username, the date, and the section they're looking at are all stored in the user_access table. The sample data that follow show a few accesses over time:

```
mysql> SELECT * FROM user_access;
+----+----------+------------+--------------+
| id | username | access_date | accessed_area |
+----+----------+------------+--------------+
|  1 | jimbo    | 2001-12-24 | products     |
|  2 | jimbo    | 2001-12-24 | products     |
|  3 | john     | 2001-12-25 | contacts     |
|  4 | alice    | 2001-12-24 | store        |
|  5 | john     | 2002-01-10 | products     |
|  6 | alice    | 2002-01-10 | store        |
|  7 | alice    | 2002-01-10 | contacts     |
|  8 | john     | 2002-01-12 | store        |
|  9 | jimbo    | 2002-01-11 | products     |
| 10 | jimbo    | 2002-01-08 | contacts     |
| 11 | john     | 2002-01-02 | contacts     |
| 12 | jimbo    | 2002-01-12 | products     |
| 13 | jimbo    | 2002-01-13 | products     |
| 14 | jimbo    | 2002-01-14 | contacts     |
| 15 | alice    | 2002-01-14 | contacts     |
| 16 | jimbo    | 2002-01-03 | products     |
| 17 | jimbo    | 2002-01-11 | contacts     |
+----+----------+------------+--------------+
17 rows in set (0.00 sec)
```

Results of this type are perfect for a GROUP BY clause to help discern something meaningful from the numbers. Suppose you want to see which user is accessing a particular section most often. If you used ORDER BY in your SELECT statement, you could sort the rows by accessed_area and then by username, but that result won't really answer the question. Instead, you'd get a result like this:

```
mysql> SELECT * FROM user_access ORDER BY accessed_area, username;
+----+----------+------------+--------------+
| id | username | access_date | accessed_area |
+----+----------+------------+--------------+
|  7 | alice    | 2002-01-10 | contacts     |
| 15 | alice    | 2002-01-14 | contacts     |
| 10 | jimbo    | 2002-01-08 | contacts     |
| 14 | jimbo    | 2002-01-14 | contacts     |
| 17 | jimbo    | 2002-01-11 | contacts     |
|  3 | john     | 2001-12-25 | contacts     |
| 11 | john     | 2002-01-02 | contacts     |
|  1 | jimbo    | 2001-12-24 | products     |
```

```
|  2 | jimbo   | 2001-12-24 | products      |
|  9 | jimbo   | 2002-01-11 | products      |
| 12 | jimbo   | 2002-01-12 | products      |
| 13 | jimbo   | 2002-01-13 | products      |
| 16 | jimbo   | 2002-01-03 | products      |
|  5 | john    | 2002-01-10 | products      |
|  4 | alice   | 2001-12-24 | store         |
|  6 | alice   | 2002-01-10 | store         |
|  8 | john    | 2002-01-12 | store         |
+----+---------+------------+---------------+
17 rows in set (0.00 sec)
```

If you glance at the result set, you can see that alice and john both accessed the contacts area twice, and jimbo accessed the contacts area three times. But when you have more than 17 rows, eyeballing the results is not an option!

For starters, you use a GROUP BY clause to condense the result set, in this case from 17 to 7 rows:

```
mysql> SELECT username, accessed_area FROM user_access
    -> GROUP BY username, accessed_area;
+----------+---------------+
| username | accessed_area |
+----------+---------------+
| alice    | contacts      |
| alice    | store         |
| jimbo    | contacts      |
| jimbo    | products      |
| john     | contacts      |
| john     | products      |
| john     | store         |
+----------+---------------+
7 rows in set (0.00 sec)
```

Now, all the accesses for alice in the contacts section are grouped together, all of her accesses in the store section are grouped together, and so on for each user in each section. However, this is the bare minimum result of the GROUP BY clause—lumping together results. The question of "how many" still has not been answered.

So use a GROUP BY clause with a COUNT() function thrown in for good measure to answer the question at hand:

```
mysql> SELECT count(accessed_area) as access_count, username, accessed_area
    -> FROM user_access GROUP BY username, accessed_area
    -> ORDER BY access_count DESC;
+--------------+----------+---------------+
| access_count | username | accessed_area |
+--------------+----------+---------------+
|            6 | jimbo    | products      |
|            3 | jimbo    | contacts      |
```

11

```
|      2 | john     | contacts    |
|      2 | alice    | store       |
|      2 | alice    | contacts    |
|      1 | john     | products    |
|      1 | john     | store       |
+--------------+----------+---------------+
7 rows in set (0.00 sec)
```

The answer is now clear: jimbo accessed the products area six times, more than any other user accessed any other section.

When using a GROUP BY clause, the HAVING clause comes into play in any instance where you would use a WHERE clause. WHERE clauses are not allowed when using GROUP BY, so HAVING takes its place. For example, if you took the SQL statement above and wanted to modify it to show only jimbo's accesses, using WHERE would produce an error:

```
mysql> SELECT count(accessed_area) as access_count, username, accessed_area FROM
    -> user_access GROUP BY username, accessed_area  WHERE username = 'jimbo';
ERROR 1064: You have an error in your SQL syntax near 'WHERE username = 'jimbo''
at line 1
```

Replacing the WHERE clause with the HAVING clause that follows produces the results you're looking for:

```
mysql> SELECT count(accessed_area) as access_count, username, accessed_area FROM
    -> user_access GROUP BY username, accessed_area  HAVING username = 'jimbo';
+--------------+----------+---------------+
| access_count | username | accessed_area |
+--------------+----------+---------------+
|            3 | jimbo    | contacts      |
|            6 | jimbo    | products      |
+--------------+----------+---------------+
2 rows in set (0.00 sec)
```

Using SELECT Within INSERT Statements

You can use a SELECT statement as part of an INSERT statement to essentially copy the contents of one table into another table with the same structure. When a SELECT statement takes the place of a list of values in an INSERT statement, you can also use a WHERE clause to pick and choose which records to copy.

The syntax of this structure, commonly referred to as an INSERT ... SELECT statement, is

```
INSERT INTO table_name (columns) SELECT_STATEMENT
```

Suppose you have a table in your contact management system called old_master_name, which has exactly the same structure as the master_name table. If you want to copy all the records from master_name directly into old_master_name, you would use the following statement:

```
mysql> INSERT INTO old_master_name (name_id, name_dateadded, name_datemodified,
    -> firstname, lastname) SELECT * FROM master_name;
Query OK, 10 rows affected (0.03 sec)
Records: 10  Duplicates: 0  Warnings: 0
```

> When you use INSERT with SELECT, you will see another status message from
> MySQL after the "Query OK" line. This message provides additional informa-
> tion about the import of data, which is essentially what INSERT with SELECT
> is doing.

If you are using all the columns from the table specified in the SELECT statement, you do
not have to specify the column names in the INSERT portion of the statement. For example, this statement works just as well:

```
mysql> INSERT INTO old_master_name SELECT * FROM master_name;
Query OK, 10 rows affected (0.00 sec)
Records: 10  Duplicates: 0  Warnings: 0
```

However, if you are simply inserting one column per record from master_name into
old_master_name and don't indicate the column in the INSERT portion of the statement,
you'll get an error:

```
mysql> INSERT INTO old_master_name SELECT name_id from master_name;
ERROR 1136: Column count doesn't match value count at row 1
```

You can use any sort of SELECT statement in order to retrieve just the columns and
records you wish to INSERT into the new table. For example, you can use a WHERE clause
to determine all the records that were modified before a particular date and only insert
those into the new table:

```
mysql> INSERT INTO old_master_name SELECT * FROM master_name
    -> WHERE name_datemodified < '2001-11-01';
Query OK, 5 rows affected (0.00 sec)
Records: 5  Duplicates: 0  Warnings: 0
```

Using SELECT within INSERT statements is a quick way to copy records from one table to
another. Just remember that the table(s) named in the SELECT statement must be different
than the table named in the INSERT statement.

Selecting from Multiple Tables

You're not limited to selecting only from one table at a time. That would certainly make
application programming a long and tedious task! When you select from more than one
table in one SELECT statement, you are said to be joining the tables together.

Suppose you have two tables, `fruit` and `color`. You can select all rows from each of the two tables, using two separate SELECT statements:

```
mysql> SELECT * FROM fruit;
+----+-----------+
| id | fruitname |
+----+-----------+
|  1 | apple     |
|  2 | orange    |
|  3 | grape     |
|  4 | banana    |
+----+-----------+
4 rows in set (0.00 sec)

mysql> SELECT * FROM color;
+----+-----------+
| id | colorname |
+----+-----------+
|  1 | red       |
|  2 | orange    |
|  3 | purple    |
|  4 | yellow    |
+----+-----------+
4 rows in set (0.00 sec)
```

When you want to select from both tables at once, there are a few differences in the syntax of the SELECT statement. First, you must ensure that all the tables you're using in your query appear in the FROM clause of the SELECT statement. Using the `fruit` and `color` example, if you simply want to select all columns and rows from both tables, you might think you would use the following SELECT statement:

```
mysql> SELECT * FROM fruit, color;
+----+-----------+----+-----------+
| id | fruitname | id | colorname |
+----+-----------+----+-----------+
|  1 | apple     |  1 | red       |
|  2 | orange    |  1 | red       |
|  3 | grape     |  1 | red       |
|  4 | banana    |  1 | red       |
|  1 | apple     |  2 | orange    |
|  2 | orange    |  2 | orange    |
|  3 | grape     |  2 | orange    |
|  4 | banana    |  2 | orange    |
|  1 | apple     |  3 | purple    |
|  2 | orange    |  3 | purple    |
|  3 | grape     |  3 | purple    |
|  4 | banana    |  3 | purple    |
|  1 | apple     |  4 | yellow    |
|  2 | orange    |  4 | yellow    |
```

```
|  3 | grape    |  4 | yellow    |
|  4 | banana   |  4 | yellow    |
+----+----------+----+-----------+
16 rows in set (0.00 sec)
```

Sixteen rows of repeated information is probably not what you were going for! What this query did is literally join a row in the color table to each row in the fruit table. Since there are four records in the fruit table and four entries in the color table, that's 16 records returned to you.

When you select from multiple tables, you must build proper WHERE clauses to ensure you really get what you want. In the case of the fruit and color tables, what you really want is to see the fruitname and colorname records from these two tables where the IDs of each match up. This brings us to the next nuance of the query—how to indicate exactly which field you want when the fields are named the same in both tables!

Simply, you append the table name to the field name, like this:

```
tablename.fieldname
```

So the query for selecting fruitname and colorname from both tables where the IDs match would be:

```
mysql> SELECT fruitname, colorname FROM fruit, color WHERE fruit.id = color.id;
+-----------+-----------+
| fruitname | colorname |
+-----------+-----------+
| apple     | red       |
| orange    | orange    |
| grape     | purple    |
| banana    | yellow    |
+-----------+-----------+
4 rows in set (0.00 sec)
```

This was a basic example of joining two tables together for use in a single SELECT query. The JOIN keyword is an actual part of SQL, which allows you to build more complex queries.

Using JOIN

There are several types of JOINs that can be used in MySQL, all of which refer to the order in which the tables are put together and the results are displayed. The type of JOIN used with the fruit and color tables is called an INNER JOIN, although it wasn't written explicitly as such. To rewrite the SQL statement using the proper INNER JOIN syntax, you would use

```
mysql> SELECT fruitname, colorname FROM fruit INNER JOIN color
    -> ON fruit.id = color.id;
+-----------+-----------+
| fruitname | colorname |
+-----------+-----------+
| apple     | red       |
| orange    | orange    |
| grape     | purple    |
| banana    | yellow    |
+-----------+-----------+
4 rows in set (0.00 sec)
```

The ON clause replaced the WHERE clause, in this instance telling MySQL to join together the rows in the tables where the IDs match each other. When joining tables using ON clauses, you may use any conditions that you would use in a WHERE clause, including all the various logical and arithmetic operators.

Another common type of JOIN is the LEFT JOIN. When joining two tables with LEFT JOIN, all rows from the first table will be returned, no matter if there are matches in the second table or not. A great example of this is selecting all names and e-mail addresses from the master_name and email tables in contactDB when not every entry in master_name has a corresponding e-mail address, as shown in the following example:

```
mysql> SELECT name_id, firstname, lastname FROM master_name;
+---------+-----------+----------+
| name_id | firstname | lastname |
+---------+-----------+----------+
|       1 | John      | Smith    |
|       2 | Jane      | Smith    |
|       3 | Jimbo     | Jones    |
|       4 | Andy      | Smith    |
|       7 | Chris     | Jones    |
|      45 | Anna      | Bell     |
|      44 | Jimmy     | Carr     |
|      43 | Albert    | Smith    |
|      42 | John      | Doe      |
+---------+-----------+----------+
9 rows in set (0.00 sec)

mysql> SELECT name_id, email FROM email;
+---------+------------------+
| name_id | email            |
+---------+------------------+
|      42 | jdoe@yahoo.com   |
|      45 | annabell@aol.com |
+---------+------------------+
2 rows in set (0.00 sec)
```

Using LEFT JOIN on these two tables, you can see that if a value from the email table doesn't exist, NULL will appear in place of an e-mail address:

```
mysql> SELECT firstname, lastname, email FROM master_name LEFT JOIN email
    -> ON master_name.name_id = email.name_id;
+-----------+----------+-------------------+
| firstname | lastname | email             |
+-----------+----------+-------------------+
| John      | Smith    | NULL              |
| Jane      | Smith    | NULL              |
| Jimbo     | Jones    | NULL              |
| Andy      | Smith    | NULL              |
| Chris     | Jones    | NULL              |
| Anna      | Bell     | annabell@aol.com  |
| Jimmy     | Carr     | NULL              |
| Albert    | Smith    | NULL              |
| John      | Doe      | jdoe@yahoo.com    |
+-----------+----------+-------------------+
9 rows in set (0.01 sec)
```

A RIGHT JOIN works like LEFT JOIN but with the table order reversed. In other words, when using a RIGHT JOIN, all rows from the second table will be returned, no matter whether there are matches in the first table or not. However, in the case of the master_name and email tables, there are only two rows in the email table, whereas there are nine rows in the master_name table. This means that only two of the nine rows will be returned:

```
mysql> SELECT firstname, lastname, email FROM master_name RIGHT JOIN email
    -> ON master_name.name_id = email.name_id;
+-----------+----------+-------------------+
| firstname | lastname | email             |
+-----------+----------+-------------------+
| John      | Doe      | jdoe@yahoo.com    |
| Anna      | Bell     | annabell@aol.com  |
+-----------+----------+-------------------+
2 rows in set (0.00 sec)
```

There are several different types of JOINs available in MySQL, and you've learned about the most common types. To learn more about JOINs such as CROSS JOIN, STRAIGHT JOIN, and NATURAL JOIN, please visit the MySQL Manual at http://www.mysql.com/doc/J/O/JOIN.html.

Summary

Using the GROUP BY clause within your SELECT statements will help you to produce more meaningful results than simply using ORDER BY to put results in an ascending or descending order. Instead, the GROUP BY clause puts matching sets of records together without repeating unnecessary information. The use of the GROUP BY clause requires that you think through your result sets and just what it is that you want to find out from your tables. Additional clauses, such as ORDER BY and HAVING, will help pinpoint the exact information you need.

11

Using a SELECT query within an INSERT statement is an advanced use of the SELECT statement and a very handy one at that. In this manner, you can quickly copy records from one table to a secondary table of the same structure, using a WHERE clause in the SELECT query to extract just the records you want to insert rather than all of them at once.

Selecting records from multiple tables within one statement is as advanced as it gets, as these types of statements—called JOIN—require forethought and planning in order to produce correct results. Common types of JOIN are INNER JOIN, LEFT JOIN, and RIGHT JOIN, although MySQL supports many different kinds of JOIN.

Workshop

The Workshop is designed to help you anticipate possible questions, review what you've learned, and begin learning how to put your knowledge into practice.

Quiz

1. Provide the SQL statement to insert all records from table2 into a table called table1. Assume these tables have exactly the same structure.

2. How would you explicitly refer to a field called id in a table called table1?

3. Write a SQL statement that joins two tables, orders and items_ordered, with a primary key in each of order_id. From the orders table, select the following fields: order_name and order_date. From the items_ordered table, select the item_description field.

Answers

1. INSERT INTO table1 SELECT * FROM table2

2. Use table1.id instead of id in your query.

3. SELECT order_name, order_date, item_description FROM orders LEFT JOIN items_ordered ON orders.order_id = items_ordered.id

Activity

Using the relational tables in contactDB, practice using LEFT JOIN and RIGHT JOIN to produce results. The master_name table should be the primary table, and the secondary tables, such as email, address and telephone, should be the ones in the JOIN clause.

Hour **12**

Modifying and Deleting Data

The time will come when you'll want to modify items in your tables, and there are several ways of doing this with MySQL. You can replace entire rows, or you can just update particular fields. Also, you'll eventually want (or need) to delete records from your database tables—there's no rule that says you have to keep all records until the end of time!

In this hour, you will learn

- How to use the UPDATE and REPLACE commands to modify existing records
- How to use the DELETE command
- How to conditionally delete records

Using the **UPDATE** Command to Modify Records

UPDATE is the SQL command used to modify the contents of one or more columns in an existing record. The most basic UPDATE syntax looks like this:

```
UPDATE table_name
SET column1='new value',
column2='new value2'
[WHERE some_condition_is_true]
```

The guidelines for updating a record are similar to those used when inserting a record—the data you're entering must be appropriate to the datatype of the field, and you must enclose your strings in single- or double-quotes, escaping where necessary.

For example. assume you have a table called fruit containing an ID, a fruit name, and the status of the fruit (ripe or rotten):

```
mysql> SELECT * FROM fruit;
+----+------------+--------+
| id | fruit_name | status |
+----+------------+--------+
|  1 | apple      | ripe   |
|  2 | pear       | rotten |
|  3 | banana     | ripe   |
|  4 | grape      | rotten |
+----+------------+--------+
4 rows in set (0.00 sec)
```

To update the status of the fruit to ripe, use

```
mysql> UPDATE fruit SET status = 'ripe';
Query OK, 2 rows affected (0.00 sec)
Rows matched: 4  Changed: 2  Warnings: 0
```

Take a look at the result of the query. It was successful, as you can tell from the Query OK message. Also note that only two rows were affected—if you try to set the value of a column to the value it already is, the update won't occur for that column.

The second line of the response shows that four rows were matched and only two were changed. If you're wondering "matched what?" the answer is simple—since you did not specify a particular condition for matching, the match would be on all rows.

You must be very careful and use a condition when updating a table, unless you really intend to change all the columns for all records to the same value. For the sake of argument, assume that "grape" is spelled incorrectly in the table and you want to use UPDATE to correct this mistake. This query would have horrible results:

```
mysql> UPDATE fruit SET fruit_name = 'grape';
Query OK, 4 rows affected (0.00 sec)
Rows matched: 4  Changed: 4  Warnings: 0
```

When you read the result, you should be filled with dread: four of four records were changed, meaning your fruit table now looks like this:

```
mysql> SELECT * FROM fruit;
+----+------------+--------+
| id | fruit_name | status |
+----+------------+--------+
|  1 | grape      | ripe   |
|  2 | grape      | ripe   |
|  3 | grape      | ripe   |
|  4 | grape      | ripe   |
+----+------------+--------+
4 rows in set (0.00 sec)
```

All of your fruit records are now grapes. Through attempting to correct the spelling of one field, all fields were changed because no condition was specified! When doling out UPDATE privileges to your users, think about the responsibility you're giving to someone—one wrong move and your entire table could be grapes.

Conditional UPDATE

Making a conditional UPDATE means that you are using WHERE clauses to match specific records. Using WHERE clauses in an UPDATE statement is just like using WHERE clauses in a SELECT statement. All of the same comparison and logical operators can be used, such as equal to, greater than, OR, AND—the whole nine yards. Using WHERE in your UPDATE statements will greatly reduce errors!

Assume your fruit table has not been completely filled with grapes but instead contains four records, one with a spelling mistake ("grappe" instead of "grape"). The UPDATE statement to fix the spelling mistake would be

```
mysql> UPDATE fruit SET fruit_name = 'grape' WHERE fruit_name = 'grappe';
Query OK, 1 row affected (0.00 sec)
Rows matched: 1  Changed: 1  Warnings: 0
```

In this case, only one row was matched and one row was changed. Your fruit table should be intact, and all fruit names should be spelled properly:

```
mysql> SELECT * FROM fruit;
+----+------------+--------+
| id | fruit_name | status |
+----+------------+--------+
|  1 | apple      | ripe   |
|  2 | pear       | ripe   |
|  3 | banana     | ripe   |
|  4 | grape      | ripe   |
+----+------------+--------+
4 rows in set (0.00 sec)
```

12

Using Existing Column Values with UPDATE

Another feature of UPDATE is the ability to use the current value in the record as the base value. For example, assume that you have an inventory table as part of a shopping application:

```
mysql> SELECT * FROM inventory;
+----+-------------------------+----------+
| id | item_name               | in_stock |
+----+-------------------------+----------+
|  1 | Fuzzy Hat               |       10 |
|  2 | Warm Slippers           |      100 |
|  3 | Cowboy & Indian Pajamas |        4 |
+----+-------------------------+----------+
3 rows in set (0.00 sec)
```

When someone purchases a Fuzzy Hat, the inventory table should be updated accordingly. However, you won't know exactly what number to enter in the in_stock column, just that you sold one. In this case, use the current value of the column and subtract one:

```
mysql> UPDATE inventory SET in_stock = in_stock - 1 WHERE id = 1;
Query OK, 1 row affected (0.01 sec)
Rows matched: 1  Changed: 1  Warnings: 0
```

This should give you a new value of 9 in the in_stock column, and indeed it does:

```
mysql> SELECT * FROM inventory;
+----+-------------------------+----------+
| id | item_name               | in_stock |
+----+-------------------------+----------+
|  1 | Fuzzy Hat               |        9 |
|  2 | Warm Slippers           |      100 |
|  3 | Cowboy & Indian Pajamas |        4 |
+----+-------------------------+----------+
3 rows in set (0.00 sec)
```

Using Functions in UPDATE Statements

Another shortcut for updating data is to use functions. The NOW() function, which you learned to use during INSERT, works equally as well during UPDATE.

In your contact management system tables, your records may contain many default values if you imported data from outside sources. A prime example of this is the presence of the 0000-00-00 00:00:00 default date in the *_dateadded and *_datemodified fields throughout your tables.

You can use an UPDATE statement with NOW( ) to bring all the entries up to speed:

```
mysql> UPDATE master_name SET
    -> name_dateadded = NOW(),
    -> name_datemodified = NOW()
    -> WHERE
    -> ((name_dateadded = '0000-00-00 00:00:00')
    -> AND (name_datemodified = '0000-00-00 00:00:00'));
Query OK, 4 rows affected (0.01 sec)
Rows matched: 4  Changed: 4  Warnings: 0
```

In this case, four records were updated, and now all of the records in master_name have real values in the date fields:

```
mysql> select * from master_name;
+---------+---------------------+---------------------+-----------+----------+
| name_id | name_dateadded      | name_datemodified   | firstname | lastname |
+---------+---------------------+---------------------+-----------+----------+
|       1 | 2001-10-29 13:11:00 | 2001-10-29 13:11:00 | John      | Smith    |
|       2 | 2001-10-29 13:11:00 | 2001-10-29 13:11:00 | Jane      | Smith    |
|       3 | 2001-10-29 13:11:00 | 2001-10-29 13:11:00 | Jimbo     | Jones    |
|       4 | 2001-10-29 13:11:00 | 2001-10-29 13:11:00 | Andy      | Smith    |
|       7 | 2001-10-29 14:16:21 | 2001-10-29 14:16:21 | Chris     | Jones    |
|      45 | 2001-11-05 10:12:02 | 2001-11-05 10:12:02 | Anna      | Bell     |
|      44 | 2001-11-05 10:12:02 | 2001-11-05 10:12:02 | Jimmy     | Carr     |
|      43 | 2001-11-05 10:12:02 | 2001-11-05 10:12:02 | Albert    | Smith    |
|      42 | 2001-11-05 10:12:02 | 2001-11-05 10:12:02 | John      | Doe      |
+---------+---------------------+---------------------+-----------+----------+
9 rows in set (0.01 sec)
```

Using the REPLACE Command

12

Another method for modifying records is to use the REPLACE command, which is remarkably similar to the INSERT command.

```
REPLACE INTO table_name (column list) VALUES (column values);
```

The REPLACE statement works like this: if the record you are inserting into the table contains a primary key value that matches a record already in the table, the record in the table will be deleted and the new record inserted in its place.

> The REPLACE command is a MySQL-specific extension to ANSI SQL. This command mimics the action of a DELETE and re-INSERT of a particular record. In other words, you get two commands for the price of one.

Using the company table as an example, first take a look at the records (your values may differ):

```
mysql> SELECT * FROM company;
+------------+---------------------+---------------------+------------------+
| company_id | company_dateadded   | company_datemodified | companyname      |
+------------+---------------------+---------------------+------------------+
|          1 | 2001-11-05 08:33:00 | 2001-11-05 08:33:00 | Sun Microsystems |
|          2 | 2001-11-05 08:33:21 | 2001-11-05 08:33:21 | Joe's Steakhouse |
|          3 | 2001-11-05 08:33:33 | 2001-11-05 08:33:33 | Sams Publishing  |
|          4 | 2001-11-05 08:33:37 | 2001-11-05 08:33:37 | NASA             |
+------------+---------------------+---------------------+------------------+
4 rows in set (0.00 sec)
```

The following command will replace the entry for Joe's Steakhouse:

```
mysql> REPLACE INTO company VALUES (2,NOW(),NOW(), 'Joe\'s Steak House');
Query OK, 2 rows affected (0.00 sec)
```

In the query result, notice that the result states two rows are affected. In this case, since company_id is a primary key that had a matching value in the company table, the original row was deleted and the new row inserted—two rows affected.

Select the records to verify that the entry is correct, which it is:

```
mysql> SELECT * FROM company;
+------------+---------------------+---------------------+------------------+
| company_id | company_dateadded   | company_datemodified | companyname      |
+------------+---------------------+---------------------+------------------+
|          1 | 2001-11-05 08:33:00 | 2001-11-05 08:33:00 | Sun Microsystems |
|          2 | 2001-11-05 10:32:06 | 2001-11-05 10:32:06 | Joe's Steak House |
|          3 | 2001-11-05 08:33:33 | 2001-11-05 08:33:33 | Sams Publishing  |
|          4 | 2001-11-05 08:33:37 | 2001-11-05 08:33:37 | NASA             |
+------------+---------------------+---------------------+------------------+
4 rows in set (0.00 sec)
```

> The REPLACE command used to change the name of the company to Joe's Steak House could also have been written as the following UPDATE command:
>
> ```
> UPDATE company SET
> companyname = 'Joe\'s Steak House',
> company_datemodified = NOW()
> WHERE company_id = 2;
> ```

If you use a REPLACE statement and the value of the primary key in the new record does not match a value for a primary key already in the table, the record would simply be inserted, and only one row would be affected.

Using the DELETE Command

Before learning about the DELETE command, here's a reminder—always back up your data! Once you delete data from a table, it's gone for good. As you learned in Hour 4, "Using the MySQL Client," a good way to back up your data is to use the mysqldump utility to produce an external file.

> If you are using a transactions-aware version of MySQL, you can roll back a DELETE statement and in that case you do have a method for fixing an errant DELETE command. You will learn more about transactions in Hour 18, "Transactions Overview."

The basic DELETE syntax is

```
DELETE FROM table_name
[WHERE some_condition_is_true]
[LIMIT rows]
```

Notice there is no column specification in the delete command—when you use DELETE, the entire record is removed. You may recall the fiasco in the previous hour, when updating a table without specifying a condition caused all records to be updated; you must be similarly careful when using DELETE.

> Be very wary of who you assign DELETE privileges to—not everyone on your database administration team should have the ability to wipe out all records.

12

Assuming the structure and data in a table called fruit:

```
mysql> SELECT * FROM fruit;
+----+------------+--------+
| id | fruit_name | status |
+----+------------+--------+
|  1 | apple      | ripe   |
|  2 | pear       | rotten |
|  3 | banana     | ripe   |
|  4 | grape      | rotten |
+----+------------+--------+
4 rows in set (0.00 sec)
```

This statement will remove all records in the table:

```
mysql> DELETE FROM fruit;
Query OK, 0 rows affected (0.00 sec)
```

Don't be concerned that the query result states "0 rows affected"—this is the expected result in MySQL 3.23, when a WHERE or LIMIT clause is not specified. You can always verify the deletion by attempting to SELECT data from the table:

```
mysql> SELECT * FROM fruit;
Empty set (0.00 sec)
```

Optimizing DELETE Queries

If your table is very large, you can speed up the query a few different ways. The first method is to add a LIMIT clause to your DELETE command:

```
DELETE FROM table_name
[LIMIT rows]
```

In a sample table called test_table, 2945 records exist that all look like this:

```
+----+-----------------------+
| id | test_text             |
+----+-----------------------+
|  1 | This is a test string. |
|  2 | This is a test string. |
|  3 | This is a test string. |
|  4 | This is a test string. |
|  5 | This is a test string. |
+----+-----------------------+
```

To delete only 1000 records, use

```
mysql> DELETE FROM test_table LIMIT 1000;
Query OK, 1000 rows affected (0.04 sec)
```

The query result says that 1000 rows were affected, which means that 1000 rows were deleted. You can verify this by counting the rows again:

```
mysql> SELECT COUNT(id) from test_table;
+-----------+
| COUNT(id) |
+-----------+
|      1945 |
+-----------+
1 row in set (0.00 sec)
```

Success! You should see that 1000 rows were deleted. A LIMIT clause helps optimize DELETE because you are slicing off large chunks of information at one time instead of issuing a command that may take some time to execute in the case of a large table. You can simply repeat the statement using the LIMIT clause until all rows are deleted.

Another optimized method for deleting all records in a table is the TRUNCATE command:

```
TRUNCATE TABLE table_name
```

Instead of removing records from a table, TRUNCATE drops the entire table and then recreates it without any records. This example uses the sample table (test_table) with 2945 records to show the speed of the TRUNCATE command:

```
mysql> TRUNCATE TABLE test_table;
Query OK, 0 rows affected (0.01 sec)
```

MySQL took all of one hundredth of a second to drop a table and recreate it without records.

Conditional DELETE

A conditional DELETE statement, just like a conditional SELECT or UPDATE statement, means you are using WHERE clauses to match specific records. You have the full range of comparison and logical operators available to you, so you can pick and choose which records you want to delete.

A prime example would be to remove all records for rotten fruit from the fruit table:

```
mysql> DELETE FROM fruit WHERE status = 'rotten';
Query OK, 2 rows affected (0.00 sec)
```

Two records were deleted, and only ripe fruit remains:

```
mysql> SELECT * FROM fruit;
+----+------------+--------+
| id | fruit_name | status |
+----+------------+--------+
|  1 | apple      | ripe   |
|  3 | banana     | ripe   |
+----+------------+--------+
2 rows in set (0.00 sec)
```

For users of MySQL 4.0 (or later), you can also use ORDER BY clauses in your DELETE statements. Take a look at the basic DELETE syntax with the ORDER BY clause added to its structure:

```
DELETE FROM table_name
[WHERE some_condition_is_true]
[ORDER BY some_column [ASC | DESC]]
[LIMIT rows]
```

At first glance, you may wonder, "Why does it matter in what order I delete records?" The ORDER BY clause isn't for the deletion order, it's for the sorting order of records.

12

In this example, a table called `access_log` shows access time and username:

```
mysql> SELECT * FROM access_log;
+----+---------------------+----------+
| id | date_accessed       | username |
+----+---------------------+----------+
|  1 | 2001-11-06 06:09:13 | johndoe  |
|  2 | 2001-11-06 06:09:22 | janedoe  |
|  3 | 2001-11-06 06:09:39 | jsmith   |
|  4 | 2001-11-06 06:09:44 | mikew    |
+----+---------------------+----------+
4 rows in set (0.00 sec)
```

To remove the oldest record, first use ORDER BY to sort the results appropriately, and then use LIMIT to remove just one record:

```
mysql> DELETE FROM access_log ORDER BY date_accessed DESC LIMIT 1;
Query OK, 1 row affected (0.01 sec)
```

Select the record from `access_log` and verify that only three records exist:

```
mysql> SELECT * FROM access_log;
+----+---------------------+----------+
| id | date_accessed       | username |
+----+---------------------+----------+
|  2 | 2001-11-06 06:09:22 | janedoe  |
|  3 | 2001-11-06 06:09:39 | jsmith   |
|  4 | 2001-11-06 06:09:44 | mikew    |
+----+---------------------+----------+
3 rows in set (0.00 sec)
```

Summary

The UPDATE and REPLACE commands are used to modify existing data in your MySQL tables. UPDATE is good for changing values in specific columns or for changing values in multiple records based on specific conditions. REPLACE is a variation of INSERT that deletes and then re-inserts a record with a matching primary key.

Be very careful when using UPDATE to change values in a column because failure to add a condition will result in the given column being updated throughout all records in the table. Not a good result if all you were trying to do was fix a spelling mistake or decrement inventory amounts!

When you're ready to delete a large portion of records from a table, be sure to backup your data using a utility, such as mysqldump. The DELETE command is a simple one—it simply removes whole records from tables. This also makes it very dangerous, so be sure you only give DELETE privileges to users who can handle the responsibility.

You can specify conditions when using DELETE so that records are removed only if a particular expression in a WHERE clause is true. Also, you can delete smaller portions of the records in your table using a LIMIT clause. If you have an exceptionally large table, deleting portions is less resource-intensive than deleting each record in a huge table.

Workshop

The Workshop is designed to help you anticipate possible questions, review what you've learned, and begin learning how to put your knowledge into practice.

Quiz

1. Given the following table named inventory, how would you reflect an influx of 15 Cowboy & Indian Pajamas?

```
+----+-------------------------+----------+
| id | item_name               | in_stock |
+----+-------------------------+----------+
|  1 | Fuzzy Hat               |       10 |
|  2 | Warm Slippers           |      100 |
|  3 | Ski Pants               |        7 |
|  4 | Ski Jacket              |        5 |
|  5 | Cowboy & Indian Pajamas |        4 |
+----+-------------------------+----------+
```

2. Given a table called prices containing the structure and data below, what would be the DELETE command to remove all records where the price of an item is less than 50.00 dollars?

```
+----+-------------------------+------------+
| id | item_name               | item_price |
+----+-------------------------+------------+
|  1 | Fuzzy Hat               |       9.99 |
|  2 | Warm Slippers           |      19.99 |
|  3 | Ski Pants               |      69.99 |
|  4 | Ski Jacket              |      59.99 |
|  5 | Cowboy & Indian Pajamas |      29.99 |
+----+-------------------------+------------+
```

3. Using the same table structure as in Question 2, what would be the REPLACE statement used to change the name of the Warm Slippers to "Pair of Warm Slippers" and the price to $100?

Answers

1. UPDATE inventory SET in_stock = in_stock + 15 WHERE id = 5;

2. DELETE FROM prices WHERE item_price < 50;

3. REPLACE INTO inventory VALUES ('2', 'Pair of Warm Slippers', 100);

Activity

Using the UPDATE command, place the relevant name_id value in all records in job_function, address, telephone, fax, email, and personal_notes tables in the contactDB database. This is the final step to tying all your tables together in a normalized fashion.

Hour 13

More About DELETE

Deleting records from a table is one thing, but removing the whole kit and kaboodle is another! The same rule applies in this hour—backup all your data—before removing entire tables and databases.

In this hour, you will learn

- How to remove related records from multiple tables successfully by using DELETE
- Two methods for listing tables and databases
- How to DROP tables and databases

Deleting Related Records

If you are coming to MySQL from the world of Oracle or any other database system with foreign key constraints, you may know about "cascading dele-tion" of records. Basically, when you have multiple tables containing records that are related to each other using a foreign key, if you delete the master record, all of its little related records are deleted as well. This method ensures that you won't have straggly records filled with unrelated data floating around.

However, MySQL does not currently support such a thing, so you must build that type of logic into your application using multiple DELETE statements. In fact, this set of DELETE statements is a prime candidate for a transaction!

> If you cannot use a transaction in this instance due to limitations of your installation, you can still perform multiple DELETE statements within a logical order to achieve the same goal of deleting related records.

In Hour 19, "Practical Transaction Usage," three tables in contactDB will be modified to become transaction-safe tables: master_name, email, and telephone. This is done so that a transaction can be created to add records to all required tables; an entry in the database will only be considered "complete" if it contains records in master_name, email, and telephone. If an entry is only complete if it contains those three parts, when one of the parts is deleted, the remaining parts must be deleted as well. This is where the transaction comes in, as shown below. You may want to come back to this section later, with a full understanding of transactions.

Just as the order of insertion is important, the order of deletion is important. When first adding the records, you add the master record and then the related records in other tables. When deleting related records, you'll want to tackle deleting the related records first and then the master record at the end. This way, the worst-case scenario if not using a transaction is a master record without additional related records (one straggly item) rather than several straggly records without a master.

The listing that follows is an approximation of the steps you might take, within a transaction, to delete a set of related records. The lines that are commented out (preceded with //) would be replaced by actual application programming in the language of your choice.

```
BEGIN WORK;
SELECT name_id FROM master_name WHERE (your criteria here);

// If failure occurs:
    // display error to user and exit

// If successful:
    DELETE FROM telephone WHERE name_id = (the id);

        // If failure occurs:
            // ROLLBACK the transaction
            // display error to user and exit

        // If successful:
            DELETE FROM email WHERE name_id = (the id);
```

```
// If failure occurs:
    // ROLLBACK the transaction
    // display error to user and exit

// If successful:
    DELETE FROM master_name WHERE name_id = (the id);

    //If failure occurs:
        // ROLLBACK the transaction
        // display error to user and exit

    // If successful:
        COMMIT;
        // display success message to user
```

Listing Tables and Databases Before Deleting Them

Before you start removing large structures like tables and databases, there are a few commands you can use to see the actual names of these things. You may know that your own tables are named inventory, fruit, or whatever they may be, but if you just inherited a database and your boss says, "get rid of that table we use for customer comments," you need to know where to start looking. You can start looking by listing the names of the structures.

Using command-line tools, there are several different ways you can list the names of structures. Some are easier than others: one within the MySQL monitor and one using a MySQL utility script called mysqlshow that's part of the installation.

Using mysqlshow

The mysqlshow utility, like other MySQL command-line utilities you've used, requires a username, and password in order to make a connection and issue commands. In the example below, substitute your own information for username, and password.

If a database is not specified when using mysqlshow, all databases on the server will be listed.

```
#prompt:> mysqlshow -u supercontact -psomepass
+------------------+
|    Databases     |
+------------------+
| contactDB        |
| mysql            |
| test_database    |
+------------------+
```

13

If a database name is specified, all tables in the database will be listed if the user has permissions for them.

```
#prompt:> mysqlshow   -u supercontact -psomepass contactDB
Database: contactDB
+------------------+
|      Tables      |
+------------------+
| address          |
| company          |
| email            |
| fax              |
| job_function     |
| master_name      |
| name_company_map |
| personal_notes   |
| telephone        |
| test_table       |
+------------------+
```

Using the SHOW Command

If you do not have access to the mysqlshow utility, or just prefer to issue commands through the MySQL monitor, you can achieve the same results using the SHOW TABLES and SHOW DATABASES commands.

SHOW TABLES lists all the tables within the database currently in use for which the user has permissions:

```
mysql> SHOW TABLES;
+---------------------+
| Tables_in_contactDB |
+---------------------+
| address             |
| company             |
| email               |
| fax                 |
| job_function        |
| master_name         |
| name_company_map    |
| personal_notes      |
| telephone           |
| test_table          |
+---------------------+
10 rows in set (0.00 sec)
```

SHOW DATABASES lists all the databases on the server:

```
mysql> SHOW DATABASES;
+------------------+
| Database         |
+------------------+
| contactDB        |
| mysql            |
| test_database    |
+------------------+
3 rows in set (0.00 sec)
```

Knowing the names of the structures you're working with will greatly reduce the errors caused by random name-guessing when dropping tables and databases!

Using the DROP Command

Remember the difference between DELETE and DROP—although DELETE and DROP are both used to remove items, DELETE is used for records and DROP is for structures.

Take a moment to back up your data and table structures before going off and deleting things. Just like removing records, once a table or database is dropped, it's gone.

DROP TABLE

The DROP TABLE syntax is very simple:

```
DROP TABLE [IF EXISTS] table_name
```

The IF EXISTS clause checks to see whether the named table exists before deleting it. You can use IF EXISTS to limit error messages. For example, these next two commands attempt to drop a table called inventory, which does not exist:

```
mysql> DROP TABLE inventory;
ERROR 1051: Unknown table 'inventory'
mysql> DROP TABLE IF EXISTS inventory;
Query OK, 0 rows affected (0.00 sec)
```

An error occurred when using the first command because the inventory table doesn't exist. Although the table still doesn't exist when the second command is issued, no error occurs because the IF EXISTS clause was used.

When you drop a table that does exist, such as test_table in the example below, the query result will return 0 rows affected, even if your table contains data:

```
mysql> DROP TABLE IF EXISTS test_table;
Query OK, 0 rows affected (0.00 sec)
```

13

The only way to ensure the table was really dropped is to use SHOW TABLES and see whether the table name is in the list:

```
mysql> SHOW TABLES;
+---------------------+
| Tables_in_contactDB |
+---------------------+
| address             |
| company             |
| email               |
| fax                 |
| job_function        |
| master_name         |
| name_company_map    |
| personal_notes      |
| telephone           |
+---------------------+
9 rows in set (0.00 sec)
```

Since test_table is no longer in the list, safely assume it has been dropped.

DROP DATABASE

The DROP DATABASE command is as simple as the DROP TABLE command:

```
DROP DATABASE [IF EXISTS] db_name
```

As with DROP TABLE, the IF EXISTS clause will avoid an error message should the database you're attempting to drop not exist.

When you drop a database, changes are actually made to your filesystem. When a database is dropped, not only are the relevant entries removed from the tables in the mysql database, but its files and directories are also removed from the filestystem.

> As you learned in Hour 2, "Understanding Database Terminology," MySQL creates three files per table on your filesystem. These files contain the definition of the table, the data itself, and the indexes used in the table. It is these files that are removed when a table is dropped.

Take the example of a database called `test_database`, which contains one table:

```
mysql> SHOW TABLES;
+-----------------------+
| Tables_in_test_database |
+-----------------------+
| test_table            |
+-----------------------+
1 row in set (0.00 sec)
```

The one table corresponds to three files in the data directory for that database. Issue the DROP DATABASE command:

```
mysql> DROP DATABASE IF EXISTS test_database;
Query OK, 3 rows affected (0.00 sec)
```

You see that the query result shows `3 rows affected`. This actually means "3 files were deleted from that data directory because you had one table in the database." If the `test_database` database contained two tables, the query result would have been `6 rows affected`.

The query results for DROP DATABASE are more meaningful than the DROP TABLE results, but it's always a good idea to verify your actions:

```
mysql> SHOW DATABASES;
+------------------+
| Database         |
+------------------+
| contactDB        |
| mysql            |
+------------------+
2 rows in set (0.00 sec)
```

The `test_database` database is gone, so consider the DROP DATABASE exercise a success!

Summary

MySQL does not support automatic cascading deletions of related records, so to perform this type of action, you must write your own logic for it in your application. If possible, use a transaction to handle ROLLBACK occurrences to limit the amount of unrelated records in your system.

Sometimes the simplest commands are the most powerful, as seen by the DROP TABLE and DROP DATABASE commands! Three words can completely wreck your application if you're not careful. So before ever venturing into removing structures, back everything up!

13

To verify the tables in the current database, issue the SHOW TABLES command. You can also use the mysqlshow utility from the command line to achieve the same results—a list of tables. To see the list of databases on the MySQL server, issue the SHOW DATABASES command. Again, you can use mysqlshow to retrieve a list of databases.

Once you know the proper names of structures, you can delete them using the DROP TABLE or DROP DATABASE command. You can avoid errors by using the IF EXISTS clause with either command. Once a table is dropped, its data is gone. Once a database is dropped, all of its related files are removed from the filesystem.

Q&A

Q Can you drop a database using a MySQL command-line utility, or do you have to use the MySQL monitor?

A With the proper permissions, you can use mysqladmin to drop a database:

```
#prompt:> mysqladmin -u supercontact -psomepass drop test_database;
Dropping the database is potentially a very bad thing to do.
Any data stored in the database will be destroyed.

Do you really want to drop the 'test_database' database [y/N] y
Database "test_database" dropped
```

Q When logged into the MySQL monitor, can you drop a database you're currently using?

A Yes, but when the database has been dropped, you'll have to issue another USE database_name command to switch to a new database.

Workshop

The Workshop is designed to help you anticipate possible questions, review what you've learned, and begin learning how to put your knowledge into practice.

Quiz

1. How would you verify the existence of, remove, and then verify the removal of a table called fruit?

2. How would you list databases using mysqlshow?

3. When a database is dropped, what filesystem changes occur?

Answers

1. First issue the SHOW TABLES command to see that it's there and is actually called fruit, then issue the DROP TABLE IF EXISTS fruit command, followed by SHOW TABLES again to verify it's not in the list.

2. `mysqlshow -u someuser -psomepass`

3. When a database is dropped, the files corresponding to the tables in the database are removed, and the database directory is also removed.

Activities

1. Delete a few entries from your contact management system. This isn't as simple as it seems—not only must you delete a record from the master_name table but also from all other tables in which the name_id of the deleted record appears. Use a transaction if possible.

2. Create a sample database with several sample tables, and then drop a few of the tables and finally the sample database. Use the SHOW command at each step to get in the habit of verifying, removing, and verifying again major administrative tasks like removing structures.

13

Hour **14**

Modifying Table Structure

Making changes to your table structure is inevitable, and there are a few SQL commands designed for adding new fields, changing the type of an existing field, or simply renaming the table.

In this hour, you will learn

- How to view your table structure
- How to rename tables
- How to add fields, indexes, and keys
- How to change the definition of a field
- How to remove fields, indexes, and keys

Using DESCRIBE to View Table Structure

The DESCRIBE command displays the following information about an existing table:

- The field names
- The field types
- If the column can hold a NULL value
- If the column is a key and which type
- Any default values
- Any extra information, such as auto_increment

> DESCRIBE is actually a shortcut for the SHOW COLUMNS FROM command, which does exactly the same thing but is indeed shorter to type! The SHOW COLUMNS FROM command is part of the SHOW family of commands, which you'll learn about in Hour 22, "Basic Administrative Commands."

The syntax for DESCRIBE is:

```
DESCRIBE table_name [column_name]
```

For example, to show the table structure for the master_name table in your contact management database, use

```
mysql> DESCRIBE master_name;
```

You should see a result like that in Figure 14.1.

FIGURE 14.1

Using DESCRIBE to display information about an entire table.

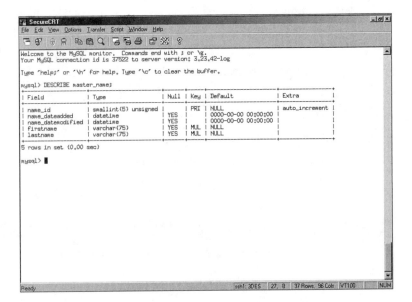

If you only need a description of the name_id field, use

```
mysql> DESCRIBE master_name name_id;
```

You should see a result like that in Figure 14.2.

FIGURE 14.2

Using DESCRIBE to display information about a single field in a table.

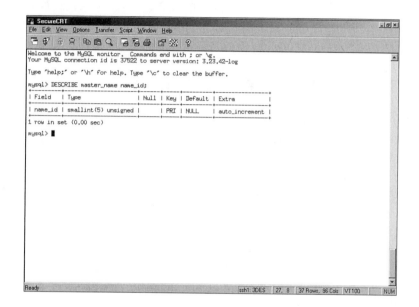

Using DESCRIBE before and after any changes to a table structure will help you to issue the correct statements, as well as verify your actions.

Renaming Tables

The RENAME command is a quick way to rename one or more tables. The syntax is

```
RENAME TABLE old_name TO new_name [, old_name2 TO new_name2]
```

So to rename a table named inventory to a table named product_stock, the query would be

```
RENAME TABLE inventory TO product_stock
```

If you are renaming more than one table during a single query, the action occurs from left to right. This means that the following query will rename a table and then give it its old name back:

```
mysql> RENAME TABLE address TO old_address, old_address TO address;
Query OK, 0 rows affected (0.00 sec)
```

14

You can also essentially move a table from one database to another, as long as both databases are on the same filesystem:

```
RENAME TABLE old_database.table_name TO new_database.table_name
```

RENAME is wonderful for a quick name change or move to a different database, but for more advanced modifications to tables and their structures, the ALTER command is what you'll need.

Using the ALTER Command

The ALTER command has more variations than any SQL command you've seen so far because you can perform several different types of actions using ALTER. You can use ALTER to add to, modify, or delete from your tables.

To use the ALTER command, your user must have ALTER privileges. The privileges for the contactDB sample database allow supercontact to use ALTER commands, but not the user named simpleuser.

To modify privileges for a user, use the GRANT command you learned about in Hour 6, "Planning and Creating Your Database."

When issuing an ALTER command, MySQL makes a temporary copy of the original table. The action in the ALTER command is performed on the copy of the table, and then the original table is deleted, and the temporary table is given the name of the original table. While all of this is going on, the original table can still be read from (SELECT), but any additions or modifications (INSERT or UPDATE) are held in check until the new table is ready for action. Bear in mind that changes with ALTER often take less than a second, but it's important to understand the process.

The basic ALTER syntax is

```
ALTER TABLE table_name alter_specification
```

The ALTER specifications can be broken into three groups: adding, modifying, and deleting elements within a table, such as fields, keys, indexes, and so forth. In the next few sections, you'll learn more about each specification group.

Adding Fields, Indexes, and Keys

The ALTER specifications for adding structures to your tables are

- ADD COLUMN (create_definition) [FIRST | AFTER column_name]
- ADD INDEX [index_name] (index_col_name)
- ADD PRIMARY KEY (index_col_name)
- ADD UNIQUE [index_name] (index_col_name)

You'll notice that the ALTER specifications look suspiciously like parts of the CREATE TABLE statements. If you understood the CREATE TABLE syntax, you'll have no problem with the ALTER specifications for adding to your structures because all you're doing is taking pieces from the table creation syntax.

For example, to add a column called middle_initial to your master_name table, defined as char(1), use

```
mysql> ALTER TABLE master_name ADD COLUMN middle_initial char(1);
Query OK, 9 rows affected (0.07 sec)
Records: 9  Duplicates: 0  Warnings: 0
```

Because the master_name table included 9 rows and you added to the structure of the table by adding a field, 9 rows affected is accurate. Starting with MySQL version 3.22, you can tell MySQL where to add new columns using the FIRST or ADD...AFTER column_name clauses. If you do not specify a placement, the field will be added at the end of the list.

Using ALTER to add keys and indexes also follows the same syntax as the CREATE TABLE command. To illustrate, first create a sample table called test_table with two fields, test_id and test_field:

```
mysql> CREATE TABLE test_table (test_id int not null, test_field varchar(150));
Query OK, 0 rows affected (0.00 sec)
```

This sample table currently has no keys or indexes, but the test_id field can quickly become a primary key:

```
mysql> ALTER TABLE test_table ADD PRIMARY KEY (test_id);
Query OK, 0 rows affected (0.00 sec)
Records: 0  Duplicates: 0  Warnings: 0
```

14

Use DESCRIBE to check the structure of your table and you'll see that test_id is indeed listed as a primary key:

```
mysql> DESCRIBE test_table;
+------------+-------------+------+-----+---------+-------+
| Field      | Type        | Null | Key | Default | Extra |
+------------+-------------+------+-----+---------+-------+
| test_id    | int(11)     |      | PRI | 0       |       |
| test_field | varchar(150)| YES  |     | NULL    |       |
+------------+-------------+------+-----+---------+-------+
2 rows in set (0.00 sec)
```

If you add another field to test_table, you can then add a unique key. First, the new field:

```
mysql> ALTER TABLE test_table ADD COLUMN test_unique int not null;
Query OK, 0 rows affected (0.01 sec)
Records: 0  Duplicates: 0  Warnings: 0
```

As an afterthought, make the new field unique:

```
mysql> ALTER TABLE test_table ADD UNIQUE (test_unique);
Query OK, 0 rows affected (0.01 sec)
Records: 0  Duplicates: 0  Warnings: 0
```

You can also indicate a UNIQUE key when adding the new field, thus saving a step. You can read more about UNIQUE keys in Hour 8, "Creating Your Database Tables—Part II."

To use ALTER to add an index, first select a field that isn't already indexed. Remember, primary keys are automatically indexed. From the test_table, add an index on test_field called idx_test_field:

```
mysql> ALTER TABLE test_table ADD INDEX idx_test_field (test_field);
Query OK, 0 rows affected (0.01 sec)
Records: 0  Duplicates: 0  Warnings: 0
```

To verify the appearance of indexes in your table, you can use the SHOW INDEX FROM command:

```
mysql> SHOW INDEX FROM test_table;
```

This will return a table with various types of information about indexes on a table, including the index names. You'll learn more about this command in Hour 22.

Adding new fields, keys, and indexes is a breeze, so if you think you've painted yourself into a corner by incorrectly defining tables the first time around, just fire off a few ALTER statements and get back on track.

Modifying Field Definitions

The ALTER specifications for modifying existing table structures are

- ALTER COLUMN col_name {SET DEFAULT default_value | DROP DEFAULT}
- CHANGE COLUMN old_column create_definition [FIRST | AFTER column_name]
- MODIFY COLUMN create_definition [FIRST | AFTER column_name]

When you create a table, you may or may not specify default values for particular fields. During the creation of the tables in the contactDB database, the date-related columns were given default values of 0000-00-00 00:00:00. If you don't define a default value during table creation, you can use ALTER to fix this oversight.

For example, to add a default value of "I Love MySQL" to the test_field column in the sample table called test_table, use

```
mysql> ALTER TABLE test_table ALTER test_field SET DEFAULT "I Love MySQL";
Query OK, 0 rows affected (0.00 sec)
Records: 0  Duplicates: 0  Warnings: 0
```

Use DESCRIBE to verify the change and you'll see the default value listed for the test_field column:

```
mysql> DESCRIBE test_table;
+-------------+--------------+------+-----+--------------+-------+
| Field       | Type         | Null | Key | Default      | Extra |
+-------------+--------------+------+-----+--------------+-------+
| test_id     | int(11)      |      | PRI | 0            |       |
| test_field  | varchar(150) | YES  | MUL | I Love MySQL |       |
| test_unique | int(11)      |      | UNI | 0            |       |
+-------------+--------------+------+-----+--------------+-------+
3 rows in set (0.00 sec)
```

You can remove a default value in much the same way as adding it:

```
mysql> ALTER TABLE test_table ALTER test_field DROP DEFAULT;
Query OK, 0 rows affected (0.00 sec)
Records: 0  Duplicates: 0  Warnings: 0
```

14

If you have populated your table with records that used the default value of a field, that field will still contain its value even if you remove the DEFAULT value. Subsequent use of INSERT to add records into the table will not contain a default value in the field. If you remove the use of DEFAULT and don't want your old records to contain this value, you can use an UPDATE statement to change the value of that field.

The next type of field modification is to use the CHANGE or MODIFY clauses. These clauses are quite similar—both modify the definition of a particular field. The difference is that the CHANGE clause requires two column names during the definition and MODIFY (available starting with MySQL version 3.22) only requires one column name.

For example, to change the type of the test_field column in test_table, you can use

```
mysql> ALTER TABLE test_table CHANGE test_field test_field char(5);
Query OK, 0 rows affected (0.01 sec)
Records: 0  Duplicates: 0  Warnings: 0
```

Or you could use

```
mysql> ALTER TABLE test_table MODIFY test_field char(5);
Query OK, 0 rows affected (0.00 sec)
Records: 0  Duplicates: 0  Warnings: 0
```

When you change the type of a field within a table that already contains records, MySQL will attempt to convert the existing data in the changed field to the new datatype. In the sample table, a 150-character varchar field was changed to a 5-character char field. Any data in that field will be truncated to 5 characters, and you can't get that data back should you find you made a mistake.

Deleting Fields, Indexes, and Keys

The ALTER specifications for removing existing fields, indexes, and keys are

- DROP COLUMN col_name
- DROP INDEX index_name
- DROP PRIMARY KEY

These three ALTER clauses are quite simple and self-explanatory; in Hour 13, "More About DELETE," you learned that DROP essentially means "goes away completely and forever." If you want to remove a column and all its data from a table, use the DROP COLUMN clause:

```
mysql> ALTER TABLE master_name DROP COLUMN middle_initial;
Query OK, 9 rows affected (0.01 sec)
Records: 9  Duplicates: 0  Warnings: 0
```

> As with any structural changes, you can use DESCRIBE to verify the removal of this column from your table structure.

When you remove a column from a table, that column's data are also removed from any relevant indexes in that table. If a dropped column makes up an entire index, that index is dropped as well.

If you need to remove only an index from a table, the DROP INDEX clause in the ALTER command is the way to go:

```
mysql> ALTER TABLE test_table DROP INDEX idx_test_field;
Query OK, 0 rows affected (0.01 sec)
Records: 0  Duplicates: 0  Warnings: 0
```

Finally, if you want to remove a primary key from a table, simply use the DROP PRIMARY KEY clause:

```
mysql> ALTER TABLE test_table DROP PRIMARY KEY;
Query OK, 0 rows affected (0.01 sec)
Records: 0  Duplicates: 0  Warnings: 0
```

Dropping a primary key will also remove the index created using that primary key column.

Summary

Before making any modifications to table structures, use the DESCRIBE command. The result of this command is a table full of information about the table, including field names and definitions.

If you want to rename your table, use the RENAME command to change the name from an old name to a new name. You can also use RENAME to move a table to a different database altogether, provided the databases are on the same filesystem.

To make any changes to the structure of an existing table, use the ALTER command and its various specifications to add, modify, or remove columns, keys, and indexes. Using ADD clauses in the ALTER command, you can create additional fields, indexes, and keys in a given table. The ADD syntax is much like the CREATE TABLE syntax, just one field at a time.

14

You can change the definition of a field using the CHANGE or MODIFY clauses in the ALTER command by specifying the new definition. Also, the ALTER clause of the ALTER command allows you to set or remove default values from a field.

If you decide to remove a column, index, or key altogether from your table, the DROP clause of the ALTER command is used for these actions.

Q&A

Q What happens if I add a new field or modify an existing field to include an auto_increment value—and records already exist in that table?

A If you have records in a table and you add an auto_increment field to that table, those fields will be populated with automatically incremented values. For example, if you have ten records, the values will be from 1 to 10.

Workshop

The Workshop is designed to help you anticipate possible questions, review what you've learned, and begin learning how to put your knowledge into practice.

Quiz

1. What would be the syntax to rename a table from test_table to new_table?
2. What would be the syntax to add an index called idx_fruitname to a table called fruit on a column called fruitname?
3. If fruitname in the fruit table is a varchar(20) field, how would you change it to a 10 character varchar field and what would happen to the data?

Answers

1. RENAME TABLE test_table TO new_table;
2. ALTER TABLE fruit ADD INDEX idx_fruitname (fruitname);
3. ALTER TABLE fruit CHANGE fruitname fruitname varchar(10);

   or

   ALTER TABLE fruit MODIFY fruitname varchar(10);

   Any data in that column longer than 10 characters will be truncated.

Activity

Create indexes on multiple fields in the tables in your contactDB database. Use SHOW INDEX commands to view the indexes on your tables.

PART V

Using Built-in Functions in MySQL Queries

Hour

HOUR 15

Using MySQL String Functions

Over the next few hours, you'll learn about some of the more popular and useful functions built into MySQL. The more programming you can work into your SQL statements, the less work that has to be done by your application. This hour contains descriptions and examples of string-related functions.

In this hour, you will learn

- How to use built-in functions for working with strings in MySQL in order to put strings together or to extract pieces of strings
- How to create variations of original strings
- How to find alternate representations of strings in different bases

Frequently Used String Functions

MySQL's built-in string-related functions can be used several ways. You can use functions in SELECT statements without specifying a table in order to retrieve a result of the function. Or, you can use functions to enhance your SELECT results by concatenating two fields to form a new string.

Even if you never use these functions in your applications, it's good to know they exist, and if nothing else, you'll get some good practice in this hour using the MySQL monitor's command line interface.

Length and Concatenation Functions

This group of functions focuses on the length of strings and concatenating strings together. Length-related functions include LENGTH(), OCTET_LENGTH(), CHAR_LENGTH(), and CHARACTER_LENGTH(), which do virtually the same thing—count characters in a string.

```
mysql> SELECT LENGTH('This is cool!');
+-------------------------+
| LENGTH('This is cool!') |
+-------------------------+
|                      13 |
+-------------------------+
1 row in set (0.00 sec)
```

The fun begins with the CONCAT() function, which is used to concatenate two or more strings:

```
mysql> SELECT CONCAT('My', 'S', 'QL');
+-------------------------+
| CONCAT('My', 'S', 'QL') |
+-------------------------+
| MySQL                   |
+-------------------------+
1 row in set (0.00 sec)
```

Imagine using this with your master_name table. Instead of using two strings, use two field names to concatenate the firstname and the lastname fields. By concatenating the fields, it reduces the lines of code necessary to achieve the same result in your application:

```
mysql> SELECT CONCAT(firstname, lastname) FROM master_name;
+-----------------------------+
| CONCAT(firstname, lastname) |
+-----------------------------+
| JohnSmith                   |
| JaneSmith                   |
| JimboJones                  |
| AndySmith                   |
| ChrisJones                  |
| AnnaBell                    |
| JimmyCarr                   |
| AlbertSmith                 |
| JohnDoe                     |
+-----------------------------+
9 rows in set (0.00 sec)
```

If you're using a field name and not a string in a function, don't enclose the field name within quotation marks. If you do, MySQL will interpret the string literally. In the `CONCAT()` example, you'd get the following result:

```
mysql> SELECT CONCAT('firstname', 'lastname') FROM master_name;
+---------------------------------+
| CONCAT('firstname', 'lastname') |
+---------------------------------+
| firstnamelastname               |
| firstnamelastname               |
| firstnamelastname               |
| firstnamelastname               |
| firstnamelastname               |
| firstnamelastname               |
| firstnamelastname               |
| firstnamelastname               |
| firstnamelastname               |
+---------------------------------+
9 rows in set (0.00 sec)
```

The `CONCAT()` function would be useful if there were some sort of separator between the names, and that's where the next function comes in: `CONCAT_WS()`.

As you probably figured out, `CONTACT_WS()` stands for "concatenate with separator." The separator can be anything you choose, but the following example uses whitespace:

```
mysql> SELECT CONCAT_WS(' ', firstname, lastname) FROM master_name;
+-------------------------------------+
| CONCAT_WS(' ', firstname, lastname) |
+-------------------------------------+
| John Smith                          |
| Jane Smith                          |
| Jimbo Jones                         |
| Andy Smith                          |
| Chris Jones                         |
| Anna Bell                           |
| Jimmy Carr                          |
| Albert Smith                        |
| John Doe                            |
+-------------------------------------+
9 rows in set (0.00 sec)
```

If you want to clean up your result table, you can use `AS` to name the custom result field:

```
mysql> SELECT CONCAT_WS(' ', firstname, lastname) AS fullname FROM master_name;
+------------+
| fullname   |
+------------+
| John Smith |
```

```
| Jane Smith    |
| Jimbo Jones   |
| Andy Smith    |
| Chris Jones   |
| Anna Bell     |
| Jimmy Carr    |
| Albert Smith  |
| John Doe      |
+---------------+
9 rows in set (0.00 sec)
```

Trimming and Padding Functions

MySQL provides several functions for adding and removing extra characters (including whitespace) from strings. The RTRIM() and LTRIM() functions remove whitespace from either the right or left side of a string:

```
mysql> select RTRIM('stringstring    ');
+------------------------+
| RTRIM('stringstring  ') |
+------------------------+
| stringstring           |
+------------------------+
1 row in set (0.00 sec)

mysql> select LTRIM('  stringstring');
+------------------------+
| LTRIM('  stringstring') |
+------------------------+
| stringstring           |
+------------------------+
1 row in set (0.00 sec)
```

You may have padded strings to trim if the string is coming out of a fixed-width field and either doesn't need to carry along the additional padding or is being inserted into a varchar or other nonfixed-width field. If your strings are padded with a character besides whitespace, use the TRIM() function to name the characters you want to remove. For example, to remove the leading "X" characters from the string XXXneedleXXX, use

```
mysql> SELECT TRIM(LEADING 'X' from 'XXXneedleXXX');
+--------------------------------------+
| TRIM(LEADING 'X' from 'XXXneedleXXX') |
+--------------------------------------+
| needleXXX                            |
+--------------------------------------+
1 row in set (0.00 sec)
```

Use TRAILING to remove the characters from the end of the string:

```
mysql> SELECT TRIM(TRAILING 'X' from 'XXXneedleXXX');
+----------------------------------------+
| TRIM(TRAILING 'X' from 'XXXneedleXXX') |
+----------------------------------------+
| XXXneedle                              |
+----------------------------------------+
1 row in set (0.00 sec)
```

If neither LEADING nor TRAILING are indicated, both are assumed:

```
mysql> SELECT TRIM('X' from 'XXXneedleXXX');
+------------------------------+
| TRIM('X' from 'XXXneedleXXX') |
+------------------------------+
| needle                       |
+------------------------------+
1 row in set (0.00 sec)
```

Just like RTRIM() and LTRIM() remove padding characters, RPAD() and LPAD() will add characters to a string. For example, you may want to add specific identification characters to a string that is part of an order number in a database used for sales. When using the padding functions, the required elements are the string, the target length, and the padding character. For example, pad the string "needle" with the "X" character until the string is 10 characters long:

```
mysql> SELECT RPAD('needle', 10, 'X');
+------------------------+
| RPAD('needle', 10, 'X') |
+------------------------+
| needleXXXX             |
+------------------------+
1 row in set (0.00 sec)
```

```
mysql> SELECT LPAD('needle', 10, 'X');
+------------------------+
| LPAD('needle', 10, 'X') |
+------------------------+
| XXXXneedle             |
+------------------------+
1 row in set (0.00 sec)
```

Location and Position Functions

This group contains useful functions for finding parts of strings within other strings. The LOCATE() function will return the position of the first occurrence of a given substring within the target string. For example, looking for a needle in a haystack

```
mysql> SELECT LOCATE('needle', 'haystackneedlehaystack');
+-------------------------------------------+
| LOCATE('needle', 'haystackneedlehaystack') |
```

```
+-------------------------------------------+
|                                         9 |
+-------------------------------------------+
1 row in set (0.00 sec)
```

The substring `needle` begins at position 9 in the target string. If the substring cannot be found in the target string, MySQL returns 0 as a result.

 Unlike counting in arrays, which starts at 0, string position counting starts at 1.

An extension of the `LOCATE()` function is to use a third argument for starting position. If you start looking for `needle` in `haystack` before position 9, you'll receive a result. Otherwise, because `needle` starts at position 9, you'll receive a 0 result if you specify a greater starting position:

```
mysql> SELECT LOCATE('needle', 'haystackneedlehaystack',6);
+-------------------------------------------+
| LOCATE('needle', 'haystackneedlehaystack',9) |
+-------------------------------------------+
|                                         9 |
+-------------------------------------------+
1 row in set (0.00 sec)
mysql> SELECT LOCATE('needle', 'haystackneedlehaystack',12);
+-------------------------------------------+
| LOCATE('needle', 'haystackneedlehaystack',12) |
+-------------------------------------------+
|                                         0 |
+-------------------------------------------+
1 row in set (0.00 sec)
```

Substring Functions

If the goal is to extract a substring from a target string, there are several functions that fit the bill. Given a string, a starting position, and a length, you can use the `SUBSTRING()` function. This example gets three characters from the string `MySQL`, starting at position 2:

```
mysql> SELECT SUBSTRING("MySQL", 2, 3);
+------------------------+
| SUBSTRING("MySQL", 2, 3) |
+------------------------+
| ySQ                    |
+------------------------+
1 row in set (0.00 sec)
```

If you just want a few characters from the left or right ends of a string, use the `LEFT()` and `RIGHT()` functions:

15

```
mysql> SELECT LEFT("MySQL", 2);
+------------------+
| LEFT("MySQL", 2) |
+------------------+
| My               |
+------------------+
1 row in set (0.00 sec)

mysql> SELECT RIGHT("MySQL", 3);
+-------------------+
| RIGHT("MySQL", 3) |
+-------------------+
| SQL               |
+-------------------+
1 row in set (0.00 sec)
```

One of the many, many common uses of substring functions is to extract parts of order numbers in order to find out who placed the order. In some applications, the system will be designed to automatically generate an order number, containing a date, customer identification, and other information. If this order number always follows a particular pattern, such as XXXX-YYYYY-ZZ, you can use substring functions to extract the individual parts of the whole. For example, if ZZ always represents the state to which the order was shipped, you can use the RIGHT() function to extract these characters and to report the number of orders shipped to a particular state.

String Modification Functions

Your programming language of choice likely has functions to modify the appearance of strings, but if you can perform the task as part of the SQL statement, all the better.

The MySQL LCASE() and UCASE() functions will transform a string into lowercase or uppercase:

```
mysql> SELECT LCASE('MYSQL');
+----------------+
| LCASE('MYSQL') |
+----------------+
| mysql          |
+----------------+
1 row in set (0.00 sec)

mysql> SELECT UCASE('mysql');
+----------------+
| UCASE('mysql') |
+----------------+
| MYSQL          |
+----------------+
1 row in set (0.00 sec)
```

Remember, if you use the functions with fieldnames, don't use quotation marks:

```
mysql> SELECT UCASE(lastname) FROM master_name;
+-----------------+
| UCASE(lastname) |
+-----------------+
| BELL            |
| CARR            |
| DOE             |
| JONES           |
| JONES           |
| SMITH           |
| SMITH           |
| SMITH           |
| SMITH           |
+-----------------+
9 rows in set (0.00 sec)
```

Another fun string manipulation function is the REPEAT() function, which does just what it sounds like—repeats a string for a given number of times:

```
mysql> SELECT REPEAT("bowwow", 4);
+--------------------------+
| REPEAT("bowwow", 4)      |
+--------------------------+
| bowwowbowwowbowwowbowwow |
+--------------------------+
1 row in set (0.00 sec)
```

The REPLACE() function will replace all occurrences of a given string with another string:

```
mysql> SELECT REPLACE('bowwowbowwowbowwowbowwow', 'wow', 'WOW');
+---------------------------------------------------+
| REPLACE('bowwowbowwowbowwowbowwow', 'wow', 'WOW') |
+---------------------------------------------------+
| bowWOWbowWOWbowWOWbowWOW                           |
+---------------------------------------------------+
1 row in set (0.00 sec)
```

Obscure String Functions

This group of functions focuses on gathering more information about characters or on converting characters to different bases—far and away the least common usage of string functions in MySQL but important nonetheless if you're into such things. The first function is the ASCII() function, which gets the ASCII code value of a given character. This example gets the ASCII value of the ampersand (&) character:

```
mysql> SELECT ASCII('&');
+------------+
| ASCII('&') |
+------------+
|         38 |
+------------+
1 row in set (0.04 sec)
```

If there are multiple characters in a string, the function gets the value of the left-most character:

```
mysql> SELECT ASCII('def');
+--------------+
| ASCII('def') |
+--------------+
|          100 |
+--------------+
1 row in set (0.00 sec)
```

In this case, "100" is the ASCII value of "d."

The next three functions return string representations of binary, octal, and hexadecimal values. Like the ASCII() function, the BIN(), OCT(), and HEX() functions do not require a table selection but will return values without a specified table.

The following example gets a string representation of the binary value of the integer 56895:

```
mysql> SELECT BIN(56895);
+------------------+
| BIN('56895')     |
+------------------+
| 1101111000111111 |
+------------------+
1 row in set (0.00 sec)
```

The following example gets a string representation of the octal value of the integer 56895:

```
mysql> SELECT OCT(56895);
+------------+
| OCT(56895) |
+------------+
| 157077     |
+------------+
1 row in set (0.00 sec)
```

The following example gets a string representation of the hexadecimal value of the integer 56895:

```
mysql> SELECT HEX(56895);
+-----------+
| HEX(56895) |
+-----------+
| DE3F      |
+-----------+
1 row in set (0.00 sec)
```

You can also use the CONV() function to convert numbers between bases. There are three parts to this function: the number, the base you're converting from, and the base you're converting to.

For example, to convert the integer 56895 from base 10 to base 8 and return its value, use

```
mysql> SELECT CONV(56895,10,8);
+-----------------+
| CONV(56895,10,8) |
+-----------------+
| 157077          |
+-----------------+
1 row in set (0.00 sec)
```

This result is equivalent to the OCT() function. Similarly, to convert an integer from base 10 to base 16

```
mysql> SELECT CONV(56895,10,16);
+------------------+
| CONV(56895,10,16) |
+------------------+
| DE3F             |
+------------------+
1 row in set (0.00 sec)
```

This result is equivalent to the HEX() function.

You can also convert from base 8 to base 16:

```
mysql> SELECT CONV(157077,8,16);
+------------------+
| CONV(157077,8,16) |
+------------------+
| DE3F             |
+------------------+
1 row in set (0.00 sec)
```

And so on. The minimum base is 2 and the maximum base is 36.

Another function for working with characters and ASCII codes is the CHAR() function, which takes a series of integers representing ASCII codes and returns a string made up of the results:

```
mysql> SELECT CHAR(84,104,105,115,32,105,115,32,99,111,111,108,33);
+-----------------------------------------------------+
| CHAR(84,104,105,115,32,105,115,32,99,111,111,108,33) |
+-----------------------------------------------------+
| This is cool!                                        |
+-----------------------------------------------------+
1 row in set (0.00 sec)
```

Summary

Using built-in MySQL functions to perform actions on strings can speed up your application by letting your database do as much work as possible.

If you have a string you want to concatenate or count characters of, you can use functions such as CONCAT(), CONCAT_WS(), and LENGTH(). To pad or remove padding from string, use RPAD(), LPAD(), TRIM(), LTRIM(), and RRIM() to get just the string you want.

To find the location of a string within another, or to return a part of a given string, the LOCATE(), SUBSTRING(),LEFT(), and RIGHT() functions are useful. Functions such as LCASE(), UCASE(), REPEAT(), and REPLACE() will also return variations of the original strings. MySQL also has numerous functions for representing strings, such as ASCII(), BIN(), OCT(), HEX(), and CONV() for converting between bases.

Q&A

Q Can I use multiple functions in one statement, such as making a concatenated string all uppercase?

A Sure—just be mindful of your opening and closing parentheses. This example shows how to uppercase the concatenated first and last names from the master name table:

```
mysql> SELECT UCASE(CONCAT_WS(' ', firstname, lastname)) FROM master_name;
+------------------------------------------+
| UCASE(CONCAT_WS(' ', firstname, lastname)) |
+------------------------------------------+
| JOHN SMITH                               |
| JANE SMITH                               |
| JIMBO JONES                              |
| ANDY SMITH                               |
| CHRIS JONES                              |
| ANNA BELL                                |
| JIMMY CARR                               |
| ALBERT SMITH                             |
| JOHN DOE                                 |
+------------------------------------------+
9 rows in set (0.00 sec)
```

15

If you wanted to uppercase just the last name, use

```
mysql> SELECT CONCAT_WS(' ', firstname, UCASE(lastname)) FROM master_name;
+-------------------------------------------+
| CONCAT_WS(' ', firstname, UCASE(lastname)) |
+-------------------------------------------+
| John SMITH                                |
| Jane SMITH                                |
| Jimbo JONES                               |
| Andy SMITH                                |
| Chris JONES                               |
| Anna BELL                                 |
| Jimmy CARR                                |
| Albert SMITH                              |
| John DOE                                  |
+-------------------------------------------+
9 rows in set (0.00 sec)
```

Workshop

The Workshop is designed to help you anticipate possible questions, review what you've learned, and begin learning how to put your knowledge into practice.

Quiz

1. Write an SQL query to return concatenated names in a field called `fullname` from the `master_name` table, ordered by last names only. Make the `lastname` uppercase.

2. Write an SQL query to find the starting position of a substring "grape" in a string "applepearbananagrape."

3. Write a query that selects the substring "grape" from the string "applepearbanana-grape."

Answers

1. `SELECT CONCAT_WS(' ', firstname, UCASE(lastname)) as fullname FROM master_name ORDER BY lastname;`

2. `SELECT LOCATE('grape', 'applepearbananagrape');`

3. `SELECT RIGHT("applepearbananagrape", 5);`

Activity

Practice using functions within functions, such as making case changes on substrings and concatenating strings using the tables in your `contactDB` database.

Hour **16**

Using MySQL Numeric Functions

MySQL has numerous built-in functions for use with numeric values, ranging from simple arithmetic to complex trigonometric functions.

In this hour, you will learn

- How to use built-in functions to perform mathematical operations
- How to use built-in trigonometric functions
- How to use built-in functions for rounding off query results

Using Numeric Functions in Queries

As with MySQL's built-in string functions, its numeric functions can be used in SELECT statements, with or without specifying a table, to retrieve a result of the function.

The next several sections group the popular numeric-related functions into logical topic groups. This hour provides more good practice for working with the MySQL monitor and learning what you can program your database to do.

Basic Arithmetic Operations

All of the basic arithmetic functions are available: add, subtract, multiply, and divide. Results will be up to 64-bit precision or the value of a BIGINT number. When you go beyond that, an error will occur, as you'll soon see within a large multiplication example. But start with the simple stuff, such as adding and subtracting.

You can use arithmetic operations without a table to get a result, such as the addition operation that follows:

```
mysql> SELECT 16+45;
+-------+
| 16+45 |
+-------+
|    61 |
+-------+
1 row in set (0.00 sec)
```

Or the subtraction operation

```
mysql> SELECT 107686-32433;
+--------------+
| 107686-32433 |
+--------------+
|        75253 |
+--------------+
1 row in set (0.00 sec)
```

Or the multiplication operation

```
mysql> SELECT 3242*4343423;
+--------------+
| 3242*4343423 |
+--------------+
|  14081377366 |
+--------------+
1 row in set (0.00 sec)
```

Or the division operation

```
mysql> SELECT 234354/323434;
+---------------+
| 234354/323434 |
+---------------+
|          0.72 |
+---------------+
1 row in set (0.00 sec)
```

And finally, there is the MOD() function, which is used to get the remainder of a division operation between two numbers. In this example, the result is the remainder when dividing 143 by 11:

```
mysql> SELECT MOD(141,11);
+-------------+
| MOD(141,11) |
+-------------+
|           9 |
+-------------+
1 row in set (0.00 sec)
```

The result is 9, because 11 goes into 141 twelve times, with 8 left over. This is rounded up to 9.

In all instances, but most applicable in the division example, results are automatically rounded to two decimal places.

Any time an arithmetic operation produces an error, the result will be 0, except in a division operation when attempting to divide by 0. In that case, the result is NULL:

```
mysql> SELECT 234354/0;
+----------+
| 234354/0 |
+----------+
|     NULL |
+----------+
1 row in set (0.00 sec)
```

The BIGINT limit comes into play with large numbers, such as attempting to multiply 18014398509481984 by 18014398509481984:

```
mysql> select 18014398509481984*18014398509481984;
+-------------------------------------+
| 18014398509481984*18014398509481984 |
+-------------------------------------+
|                                   0 |
+-------------------------------------+
1 row in set (0.00 sec)
```

The result is larger than a BIGINT can handle, so the result shown is 0.

These basic operations can be used with field names, not just literal numbers. In this example, a table called orders holds some numeric information in fields called item_total and shipping_total:

```
mysql> SELECT * from orders;
+----+------------+----------------+
| id | item_total | shipping_total |
+----+------------+----------------+
|  1 |      19.99 |           4.99 |
|  2 |      24.99 |           5.99 |
|  3 |      29.99 |           5.99 |
+----+------------+----------------+
```

```
3 rows in set (0.00 sec)
```

Use the addition operation to add two fields together to produce a new field called order_total:

```
mysql> SELECT item_total, shipping_total, (item_total+shipping_total)
    -> AS order_total FROM orders;
+------------+----------------+-------------+
| item_total | shipping_total | order_total |
+------------+----------------+-------------+
|      19.99 |           4.99 |       24.98 |
|      24.99 |           5.99 |       30.98 |
|      29.99 |           5.99 |       35.98 |
+------------+----------------+-------------+
3 rows in set (0.00 sec)
```

Recall your days in basic Algebra class, and enclose your mathematical operations within parentheses. This will ensure that your operations are performed in the proper order.

Mathematical Functions

This next group of functions runs the gamut from finding the absolute value of a number to finding the base 10 logarithm of a number. In all instances, these functions return NULL if an error occurs.

The SIGN() function gets the sign of a negative, positive, or zero number. If the sign is negative, the result is –1. A positive number returns a result of 1, and a zero number returns 0 as the result:

```
mysql> SELECT SIGN(-78);
+-----------+
| SIGN(-78) |
+-----------+
|        -1 |
+-----------+
1 row in set (0.00 sec)

mysql> SELECT SIGN(78);
+----------+
| SIGN(78) |
+----------+
|        1 |
+----------+
1 row in set (0.00 sec)

mysql> SELECT SIGN(0);
+---------+
| SIGN(0) |
+---------+
|       0 |
```

```
+----------+
1 row in set (0.00 sec)
```

Use the ABS() function to return the absolute value of a number:

```
mysql> SELECT ABS(-78);
+----------+
| ABS(-78) |
+----------+
|       78 |
+----------+
1 row in set (0.01 sec)

mysql> SELECT ABS(23543);
+------------+
| ABS(23543) |
+------------+
|      23543 |
+------------+
1 row in set (0.00 sec)
```

The next few functions deal with logarithms. To find the base 10 logarithm of a number, use the LOG10() function:

```
mysql> SELECT LOG10(34);
+-----------+
| LOG10(34) |
+-----------+
|  1.531479 |
+-----------+
1 row in set (0.00 sec)
```

To find the natural logarithm of a number, use just the LOG() function:

```
mysql> SELECT LOG(34);
+----------+
| LOG(34)  |
+----------+
| 3.526361 |
+----------+
1 row in set (0.00 sec)
```

The next two functions are more common than the logarithm functions. POW() (you can also use POWER()) will return the value of a number after raising it to a given power. In the first example, 12 is raised to the second power:

```
mysql> SELECT POW(12,2);
+------------+
| POW(12,2)  |
+------------+
| 144.000000 |
```

16

```
+------------+
1 row in set (0.00 sec)
```

In this example, 12 is raised to the 25th power:

```
mysql> SELECT POW(12,25);
+----------------------------------+
| POW(12,25)                       |
+----------------------------------+
| 9539621664406901296013298432.000000 |
+----------------------------------+
1 row in set (0.00 sec)
```

The SQRT() function returns a non-negative square root of a number:

```
mysql> SELECT SQRT(144);
+-----------+
| SQRT(144) |
+-----------+
| 12.000000 |
+-----------+
1 row in set (0.00 sec)
```

```
mysql> SELECT SQRT(9539621664406901296013298432);
+----------------------------------+
| SQRT(9539621664406901296013298432) |
+----------------------------------+
|               30886277963534.066406 |
+----------------------------------+
1 row in set (0.00 sec)
```

Trigonometric Functions

Functions in this section would commonly be used in applications using trigonometry, with your database handling as much of the load as possible.

The SIN() and COS() functions return the sine and cosine of a number, provided in radians:

```
mysql> SELECT SIN(0.5);
+----------+
| SIN(0.5) |
+----------+
| 0.479426 |
+----------+
1 row in set (0.00 sec)
```

```
mysql> SELECT COS(0.5);
+----------+
| COS(0.5) |
+----------+
| 0.877583 |
```

```
+----------+
1 row in set (0.00 sec)
```

You can also use a handy function called PI() to refer to the number 3.141593. This function, like all functions, can exist within other functions, as long as the parenthetical statements are in order:

```
mysql> SELECT SIN(PI());
+----------+
| SIN(PI()) |
+----------+
|  0.000000 |
+----------+
1 row in set (0.00 sec)
```

The TAN() function returns the tangent of a number:

```
mysql> SELECT TAN(0.5);
+----------+
| TAN(0.5) |
+----------+
| 0.546302 |
+----------+
1 row in set (0.01 sec)
```

The functions ASIN(), ACOS(), and ATAN() return the arc sine, arc cosine, and arc tangents of numbers. Unless the number is between –1 and 1, the result of these functions will be NULL.

```
mysql> SELECT ASIN(0.4353);
+--------------+
| ASIN(0.4353) |
+--------------+
|     0.450371 |
+--------------+
1 row in set (0.00 sec)
```

```
mysql> SELECT ACOS(0.4353);
+--------------+
| ACOS(0.4353) |
+--------------+
|     1.120425 |
+--------------+
1 row in set (0.00 sec)
```

```
mysql> SELECT ATAN(0.4353);
+--------------+
| ATAN(0.4353) |
+--------------+
```

```
|     0.410562 |
+--------------+
1 row in set (0.00 sec)
```

The DEGREES() function is used to convert radians to degrees, and the RADIANS() function converts degrees to radians:

```
mysql> SELECT DEGREES(PI());
+---------------+
| DEGREES(PI()) |
+---------------+
|           180 |
+---------------+
1 row in set (0.00 sec)

mysql> SELECT DEGREES(3.23);
+-----------------+
| DEGREES(3.23)   |
+-----------------+
| 185.06536782726 |
+-----------------+
1 row in set (0.00 sec)

mysql> SELECT RADIANS(180);
+-----------------+
| RADIANS(180)    |
+-----------------+
| 3.1415926535898 |
+-----------------+
1 row in set (0.00 sec)

mysql> SELECT RADIANS(185.06536782726);
+--------------------------+
| RADIANS(185.06536782726) |
+--------------------------+
|          3.2300000000001 |
+--------------------------+
1 row in set (0.00 sec)
```

If trigonometry isn't your cup of tea, don't fret. The remaining mathematical functions are more useful in everyday applications.

Rounding Functions

The most common rounding function is the simple ROUND() function, which will produce a result rounded to the nearest integer:

```
mysql> SELECT ROUND(34.2343);
+----------------+
| ROUND(34.2343) |
+----------------+
```

```
|               34 |
+-----------------+
1 row in set (0.00 sec)

mysql> SELECT ROUND(34.7676);
+-----------------+
| ROUND(34.7676) |
+-----------------+
|              35 |
+-----------------+
1 row in set (0.00 sec)
```

You can also specify a decimal precision with the ROUND() function in the second position. The following rounds the number 34.7676 to the nearest hundredth place:

```
mysql> SELECT ROUND(34.7676,2);
+------------------+
| ROUND(34.7676,2) |
+------------------+
|            34.77 |
+------------------+
1 row in set (0.00 sec)
```

If you want to round your integers in a particular way, such as always to the lowest integer or always to the highest integer, the FLOOR() and CEILING() functions do just that:

```
mysql> SELECT FLOOR(34.7676);
+-----------------+
| FLOOR(34.7676) |
+-----------------+
|              34 |
+-----------------+
1 row in set (0.00 sec)

mysql> SELECT CEILING(34.7676);
+------------------+
| CEILING(34.7676) |
+------------------+
|               35 |
+------------------+
1 row in set (0.00 sec)
```

The TRUNCATE() function does no rounding; it just lops off the extra past the decimal precision indicated:

```
mysql> SELECT TRUNCATE(34.7676,2);
+---------------------+
| TRUNCATE(34.7676,2) |
+---------------------+
```

```
|                34.76 |
+---------------------+
1 row in set (0.00 sec)

mysql> SELECT TRUNCATE(34.7676,0);
+---------------------+
| TRUNCATE(34.7676,0) |
+---------------------+
|                  34 |
+---------------------+
1 row in set (0.00 sec)
```

If you use TRUNCATE() with a specified decimal precision that is greater than the current precision of the number, MySQL will add a zero, which isn't actually a truncation, but it works:

```
mysql> SELECT TRUNCATE(34.7676,5);
+---------------------+
| TRUNCATE(34.7676,5) |
+---------------------+
|            34.76760 |
+---------------------+
1 row in set (0.00 sec)
```

Summary

MySQL's functions for working with numbers can be used in many ways throughout your database-driven application. Basic arithmetic operations are very common—addition, subtraction, multiplication, and deletion. You can also use functions to determine absolute values and logarithms of numbers.

MySQL is full of trigonometric functions. The PI() function simply returns the value of Pi, and functions exist to determine sines, cosines, tangents, arc sines, arc cosines, and arc tangents. Other functions, such as ROUND(), FLOOR(), CEILING(), and TRUNCATE(), will return numbers that are rounded up or down to integers or numbers with specific decimal precision.

Workshop

The Workshop is designed to help you anticipate possible questions, review what you've learned, and begin learning how to put your knowledge into practice.

Quiz

1. Given a field called item_total in a table called orders, write an SQL query that calculates 8% sales tax and returns it in a field called sales_tax.

2. Using multiple functions in one SQL query, find the absolute value of the result of 389.1245 divided by 28.43, rounded to the hundredth place.

3. How do the `FLOOR()` and `CEILING()` functions differ from the `ROUND()` function?

Answers

1. `SELECT (item_total * 0.08) AS sales_tax FROM orders;`

2. `SELECT ABS(ROUND(389.1245/28.43,2));`

3. `FLOOR()` and `CEILING()` will return the nearest lowest or highest integer, respectively. `ROUND()` finds the nearest number with a given decimal precision.

Activity

Create a sample table and populate it with purchase information, such as item and shipping totals. Work with the numbers using various mathematical and rounding functions, mimicking the real-life process of making a purchase. For example, use `SUM()` to add up the total of the items ordered, then use multiplication operators to find the total amount of the order plus sales tax, then add shipping costs, and finally round it all off to two decimal places.

16

HOUR 17

Using MySQL Date and Time Functions

The built-in functions used with dates and times are some of MySQL's most useful features. From displaying the current date and time to finding the amount of time between two dates, MySQL can take a lot of the programming burden off your hands.

In this hour, you will learn

- How to use date-related functions
- How to use time-related functions
- How to format date and time results
- How to find and express intervals between dates and times

Using Date and Time Functions in Queries

MySQL's built-in date-related functions can be used in SELECT statements, with or without specifying a table, to retrieve a result of the function. Or use the functions with any type of date field: date, datetime, timestamp, year. Depending on the type of field in use, the results of the date-related functions will be more or less useful.

Working with Days

The DAYOFWEEK() and WEEKDAY() functions do similar things with slightly different results. Both functions are used to find the weekday index of a date, but the difference lies in the starting day and position.

If you use DAYOFWEEK(), the first day of the week is Sunday, at position 1, and the last day of the week is Saturday, at position 7. For example:

```
mysql> SELECT DAYOFWEEK('2001-11-13');
+------------------------+
| DAYOFWEEK('2001-11-13') |
+------------------------+
|                      3 |
+------------------------+
1 row in set (0.00 sec)
```

The result shows that November 13, 2001 was weekday index 3, or Tuesday. Using the same date except with WEEKDAY() gives you a different result with the same meaning:

```
mysql> SELECT WEEKDAY('2001-11-13');
+----------------------+
| WEEKDAY('2001-11-13') |
+----------------------+
|                    1 |
+----------------------+
1 row in set (0.00 sec)
```

The result shows that November 13, 2001 was weekday index 1. Since WEEKDAY() uses Monday as the first day of the week at position 0 and Sunday as the last day at position 6, 1 is accurate: Tuesday.

The DAYOFMONTH() and DAYOFYEAR() functions are more straightforward, with only one result and a range that starts at 1 and ends at 31 for DAYOFMONTH() and 366 for DAYOFYEAR(). Some examples are shown below:

```
mysql> SELECT DAYOFMONTH('2001-11-13');
+-------------------------+
| DAYOFMONTH('2001-11-13') |
+-------------------------+
|                      13 |
+-------------------------+
1 row in set (0.00 sec)
```

```
mysql> SELECT DAYOFYEAR('2001-11-13');
+-------------------------+
| DAYOFYEAR('2001-11-13') |
+-------------------------+
|                     317 |
+-------------------------+
1 row in set (0.00 sec)
```

It may seem odd to have a function that returns the day of the month on a particular date since the day is right there in the string. But think about using these types of functions in WHERE clauses to perform comparisons on records. If you have a table that holds online orders with a field containing the date the order was placed, you can quickly get a count of the orders placed on any given day of the week or see how many orders were placed during the first half of the month versus the second half.

These two queries show how many orders were placed during the first three days of the week (throughout all months) and then the remaining days of the week:

```
mysql> SELECT COUNT(id) FROM orders WHERE DAYOFWEEK(date_ordered) < 4;
+-----------+
| COUNT(id) |
+-----------+
|         3 |
+-----------+
1 row in set (0.00 sec)

mysql> SELECT COUNT(id) FROM orders WHERE DAYOFWEEK(date_ordered) > 3;
+-----------+
| COUNT(id) |
+-----------+
|         5 |
+-----------+
1 row in set (0.00 sec)
```

Using DAYOFMONTH(), these examples show the number of orders placed during the first half of any month versus the second half:

```
mysql> SELECT COUNT(id) FROM orders WHERE DAYOFMONTH(date_ordered) < 16;
+-----------+
| COUNT(id) |
+-----------+
|         6 |
+-----------+
1 row in set (0.00 sec)

mysql> SELECT COUNT(id) FROM orders WHERE DAYOFMONTH(date_ordered) > 15;
+-----------+
| COUNT(id) |
+-----------+
|         2 |
+-----------+
1 row in set (0.00 sec)
```

17

You can throw in the DAYNAME() function to add more life to your results, as it returns the name of the weekday for any given date:

```
mysql> SELECT DAYNAME(date_ordered) FROM orders;
+----------------------+
| DAYNAME(date_ordered) |
+----------------------+
| Thursday             |
| Monday               |
| Thursday             |
| Thursday             |
| Wednesday            |
| Thursday             |
| Sunday               |
| Sunday               |
+----------------------+
8 rows in set (0.00 sec)
```

Functions aren't limited to WHERE clauses—you can use them in ORDER BY clauses as well:

```
mysql> SELECT DAYNAME(date_ordered) FROM orders
       ORDER BY DAYOFWEEK(date_ordered);
+----------------------+
| DAYNAME(date_ordered) |
+----------------------+
| Sunday               |
| Sunday               |
| Monday               |
| Wednesday            |
| Thursday             |
| Thursday             |
| Thursday             |
| Thursday             |
+----------------------+
8 rows in set (0.00 sec)
```

Working with Months and Years

Days of the week aren't the only parts of the calendar, and MySQL has functions specifically for months and years as well. Just like the DAYOFWEEK() and DAYNAME() functions, MONTH() and MONTHNAME() return the number of the month in a year and the name of the month for a given date. For example:

```
mysql> SELECT MONTH('2001-11-13'), MONTHNAME('2001-11-13');
+---------------------+-------------------------+
| MONTH('2001-11-13') | MONTHNAME('2001-11-13') |
+---------------------+-------------------------+
|                  11 | November                |
+---------------------+-------------------------+
1 row in set (0.00 sec)
```

Using MONTHNAME() on the sample orders table shows the proper results but a lot of repeating data:

```
mysql> SELECT MONTHNAME(date_ordered) FROM orders;
+-----------------------+
| MONTHNAME(date_ordered) |
+-----------------------+
| November              |
| November              |
| November              |
| November              |
| November              |
| November              |
| November              |
| October               |
+-----------------------+
8 rows in set (0.00 sec)
```

Remember, you can use DISTINCT to get non-repetitive results:

```
mysql> SELECT DISTINCT MONTHNAME(date_ordered) FROM orders;
+-----------------------+
| MONTHNAME(date_ordered) |
+-----------------------+
| November              |
| October               |
+-----------------------+
2 rows in set (0.00 sec)
```

For work with years, the YEAR() function will return the year of a given date:

```
mysql> SELECT DISTINCT YEAR(date_ordered) FROM orders;
+-------------------+
| YEAR(date_ordered) |
+-------------------+
|              2001 |
+-------------------+
1 row in set (0.00 sec)
```

Working with Weeks

Weeks can be tricky things—there can be 53 weeks in a year if Sunday is the first day of the week and December hasn't ended. For example, December 30th of 2001 is a Sunday:

```
mysql> SELECT DAYNAME('2001-12-30');
+-----------------------+
| DAYNAME('2001-12-30') |
+-----------------------+
| Sunday                |
+-----------------------+
1 row in set (0.00 sec)
```

Which would make that date part of the 53rd week of the year:

```
mysql> SELECT WEEK('2001-12-30');
+-------------------+
| WEEK('2001-12-30') |
+-------------------+
|                53 |
+-------------------+
1 row in set (0.00 sec)
```

The 53rd week contains December 30th and 31st and thus is only 2 days long; the first week of 2002 begins with January 1st.

If you want your weeks to start on Mondays but still want to find the week of the year, the optional second argument allows you to change the start day. A "1" indicates a week that starts on Monday. In the examples below, a Monday start day would make December 30th part of the 52nd week of 2001, but December 31 would still be part of the 53rd week of 2001.

```
mysql> SELECT WEEK('2001-12-30',1);
+---------------------+
| WEEK('2001-12-30',1) |
+---------------------+
|                  52 |
+---------------------+
1 row in set (0.00 sec)

mysql> SELECT WEEK('2001-12-31',1);
+---------------------+
| WEEK('2001-12-31',1) |
+---------------------+
|                  53 |
+---------------------+
1 row in set (0.00 sec)
```

Working with Hours, Minutes, and Seconds

If you are using a date that includes the exact time in it, such as datetime or timestamp, or even just a time field, there are functions to find the given hours, minutes, and seconds from that string. Not surprisingly, these functions are called HOUR(), MINUTE(), and SECOND(). HOUR() returns the hour in a given time, which is between 0 and 23. The range for MINUTE() and SECOND() is 0 to 59.

Here are some examples:

```
mysql> SELECT HOUR('2001-11-13 07:27:49') as hour,MINUTE('2001-11-13 07:27:49')
       as minute,SECOND('2001-11-13 07:27:49') as second;
+------+--------+--------+
| hour | minute | second |
```

```
+------+--------+--------+
|   7  |   27   |   49   |
+------+--------+--------+
1 row in set (0.00 sec)
```

That's a lot of queries to get at one time from a datetime field—you can put the hour and minute together and even use CONCAT_WS() to put the : between the results and get a representation of the time:

```
mysql> SELECT CONCAT_WS(':',HOUR('2001-11-13 07:27:49'),
       MINUTE('2001-11-13 07:27:49')) AS sample_time;
+-------------+
| sample_time |
+-------------+
| 7:27        |
+-------------+
1 row in set (0.00 sec)
```

If you use field names instead of strings, remember not to use quotation marks. Here's an example using the name_dateadded field of the master_name table in the contactDB database:

```
mysql> SELECT CONCAT_WS(':',HOUR(name_dateadded), MINUTE(name_dateadded))
       AS sample_time FROM master_name;
+-------------+
| sample_time |
+-------------+
| 13:11       |
| 13:11       |
| 13:11       |
| 13:11       |
| 14:16       |
| 10:12       |
| 10:12       |
| 10:12       |
| 10:12       |
+-------------+
9 rows in set (0.00 sec)
```

This is cheating because it's not the actual time—it's just two numbers stuck together to look like a time. If you used the concatenation trick on a time such as "02:02", the result would be "2:2", as shown below:

```
mysql> SELECT CONCAT_WS(':',HOUR('02:02'), MINUTE('02:02')) AS sample_time;
+-------------+
| sample_time |
+-------------+
| 2:2         |
+-------------+
1 row in set (0.00 sec)
```

17

This result is obviously not the intended result. In the next section, you'll learn how to use the DATE_FORMAT() function to properly format dates and times.

Formatting Dates and Times

The DATE_FORMAT() function will format a date, datetime, or timestamp field into a string, using options that tell it exactly how to display the results. The syntax of DATE_FORMAT() is

DATE_FORMAT(date,format)

There are many formatting options, as shown in Table 17.1.

TABLE 17.1 DATE_FORMAT() Format String Options

Option	Result
%M	Month name (January through December)
%b	Abbreviated month name (Jan through Dec)
%m	Month, padded digits (01 through 12)
%c	Month (1 through 12)
%W	Weekday name (Sunday through Saturday)
%a	Abbreviated weekday name (Sun through Sat)
%D	Day of the month using the English suffix, such as first, second, third, and so on
%d	Day of the month, padded digits (00 through 31)
%e	Day of the month (0 through 31)
%j	Day of the year, padded digits (001 through 366)
%Y	Year, 4 digits
%y	Year, 2 digits
%X	Four-digit year for the week where Sunday is the first day, used with %V
%x	Four-digit year for the week where Monday is the first day, used with %v
%w	Day of the week (0=Sunday…6=Saturday)
%U	Week (0 through 53) where Sunday is the first day of the week
%u	Week (0 through 53) where Monday is the first day of the week
%V	Week (1 through 53) where Sunday is the first day of the week, used with %X
%v	Week (1 through 53) where Monday is the first day of the week. Used with %x
%H	Hour, padded digits (00 through 23)
%k	Hour (0 through 23)
%h	Hour, padded digits (01 through 12)

continues

TABLE 17.1 Continued

Option	Result
%l	Hour (1 through 12)
%i	Minutes, padded digits (00 through 59)
%S	Seconds, padded digits (00 through 59)
%s	Seconds, padded digits (00 through 59)
%r	Time, 12-hour clock (hh:mm:ss [AP]M)
%T	Time, 24-hour clock (hh:mm:ss)
%p	AM or PM

> Any other characters used in the DATE_FORMAT() option string will appear literally.

17

To display the `02:02` result that was rigged in the previous section, you would use the `%h` and `%i` options to return the hour and minute from the date, with a : between the two options. For example:

```
mysql> SELECT DATE_FORMAT('2001-11-13 02:02:00', '%h:%i') AS sample_time;
+-------------+
| sample_time |
+-------------+
| 02:02       |
+-------------+
1 row in set (0.00 sec)
```

Following are just a few more examples of the DATE_FORMAT() function in use, but this function is best understood by practicing it yourself.

```
mysql> SELECT DATE_FORMAT('2001-11-13', '%W, %M %D, %Y') AS sample_time;
+-----------------------------+
| sample_time                 |
+-----------------------------+
| Tuesday, November 13th, 2001 |
+-----------------------------+
1 row in set (0.00 sec)
```

```
mysql> SELECT DATE_FORMAT(NOW(),'%W the %D of %M, %Y around %l o\'clock %p')
    -> AS sample_time;
+----------------------------------------------------------+
| sample_time                                              |
+----------------------------------------------------------+
| Tuesday the 13th of November, 2001 around 8 o'clock AM |
+----------------------------------------------------------+
1 row in set (0.00 sec)
```

If you are working specifically with time fields, the TIME_FORMAT() function works just like the DATE_FORMAT() function; only the format options for hours, minutes, and seconds are allowed:

```
mysql> SELECT TIME_FORMAT('02:02:00', '%h:%i') AS sample_time;
+-------------+
| sample_time |
+-------------+
| 02:02       |
+-------------+
1 row in set (0.00 sec)
```

Performing Date Arithmetic

MySQL has several functions to help perform date arithmetic. The DATE_ADD() and DATE_SUB() functions will return a result given a starting date and an interval. The syntax for both functions is

```
DATE_ADD(date,INTERVAL value type)
DATE_SUB(date,INTERVAL value type)
```

Table 17.2 shows the possible types and their expected value format.

TABLE 17.2   Values and Types in Date Arithmetic

Value	Type
Number of seconds	SECOND
Number of minutes	MINUTE
Number of hours	HOUR
Number of days	DAY
Number of months	MONTH
Number of years	YEAR
"minutes:seconds"	MINUTE_SECOND
"hours:minutes"	HOUR_MINUTE
"days hours"	DAY_HOUR
"years-months"	YEAR_MONTH
"hours:minutes:seconds"	HOUR_SECOND
"days hours:minutes"	DAY_MINUTE
"days hours:minutes:seconds"	DAY_SECOND

For example, to find the date of the current day plus 21 days you would use

```
mysql> SELECT DATE_ADD(NOW(), INTERVAL 21 DAY);
+---------------------------------+
| DATE_ADD(NOW(), INTERVAL 21 DAY) |
+---------------------------------+
| 2001-12-04 09:07:31             |
+---------------------------------+
1 row in set (0.00 sec)
```

To subtract 21 days use

```
mysql> SELECT DATE_SUB(NOW(), INTERVAL 21 DAY);
+---------------------------------+
| DATE_SUB(NOW(), INTERVAL 21 DAY) |
+---------------------------------+
| 2001-10-23 09:08:30             |
+---------------------------------+
1 row in set (0.00 sec)
```

Use the expression as it's shown in the list above, despite what may be a natural tendency to use DAYS instead of DAY. Using DAYS would result in an error:

```
mysql> SELECT DATE_ADD(NOW(), INTERVAL 21 DAYS);
ERROR 1064: You have an error in your SQL syntax near 'DAYS)' at line 1
```

If you are using DATE_ADD() or DATE_SUB() with a date value instead of a datetime value, the result will be shown as a date value unless you use expressions related to hours, minutes, and seconds. In that case, your result will be a datetime result.

For example, the result of the first query remains a date field, whereas the second becomes a datetime:

```
mysql> SELECT DATE_ADD("2001-12-31", INTERVAL 1 DAY);
+---------------------------------------+
| DATE_ADD("2001-12-31", INTERVAL 1 DAY) |
+---------------------------------------+
| 2002-01-01                            |
+---------------------------------------+
1 row in set (0.00 sec)

mysql> SELECT DATE_ADD("2001-12-31", INTERVAL 12 HOUR);
+-----------------------------------------+
| DATE_ADD("2001-12-31", INTERVAL 12 HOUR) |
+-----------------------------------------+
| 2001-12-31 12:00:00                     |
+-----------------------------------------+
1 row in set (0.00 sec)
```

Starting with MySQL version 3.23, you can also perform date arithmetic using the + and - operators instead of DATE_ADD() or DATE_SUB() functions:

17

```
mysql> SELECT "2001-12-31" + INTERVAL 1 DAY;
+-------------------------------+
| "2001-12-31" + INTERVAL 1 DAY |
+-------------------------------+
| 2002-01-01                    |
+-------------------------------+
1 row in set (0.00 sec)

mysql> SELECT "2001-12-31" - INTERVAL 14 HOUR;
+---------------------------------+
| "2001-12-31" - INTERVAL 14 HOUR |
+---------------------------------+
| 2001-12-30 10:00:00             |
+---------------------------------+
1 row in set (0.00 sec)
```

Special Functions and Conversion Features

You've previously learned about the NOW() function, which returns a current datetime result. MySQL has a few other functions that perform similar tasks.

The CURDATE() and CURRENT_DATE() functions are synonymous, and each will return just the current date in "YYYY-MM-DD" format:

```
mysql> SELECT CURDATE(), CURRENT_DATE();
+------------+----------------+
| CURDATE()  | CURRENT_DATE() |
+------------+----------------+
| 2001-11-13 | 2001-11-13     |
+------------+----------------+
1 row in set (0.00 sec)
```

Similarly, the CURTIME() and CURRENT_TIME() functions return the current time in "HH:MM:SS" format:

```
mysql> SELECT CURTIME(), CURRENT_TIME();
+-----------+----------------+
| CURTIME() | CURRENT_TIME() |
+-----------+----------------+
| 09:36:13  | 09:36:13       |
+-----------+----------------+
1 row in set (0.00 sec)
```

The NOW(), SYSDATE(), and CURRENT_TIMESTAMP() functions all return values in full datetime format ("YYYY-MM-DD HH:MM:SS"):

```
mysql> SELECT NOW(), SYSDATE(), CURRENT_TIMESTAMP();
+---------------------+---------------------+---------------------+
| NOW()               | SYSDATE()           | CURRENT_TIMESTAMP() |
+---------------------+---------------------+---------------------+
| 2001-11-13 09:41:36 | 2001-11-13 09:41:36 | 2001-11-13 09:41:36 |
+---------------------+---------------------+---------------------+
1 row in set (0.00 sec)
```

The UNIX_TIMESTAMP() function returns the current date in—or converts a given date to—UNIX timestamp format. UNIX timestamp format is in seconds since the epoch, or seconds since midnight, January 1, 1970. For example:

```
mysql> SELECT UNIX_TIMESTAMP();
+------------------+
| UNIX_TIMESTAMP() |
+------------------+
|       1005673390 |
+------------------+
1 row in set (0.00 sec)

mysql> SELECT UNIX_TIMESTAMP('1973-12-30');
+------------------------------+
| UNIX_TIMESTAMP('1973-12-30') |
+------------------------------+
|                    126086400 |
+------------------------------+
1 row in set (0.00 sec)
```

The FROM_UNIXTIME() function will perform a conversion of a UNIX timestamp to a full datetime format when used without any options:

```
mysql> SELECT FROM_UNIXTIME('1005673390');
+-----------------------------+
| FROM_UNIXTIME('1005673390') |
+-----------------------------+
| 2001-11-13 09:43:10         |
+-----------------------------+
1 row in set (0.00 sec)
```

You can use the format options from the DATE_FORMAT() functions to display a time stamp in a more appealing manner:

```
mysql> SELECT FROM_UNIXTIME(UNIX_TIMESTAMP(), '%D %M %Y at %h:%i:%s');
+--------------------------------------------------------+
| FROM_UNIXTIME(UNIX_TIMESTAMP(), '%D %M %Y at %h:%i:%s') |
+--------------------------------------------------------+
| 13th November 2001 at 09:48:00                         |
+--------------------------------------------------------+
1 row in set (0.00 sec)
```

If you are just working with a number of seconds and want to convert the seconds to a time-formatted result, you can use SEC_TO_TIME() and TIME_TO_SEC() to convert values back and forth.

For example, 1440 seconds is equal to 24 minutes and vice versa:

```
mysql> SELECT SEC_TO_TIME('1440'), TIME_TO_SEC('00:24:00');
+---------------------+-------------------------+
| SEC_TO_TIME('1440') | TIME_TO_SEC('00:24:00') |
+---------------------+-------------------------+
| 00:24:00            |                    1440 |
+---------------------+-------------------------+
1 row in set (0.01 sec)
```

17

Summary

The date and time functions built in to MySQL can definitely take some of the load off your application by internally formatting dates and times and performing the date and time arithmetic. The formatting options used for the DATE_FORMAT() function provide a simple method to produce a custom display string from any sort of date field. The DATE_ADD() and DATE_SUB() functions and their numerous available interval types help you determine dates and times in the past or future. Additionally, functions such as DAY(), WEEK(), MONTH(), and YEAR() are useful for extracting parts of dates for use in WHERE or ORDER BY clauses.

Workshop

The Workshop is designed to help you anticipate possible questions, review what you've learned, and begin learning how to put your knowledge into practice.

Quiz

1. Write a query to find the date and time exactly 8 days and 4 hours from this exact moment.

2. Write a query that finds all entries added to your master_name table within in the current month.

3. Write a query to extract the date added for each record in your master_name table in UNIX timestamp format.

Answers

1. SELECT DATE_ADD(NOW(), INTERVAL "4 8" DAY_HOUR);

2. SELECT * FROM master_name WHERE (MONTH(name_dateadded) = MONTH(NOW()));

3. SELECT UNIX_TIMESTAMP(name_dateadded) FROM master_name;

Activities

1. Practice using the DATE_FORMAT() function to return date strings. Be sure to escape any quotation marks used as part of your options, like "o'clock".

2. Work with the DATE_ADD() and DATE_SUB() functions within WHERE clauses to SELECT or DELETE records from your sample tables that have dates that fall within given intervals.

PART VI
Using Transactions

Hour

Hour **18**

Transactions Overview

Transactions are a new addition to MySQL but not to relational database systems in general. If you have used an enterprise database system, such as Oracle or Microsoft SQL Server, the transactional concept should seem familiar. If this is your first venture into relational databases, this hour will bring you up to speed and provide an overview of using transactions in MySQL.

In this hour, you will learn about

- The basic properties of transactions
- Berkeley DB, InnoDB, and Gemini table types

What Are Transactions?

A transaction is a sequential group of database manipulation operations, which is performed as if it were one single work unit. In other words, a transaction will never be complete unless each individual operation within the group is successful. If any operation within the transaction fails, the entire transaction will fail.

A good example would be a banking transaction, specifically a transfer of $100 between two accounts. In order to deposit money into one account, you must first take money from another account. Without using transactions, you would have to write SQL statements that do the following:

1. Check that the balance of the first account is greater than $100.
2. Deduct $100 from the first account.
3. Add $100 to the second account.

Additionally, you would have to write your own error-checking routines within your program, specifically to stop the sequence of events should the first account not have more than $100 or should the deduction statement fail. This all changes with transactions, for if any part of the operation fails, the entire transaction is rolled back. This means that the tables and the data inside them revert to their previous state.

Properties of Transactions

Transactions have the following four standard properties, usually referred to by the acronym ACID:

- Atomicity ensures that all operations within the work unit are completed successfully; otherwise, the transaction is aborted at the point of failure, and previous operations are rolled back to their former state.
- Consistency ensures that the database properly changes states upon a successfully committed transaction.
- Isolation enables transactions to operate independently of and transparent to each other.
- Durability ensures that the result or effect of a committed transaction persists in case of a system failure.

In MySQL, transactions begin with the statement BEGIN WORK and end with either a COMMIT or a ROLLBACK statement. The SQL commands between the beginning and ending statements form the bulk of the transaction.

COMMIT and ROLLBACK

When a successful transaction is completed, the COMMIT command should be issued so that the changes to all involved tables will take effect. If a failure occurs, a ROLLBACK command should be issued to return every table referenced in the transaction to its previous state.

In MySQL as well as NuSphere's Enhanced MySQL, you can set the value of a session variable called AUTOCOMMIT. If AUTOCOMMIT is set to 1 (the default), then each SQL statement (within a transaction or not) is considered a complete transaction, committed by default when it finishes. When AUTOCOMMIT is set to 0, by issuing the SET AUTOCOMMIT=0 command, the subsequent series of statements acts like a transaction, and no activities are committed until an explicit COMMIT statement is issued.

If transactions were not used in application development, a large amount of programming time would be spent on intricate error checking. For example, suppose your application handles customer order information, with tables holding general order information as well as line items for that order. To insert an order into the system, the process would be something like the following:

1. Insert a master record into the master order table.
2. Retrieve the ID from the master order record you just entered.
3. Insert records into the line items table for each item ordered.

If you are not in a transactional environment, you will be left with some straggly data floating around your tables; if the addition of the record into the master order table succeeds, but steps 2 or 3 fail, you are left with a master order without any line items. The responsibility then falls on you to use programming logic and check that all relevant records in multiple tables have been added or go back and delete all the records that have been added and offer error messages to the user. This is extremely time-consuming, both in man-hours as well as in program-execution time.

In a transactional environment, you'd never get to the point of childless rows, as a transaction either fails completely or is completely successful.

Row-Level Locking

Transactional table types support row-level locking, which differs from the table-level locking that is enforced in MyISAM and other nontransactional table types. With tables that support row-level locking, only the row touched by an INSERT, UPDATE, or DELETE statement is inaccessible until a COMMIT is issued.

Rows affected by a SELECT query will have shared locks, unless otherwise specified by the programmer. A shared lock allows for multiple concurrent SELECT queries of the data. However, if you hold an exclusive lock on a row, you are the only one who can read or modify that row until the lock is released. Locks are released when transactions end through a COMMIT or ROLLBACK statement.

Setting an exclusive lock requires you to add the FOR UPDATE clause to your query. In the sequence below, you can see how locks are used to check available inventory in a product catalog before processing an order. This example builds on the previous example by adding more condition-checking.

> This sequence of events is independent of the programming language used; the logical path can be created in whichever language you use to create your application.

1. Begin transaction.

   ```
   BEGIN WORK;
   ```

2. Check available inventory for a product with a specific ID, using a table called inventory and a field called qty.

   ```
   SELECT qty FROM inventory WHERE id = 'ABC-001' FOR UPDATE;
   ```

3. If the result is less than the amount ordered, rollback the transaction to release the lock.

   ```
   ROLLBACK;
   ```

4. If the result is greater than the amount ordered, continue issuing a statement that reserves the required amount for the order.

   ```
   UPDATE inventory SET qty = qty - [amount ordered] WHERE id = 'ABC-001';
   ```

5. Insert a master record into the master order table.

6. Retrieve the ID from the master order record you just entered.

7. Insert records into the line items table for each item ordered.

8. If steps 5 through 7 are successful, commit the transaction and release the lock.

   ```
   COMMIT;
   ```

While the transaction remains uncommitted and the lock remains in effect, no other users can access the record in the inventory table for the product with the ID of ABC-001. If a user requests the current quantity for the item with the ID of ABC-002, that row still operates under the shared lock rules and can be read.

Transaction-Safe Table Types in MySQL

To use transactions in MySQL, you must use a transaction-safe table type. The default MySQL table type, MyISAM, does not support transactions. BerkeleyDB and InnoDB are the transaction-safe table types available in the open source MySQL, version 3.23.34 and greater, whereas the Gemini table is used for transactions in NuSphere's Enhanced MySQL.

BerkeleyDB

BerkeleyDB is a product from Sleepycat Software (http://www.sleepycat.com/), which provides MySQL with a transaction-safe table type. Support for BerkeleyDB tables began with version 3.23.34 of the open source MySQL and requires a specific compilation parameter when compiling MySQL from source. Most users do not compile MySQL from source and instead rely on whatever has been installed by their Internet Service Provider. If this is true for you, there are two options: ask your Internet Service Provider to build a version of MySQL with support for BerkeleyDB table types, or download and install the MySQL-Max binary distribution for Windows or Linux/UNIX and work with the table type in a development environment.

If your MySQL installation supports BerkeleyDB tables, simply add a TYPE=BDB definition to the table creation statement. For example, the following code creates a BerkeleyDB table called test, with two fields:

```
mysql> CREATE TABLE test (
    -> id INT NOT NULL PRIMARY KEY AUTO_INCREMENT,
    -> sample_text VARCHAR(25)
    -> ) TYPE=BDB;
```

The BerkeleyDB table type is a usable, transaction-safe table type, but it is not the most optimized table type in the mix. BerkeleyDB tables support the basic elements of transactions as well as the AUTOCOMMIT variable, but are not as popular or as developed as the InnoDB or Gemini table types.

You can learn more about the BerkeleyDB table type in the MySQL manual at http://www.mysql.com/doc/B/D/BDB.html.

InnoDB

InnoDB is the more popular and stable transaction-safe table type in open source MySQL and was designed specifically for high performance with large volumes of data, as well as overall CPU efficiency—two very important features in Web application development. As with the BerkeleyDB table type, InnoDB is not the default table type, and support for it did not appear until version 3.23.34 of the open source MySQL.

Support for InnoDB tables requires a specific compilation parameter when compiling MySQL from source. If your MySQL version does not have InnoDB support, ask your Internet Service Provider to build a version of MySQL with support for InnoDB table types, or download and install the MySQL-Max binary distribution for Windows or Linux/UNIX and work with the table type in a development environment.

If your MySQL installation supports InnoDB tables, simply add a TYPE=InnoDB definition to the table creation statement. For example, the following code creates an InnoDB table called test2, with two fields:

18

```
mysql> CREATE TABLE test2 (
    -> id INT NOT NULL PRIMARY KEY AUTO_INCREMENT,
    -> sample_text VARCHAR(25)
    -> ) TYPE=InnoDB;
```

You can learn much more about the InnoDB table type in the MySQL manual at
`http://www.mysql.com/doc/I/n/InnoDB.html`.

Gemini

The Gemini table type is available only in NuSphere's Enhanced MySQL product and
not in the open source version of MySQL. If you have purchased Enhanced MySQL or
have access to it through your Internet Service Provider, simply add a `TYPE=Gemini` definition to the table creation statement. For example, the following code creates a Gemini
table called `test2`, with two fields:

```
mysql> CREATE TABLE test3 (
    -> id INT NOT NULL PRIMARY KEY AUTO_INCREMENT,
    -> sample_text VARCHAR(25)
    -> ) TYPE=Gemini;
```

You can learn much more about the Gemini table type in the NuSphere Tech Library, at
`http://www.nusphere.com/products/tech_library.htm`.

Summary

Transactions are groups of operations performed as one single work unit. The four basic
properties of transactions are atomicity, consistency, isolation, and durability, which form
the acronym "ACID."

To use transactions in MySQL, you must use a transaction-safe table type, such as
Berke' DB or InnoDB. If you own NuSphere Enhanced MySQL, the transaction-safe
table type is called Gemini.

A transaction fails if any operation within it fails. If none of the operations fail, then
you can COMMIT the transaction, which finalizes all the changes made while it was
active. If a transaction fails, use the ROLLBACK command to return all affected tables to
their previous state.

Workshop

The Workshop is designed to help you anticipate possible questions, review what you've learned, and begin learning how to put your knowledge into practice.

Quiz

1. What are the four basic properties of transactions? Hint: think "ACID."
2. What SQL statement should be used to indicate that subsequent statements form a transaction?
3. If query #3 of a 5-query transaction fails, what SQL command should be issued so affected tables revert to their previous state?

Answers

1. Atomicity, consistency, isolation, and durability.
2. BEGIN WORK
3. ROLLBACK

Activity

Based on the table design of your contact management system, think about how the tables relate to each other and how transactions would help maintain the integrity of your data. Think about inserting records in logical groupings, as well as deleting related records.

18

Hour 19

Practical Transaction Usage

Knowing that transactions exist and can be used in MySQL is all well and good, but there's still a thought process that must occur. You'll have to create a schema that accommodates a transactional model or possibly re-work an existing schema to use transaction-safe tables.

In this hour, you will learn

- How to convert existing tables to transaction-safe tables
- When to use transaction-safe tables
- How to integrate transactions into existing applications, specifically the contact management application

Converting Tables to Transaction-Safe Table Types

You have already learned how to create tables that support transactions by using TYPE when you issue the CREATE TABLE statement. If you have a MyISAM table (or another non-transaction-safe table) that you wish to convert to BDB, InnoDB, or Gemini, the ALTER TABLE command will do this for you. The syntax for a table type change is

```
ALTER TABLE table_name TYPE=new_type
```

For example, if you would like to convert the master_name in the contactDB database to an InnoDB table, you would use

```
mysql> ALTER TABLE master_name TYPE=InnoDB;
```

Similarly, you would use TYPE=BDB to convert to BDB tables and TYPE=Gemini to convert to Gemini tables.

 To perform any table conversions, the new table type must be enabled in your version of the open source MySQL. If you use the MySQL-Max product from MySQL AB, support for the InnoDB and Berkeley DB table types is already built in and enabled. With NuSphere's Enhanced MySQL, you can use the Gemini table type right out of the box.

Additionally, users with shell access (and permission to execute MySQL utility scripts) can use the mysql_convert_table_format script to convert a table to a particular type. Executed from the data directory of a given database, the syntax is

```
#prompt> mysql_convert_table_format  —user='username'  —password='password'
         —type='new_type' table_name
```

So, to use the mysql_convert_table_format script to convert master_name in the contactDB database to an InnoDB table, you would type

```
#prompt> mysql_convert_table_format  —user='supercontact'  —password='somepass'
         —type='InnoDB' master_name
```

Using Transactions in Your Applications

When starting to develop an application from scratch with no database schema to speak of, you can easily think ahead and create the perfect mix of transaction-safe and MyISAM (non-transaction-safe) table types for your application. After creating the tables, you then have solid ground to stand on to define and implement transactions within your actual programming code. Just like creating a database for an application without transactions, such as the original contact management database, the planning stage is the most important stage in the creation process.

When to Use Transaction-Safe Tables

Not all tables need to be transaction-safe tables, only tables whose content comes primarily from INSERT, UPDATE, or DELETE actions. In other words, if you have tables containing static content (SELECT only), these do not need to be transaction-safe tables.

 With transaction-safe tables comes an increase in the amount of system resources needed to use those table types. This transaction overhead shouldn't be welcomed into your system—if you don't need a transaction-safe table, don't use one!

Think about a database for an online store, which would contain tables relating to customer orders and a product catalog. The customer order tables would have records added to them when an order is finalized, whereas the product tables would be the home for both static and dynamic content, ranging from product descriptions to the available inventory of an item.

In a basic system of this type, you would probably store the name and address of the customer, the order number and date, and a line item for each item ordered. Some of the address information may come from static tables holding "official" names of U.S. states and other countries. Except for these static tables, all other order-related tables should be transaction-safe tables because of the dependencies and possible need for transactional rollback. For example, an order wouldn't be complete unless it had line items attached to it. In that case, if an order entry appears in a customer table without any related line items, or if line items exist without a master order attached to them, this is an indication that something has gone dreadfully wrong. If the affected tables are transaction safe, the order process could be rolled back, a message could be displayed to the user regarding the error, and no straggly records would exist in your tables.

Modifying the contactDB Schema

The basic schema for the contact management system does not contain any transaction-safe tables. By using a few ALTER TABLE commands, you can easily take care of this! Before you start changing table types, remember that not all tables need to be transaction safe. Think about the requirements of your system—it's a contact-management system, so at least one form of contact must be required when adding a record.

If you use telephone numbers and e-mail addresses for most of your contacts, make the
e-mail and telephone tables transaction-safe, as well as the master_name table. Select a
transaction-safe table type (BDB, InnoDB, or Gemini) and use the ALTER TABLE command to change the table type:

```
mysql> ALTER TABLE master_name TYPE=InnoDB;
mysql> ALTER TABLE email TYPE=InnoDB;
mysql> ALTER TABLE telephone TYPE=InnoDB;
```

The remaining tables do not need to be transaction-safe if they are ever used only in simple actions that do not break the model of your application. For example, suppose you
select a person from the master_name table and then attempt to add a new address record
for that person. If the addition of the address record fails, the master_name table is not
affected, nor is the rule regarding required entries—entries are required only in the email
and telephone tables, for each contact.

If you decide to make any of the other information (address, company, fax, job function,
or personal notes) required, those tables should be altered into transaction-safe tables.
Until then, it's fine to leave well enough alone and keep some of your tables MyISAM
while others are transaction-safe.

Programming Transactions in the Contact Management System

Based on the required information for records in your contact management system, you
can determine a logical transaction for use in the programming of the application.

NEW TERM   *Pseudocode*   When you write psuedocode, you're writing in plain English (or
your native language) a step-by-step method for solving a problem. Psuedocode
contains no actual programming code; rather, it is just the logical flow of coding events
toward a solution.

Think of the entire record addition process in pseudocode:

1. Insert first name and last name into the master_name table.

2. If successful, you'll need to get the value of name_id for the record you just added.

3. If a failure, there's no need to specifically rollback anything at this point because
    nothing was inserted in any required tables.

4. Once you have the value of the name_id, add a record to the email table.

5. If the insertion of the record in the email table fails, rollback the transaction. You
    can't have a record in the master_name table without a matching entry in the email
    table.

6. If the insertion of the record into the email table is successful, insert a record into the telephone table.

7. If the insertion of the record in the telephone table fails, rollback the transaction. You can't have a record in the master_name table without a matching entry in the telephone table, nor can a record exist in master_name and email without another in telephone.

8. If associated records were inserted successfully into the master_name, email, and telephone tables, commit the transaction.

An error-free transaction with no explicit ROLLBACK would look something like this, replacing "..." with actual values of course:

```
BEGIN WORK;
INSERT INTO master_name VALUES (...);
SELECT LAST_INSERT_ID();
INSERT INTO email VALUES (...);
INSERT INTO telephone VALUES (...);
COMMIT;
```

If any of the statements within the transaction should fail, the transaction will not be committed. Within your application programming, you should add code that will rollback the transaction at the point of failure and also inform the user of an error.

In the listing below, the error-free transaction has been modified according to the steps in the pseudocode, showing when to display an error and when to issue a ROLLBACK. The lines that are commented out (preceded with //) would be replaced by actual application programming in the language of your choice.

```
BEGIN WORK;
INSERT INTO master_name VALUES (...);

// If failure occurs:
    // display error to user and exit

// If successful:
    SELECT LAST_INSERT_ID();
    INSERT INTO email VALUES (...);

    // If failure occurs:
        // ROLLBACK the transaction
        // display error to user and exit

    // If successful:
        INSERT INTO telephone VALUES (...);
```

19

```
// If failure occurs:
    // ROLLBACK the transaction
    // display error to user and exit

// If successful:
    COMMIT;
    // display success message to user
```

Transactions are simply sets of related or dependent statements with BEGIN WORK and COMMIT/ROLLBACK wrapped around them. As long as you issue those statements in your application programming, you can use your transaction-aware tables to their fullest potential.

Summary

The process of converting existing MyISAM tables to transaction-safe table types is a simple one. The ALTER TABLE command is used to change the type, or you can use the mysql_convert_table_format utility script. Before changing the table type, be sure that your installation of MySQL supports the new type!

Not all tables need to be transaction-safe. Because of the additional overhead involved in using transaction-safe tables, only those tables that will play a role in a transaction (that is, those that may need to be rolled back at some point) should be transaction safe. Three tables from the existing contactDB were modified to become transaction safe, whereas the remaining tables did not have requirements that necessitate transactions.

When you create a transaction within your application programming, you're simply issuing sets of related or dependent statements between BEGIN WORK and COMMIT or ROLLBACK statements. Additional programming should be used to display messages explaining any errors to the user. If a transaction is rolled back, the person who made the error certainly needs to know!

Workshop

The Workshop is designed to help you anticipate possible questions, review what you've learned, and begin learning how to put your knowledge into practice.

Quiz

1. Write a SQL command used to change the type of a table named myTable to the InnoDB table type.

2. In a database used for an online store, would a table containing the acceptable abbreviations for state names be a good candidate for a transaction-safe table type? Why or why not?

3. Which MySQL function was used in the example transaction to find last inserted id in a table?

Answers

1. ALTER TABLE myTable TYPE=InnoDB

2. No; a list of states and abbreviations would be static information used for reference purposes and not dependent on anything. It would be used only for SELECT purposes, so making it transaction-safe would be overkill.

3. LAST_INSERT_ID()

Activity

Suppose that an entry is required in all of the tables in contactDB as part of your contact management system. Using pseudocode, write out all of the steps that would be taken during a record insertion transaction, including error display and commit/rollback.

19

PART VII

Administering Your MySQL Server

Hour

HOUR 20

Optimizing and Tuning Your Database

Proper care and feeding of your MySQL server will keep it running happily and without incident. The optimization of your system consists of proper hardware maintenance and software tuning, as well as the database design methods you've learned throughout this book.

In this hour, you will learn

- Basic hardware and software optimization tips for your MySQL server
- Key start-up parameters for your MySQL server
- How to use the OPTIMIZE command
- How to use the EXPLAIN command

Building an Optimized Platform

Designing a well-structured, normalized database schema is just half of the optimization puzzle. The other half is building and fine-tuning a server to run this fine database. Think about the four main components of a server: CPU, memory, hard drive, and operating system. Each of these better be up to speed, or no amount of design or programming will make your database faster!

- CPU—The faster the CPU, the faster MySQL will be able to process your data. There's no real secret to this, but a 750 MHz processor is significantly faster than a 266 MHz processor. With processor speeds now over 1 GHz, and with reasonable prices all around, it's not difficult to get a good bang for your buck.

- Memory—Put as much RAM in your machine as you can. You can never have enough, and RAM prices will be at rock bottom for the foreseeable future. Having available RAM can help balance out sluggish CPUs.

- Hard Drive—The proper hard drive will be both large enough and fast enough to accommodate your database server and its traffic. An important measurement of hard drive speed is its seek time, or the amount of time it takes for the drive to spin around and find a specific piece of information. Seek time is measured in milliseconds, and an average disk seek time is around 8 or 9 milliseconds. When buying a hard drive, make sure it's big enough to accommodate all the data you'll eventually store in your database and fast enough to find it quickly.

- Operating System—If you use an operating system that's a resource hog, you have two choices: buy enough resources (that is, RAM) so that it doesn't matter, or use an operating system that doesn't suck away all your resources just so that you can have windows and pretty colors. Also, if you are blessed with a machine with multiple processors, be sure your operating system can handle this condition and handle it well.

If you put the proper pieces together at the system level, you'll have taken several steps toward overall server optimization.

Using the `benchmark()` Function

A quick test of your server speed is to use the benchmark() MySQL function to see how long it takes to process a given expression. You can make the expression something simple, such as 10 + 10, or something more extravagant, such as extracting pieces of dates.

No matter the result of the expression, the result of benchmark() will always be 0. The purpose of benchmark() is not to retrieve the result of the expression but to see how long it takes to repeat the expression for a specific number of times. For example, the following command executes the expression 10 + 10 one million times:

```
mysql> SELECT BENCHMARK(1000000,10+10);
+--------------------------+
| BENCHMARK(1000000,10+10) |
+--------------------------+
|                        0 |
+--------------------------+
1 row in set (0.14 sec)
```

This command executes the date extraction expression, also one million times:

```
mysql> SELECT BENCHMARK(1000000, EXTRACT(YEAR FROM NOW()));
+----------------------------------------------+
| BENCHMARK(1000000, EXTRACT(YEAR FROM NOW())) |
+----------------------------------------------+
|                                            0 |
+----------------------------------------------+
1 row in set (0.20 sec)
```

The important number is the time in seconds, which is the elapsed time for the execution of the function. You may want to run the same uses of benchmark() multiple times during different times of day (when your server is under different loads) to get a better idea of how your server is performing.

MySQL Startup Options

MySQL AB provides a wealth of information regarding the tuning of server parameters, much of which the average user will never need to use. So as not to completely overwhelm you with information, this section will contain a few of the more common startup options for a finely tuned MySQL server.

When you start MySQL, a configuration file called my.cnf is loaded. This file contains information ranging from port number to buffer sizes but can be overruled by command-line startup options. At installation time, my.cnf is placed in the /etc/ directory, but you can also specify an alternate location for this file during start-up.

In the support-files sub-directory of your MySQL installation directory, you'll find four sample configuration files, each tuned for a specific range of installed memory:

- my-small.cnf—For systems with less than 64MB of RAM, where MySQL is used occasionally.

20

- `my-medium.cnf`—For systems with less than 64MB of RAM, where MySQL is the primary activity on the system, or for systems with up to 128MB of RAM, where MySQL shares the box with other processes. This is the most common configuration, where MySQL is installed on the same box as a Web server and receives a moderate amount of traffic.
- `my-large.cnf`—For a system with 128MB to 512MB of RAM, where MySQL is the primary activity.
- `my-huge.cnf`—For a system with 1GB to 2GB of RAM, where MySQL is the primary activity.

To use any of these as the base configuration file, simply copy the file of your choice to `/etc/my.cnf` (or wherever `my.cnf` is on your system) and change any system-specific information, such as port or file locations.

Key Startup Parameters

There are two primary start-up parameters that will affect your system the most: `key_buffer_size` and `table_cache`. If you get only two server parameters correctly tuned, make sure they're these two!

The value of `key_buffer_size` is the size of the buffer used with indexes. The larger the buffer, the faster the SQL command will finish and a result will be returned. Try to find the fine line between finely tuned and over-optimized; you may have a `key_buffer_size` of 256MB on a system with 512MB of RAM, but any more than 256MB could cause degraded server performance.

A simple way to check the actual performance of the buffer is to examine four additional variables: `key_read_requests`, `key_reads`, `key_write_requests`, and `key_writes`. You can find the values of these variables by issuing the SHOW STATUS command:

```
mysql> SHOW STATUS;
```

You'll learn more about the SHOW command in Hour 22, "Basic Administrative Commands."

A long list of variables and values will be returned, listed in alphabetical order. Find the rows that look something like this (your values will differ):

```
| Key_read_requests    | 602843 |
| Key_reads            | 151    |
| Key_write_requests   | 1773   |
| Key_writes           | 805    |
```

If you divide the value of `key_read` by the value of `key_reads_requests`, the result should be less than 0.01. Also, if you divide the value of `key_write` by the value of `key_writes_requests`, the result should be less than 1. Using the values above, we have results of 0.000250479809834401 and 0.454032712915962 respectively, well within the acceptable parameters. To try to get these numbers even smaller, more tuning could occur by increasing the value of `key_buffer_size`, but these numbers would be fine to leave as they are.

The other important server parameter is `table_cache`, which is the number of open tables for all threads. The default is 64, but you may need to adjust this number. Using the `SHOW STATUS` command, look for a variable called `open_tables` in the output. If this number is large, the value of `table_cache` should be increased.

The sample configuration files use various combinations of `key_buffer_size` and `table_cache`, which you can use as a baseline for any modifications you need to make. Whenever you modify your configuration, you'll be restarting your server in order for changes to take effect, sometimes with no knowledge of the consequences of your changes. In this case, be sure to try your modifications in a development environment before rolling the changes into production.

Optimizing Your Table Structure

An optimized table structure is different than a well-designed table. Table structure optimization has to do with reclaiming unused space after deletions and basically cleaning up the table after structural modifications have been made. The `OPTIMIZE` SQL command takes care of this, using the following syntax:

```
OPTIMIZE TABLE table_name[,table_name]
```

For example, if you want to optimize the `master_name` table in your contact management database, use:

```
mysql> OPTIMIZE TABLE master_name;
+---------------------+----------+----------+----------+
| Table               | Op       | Msg_type | Msg_text |
+---------------------+----------+----------+----------+
| contactDB.master_name | optimize | status   | OK       |
+---------------------+----------+----------+----------+
1 row in set (0.08 sec)
```

20

The output doesn't explicitly state what was fixed, but the text in the `Msg_text` column shows that the `master_name` table was indeed optimized. If you run the command again, the text will change, showing that it is a useful message:

```
mysql> OPTIMIZE TABLE master_name;
+----------------------+----------+----------+---------------------------+
| Table                | Op       | Msg_type | Msg_text                  |
+----------------------+----------+----------+---------------------------+
| contactDB.master_name | optimize | status   | Table is already up to date |
+----------------------+----------+----------+---------------------------+
1 row in set (0.03 sec)
```

Be aware that the table is locked while it is optimized, so if your table is large, optimize it during scheduled downtime or when little traffic is flowing to your system.

> You can use `OPTIMIZE` on only MyISAM and BDB tables.

Optimizing Your Queries

Query optimization has a lot to do with the proper use of indexes. The `EXPLAIN` command will examine a given `SELECT` statement to see whether it's optimized the best that it can be, using indexes wherever possible. This is especially useful when looking at complex queries involving `JOIN`. The syntax for `EXPLAIN` is

EXPLAIN SELECT *statement*

The output of the `EXPLAIN` command is a table of information containing the following columns:

- `table`—The name of the table.
- `type`—The join type, of which there are several.
- `possible_keys`—This column indicates which indexes MySQL could use to find the rows in this table. If the result is `NULL`, no indexes would help with this query. You should then take a look at your table structure and see whether there are any indexes that you could create that would increase the performance of this query.
- `key`—The key actually used in this query, or `NULL` if no index was used.
- `key_len`—The length of the key used, if any.
- `ref`—Any columns used with the `key` to retrieve a result.
- `rows`—The number of rows MySQL must examine to execute the query.
- `extra`—Additional information regarding how MySQL will execute the query.

There are several options, such as Using index (an index was used) and Where (a WHERE clause was used).

The following EXPLAIN command output shows a non-optimized query:

```
mysql> EXPLAIN SELECT * FROM master_name;
+-------------+------+---------------+------+---------+------+------+-------+
| table       | type | possible_keys | key  | key_len | ref  | rows | Extra |
+-------------+------+---------------+------+---------+------+------+-------+
| master_name | ALL  | NULL          | NULL |    NULL | NULL |    9 |       |
+-------------+------+---------------+------+---------+------+------+-------+
1 row in set (0.00 sec)
```

However, there's not much optimizing you can do with a "select all" query except add a WHERE clause with the primary key. The possible_keys column would then show PRIMARY, and the Extra column would show Where used.

Think back to the example in Hour 11, "Advanced Usage of SELECT Statements," where you used a RIGHT JOIN on the master_name and email tables. Using EXPLAIN, you can see that this is an optimized query:

FIGURE 20.1

EXPLAIN *output for an optimized query.*

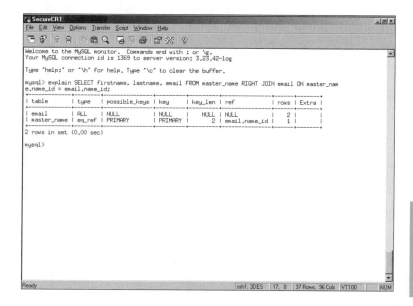

In the type column, you see the value eq_ref instead of ALL. When ALL is present, it means that all relevant tables are scanned during the course of the query for each combination of rows used. In other words, everything is looked at! On the other hand, eq_ref means that only one row will be read for each combination of rows; this indicates that indexes are being used properly and that the JOIN has done its job.

When using EXPLAIN on statements involving JOIN, a quick way to gauge the optimization of the query is to look at the values in the rows column. In the previous example, you have 2 and 1. Multiply these numbers together and you have 2 as your answer. This is the number of rows that MySQL must look at in order to produce the results of the query. You want to get this number as low as possible, and 2 is as low as it can go!

For a great deal more information on the EXPLAIN command, please visit the MySQL manual at http://www.mysql.com/doc/E/X/EXPLAIN.html.

Summary

Running an optimized MySQL server starts with the hardware and operating system in use. Your system's CPU should be sufficiently fast, and you should have enough RAM in use to pick up the slack when your CPU struggles. This is especially true if MySQL shares resources with other processes, such as a Web server. Additionally, the hard drive in use is important, as a small hard drive will limit the amount of information you can store in your database. The seek time of your hard drive is important—a slow seek time will cause the overall performance of the server to be slower. Your operating system should not overwhelm your machine and should share resources with MySQL rather than using all the resources itself.

Some key startup parameters for MySQL are the values of key_buffer_size and table_cache, among others. Baseline values can be found in sample MySQL configuration files, or you can modify the values of these variables and watch the server performance to see whether you hit on the right result for your environment.

Beyond hardware and software optimization is the optimization of tables, as well as SELECT queries. Table optimization, using the OPTIMIZE command, allows you to reclaim unused space. You can see how well (or not) optimized your queries are by using the EXPLAIN command. The resulting output will show if and when indexes are used, and whether you can use any indexes to speed up the given query.

With all optimization—hardware, software, or related to queries—try to perform the modifications and tests in a development environment rather than a production environment. Locked tables or degraded server performance should be worked out in the development environment and not during prime time!

Q&A

Q **Can MySQL take advantage of multiple CPUs in a single server?**

A Absolutely. If your operating system supports multiple CPUs, MySQL will take advantage of them. However, the performance and tuning of MySQL using multiple processors varies depending on the operating system. For more information, please see the MySQL manual section for your specific operating system:

`http://www.mysql.com/doc/O/p/Operating_System_Specific_Notes.html`

Q **What permission level must I have in order to use the OPTIMIZE command?**

A Any user with `INSERT` privileges for a table can perform `OPTIMIZE` commands. If a user has only `SELECT` permissions, the `OPTIMIZE` command will not execute.

Workshop

The Workshop is designed to help you anticipate possible questions, review what you've learned, and begin learning how to put your knowledge into practice.

Quiz

1. Which MySQL function will enable you to run an expression many times over in order to find the speed of the iterations?

2. Which four variables can help you to determine whether the value of `key_buffer_size` is adequate?

3. Which SQL command will clean up the structure of your tables?

Answers

1. The `benchmark()` function.

2. `key_read_requests`, `key_reads`, `key_write_requests`, and `key_writes`

3. `OPTIMIZE`

Activities

1. If you have root level access to your server, change the values of `key_buffer_size` and `table_cache`, and run `benchmark()` functions after each change to see how the execution times differ.

2. Use `OPTIMIZE` on all the tables in your contact management database to clean up any structural issues.

20

HOUR 21

Backing Up and Restoring Your Database

Backing up your database is a very important aspect of database administration, yet some people don't perform this simple task. They will usually learn the importance of database backups after their first disk failure, but at that point it's too late!

In this hour, you will learn

- How to use `mysqlhotcopy` to backup a database
- How to use the `BACKUP TABLE` and `RESTORE TABLE` commands
- How to use the `myisamchk` utility for table maintenance after restoring data

Database Backup Overview

Backing up your database should be done on a regular basis, just like backing up your personal files on your home computer—and it's almost as simple! When you back up your personal files, you probably just copy them to removable media of some sort or have a scheduled task do it for you.

You can do the same with your database, as your MySQL tables are stored as actual files in the MySQL installation directory. However, there are caveats to doing a backup in this manner. For example, if someone is accessing a table at the moment you try to copy the file to your tape drive (or removable media of choice), your backup won't really be complete—you'll have captured an open, perhaps partially updated file.

You can't rely on a simple "move the files to a disk" method of backup, on your own, when it comes to a live database system. To really get a good backup, you should use one of the utility programs or other methods of SQL commands that are available in MySQL. These programs and commands are designed to produce a consistent set of data that can be easily archived or restored. It's this set of data—either a dump file or a set of files—that you should put on removable media for storage.

Using `mysqlhotcopy`

Earlier in this book, you learned how to use the `mysqldump` utility to produce a file containing the SQL commands to rebuild your tables and re-insert the data. Another MySQL utility—`mysqlhotcopy`—performs a set of actions that will produce a stable set of backup files, which can then be placed on removable media. This is a "move the files to a disk" method, but it uses a built-in utility that goes through a specific sequence of events to ensure a reliable set of backup files.

To use `mysqlhotcopy`, you must first have the proper permissions for both the file system and the database. Specifically, you need to have write access to the location of the backup files (this can be your home directory, or a path to a backup drive), the ability to execute the `mysqlhotcopy` script, and SELECT and RELOAD privileges for all tables in the database.

The `mysqlhotcopy` utility is run directly from the command line, using this syntax:

```
mysqlhotcopy [options] database_name /path/to/backup/dir
```

If you want to backup the contactDB database to the /backups/ directory, you would use

```
#prompt> mysqlhotcopy -u supercontact -p somepass contactDB /backups/
```

The resulting output should be something like the following, telling you exactly what occurred:

```
Locked 11 tables in 0 seconds.
Flushed tables (contactDB.address, contactDB.company, contactDB.email,
contactDB.fax, contactDB.job_function, contactDB.master_name,
contactDB.myTest, contactDB.name_company_map, contactDB.personal_notes,
contactDB.telephone, contactDB.testTable) in 0 seconds.
Copying 33 files...
Copying indices for 0 files...
Unlocked tables.
mysqlhotcopy copied 11 tables (33 files) in 0 seconds (0 seconds overall).
```

First, `mysqlhotcopy` locks all of the tables, and then it flushes all of the tables. After ensuring that no additional updates can be made to the files, the utility copies all of the files from the original data directory to the new data directory. After copying the files, the tables are unlocked. All of this takes place in less than a second, as `contactDB` is such a small database. Larger databases will take longer, and your tables will be locked, so schedule this utility to run at a time when traffic to your system is light.

There are several command-line options for `mysqlhotcopy`, which you can learn more about in the MySQL manual, at `http://www.mysql.com/doc/m/y/mysqlhotcopy.html`

Using the BACKUP TABLE and RESTORE TABLE Commands

If you prefer to work within the MySQL monitor rather than the command line, the BACKUP TABLE and RESTORE TABLE SQL commands will create and restore files on a per-table basis. In other words, you have to list each one individually, which is cumbersome if you have more than a few tables in your database!

The BACKUP TABLE and RESTORE TABLE commands are available in MySQL 3.23.25 and later and will only work with the MyISAM table type.

This pair of commands is good for quick backups and simple restorations, such as moving a small portion of your database to a different development machine or testing against a different system configuration. The BACKUP TABLE command makes a copy of the definition and data files for a table, but it does not copy the index file—the index file is rebuilt when the RESTORE TABLE command is used.

21

The permissions for BACKUP TABLE and RESTORE TABLE are similar to those needed for mysqlhotcopy—you must have write access to the location of the backup files and SELECT and RELOAD privileges for the table you're backing up.

The syntax for the BACKUP TABLE command is

```
BACKUP TABLE table_name TO '/path/to/backup/dir'
```

If you are logged in to the MySQL monitor and are using the contactDB database, and you want to back up the master_name table to the /backups/ directory, the BACKUP TABLE command would be

```
mysql> BACKUP TABLE master_name TO '/backups/'
+----------------------+--------+----------+----------+
| Table                | Op     | Msg_type | Msg_text |
+----------------------+--------+----------+----------+
| contactDB.master_name | backup | status   | OK       |
+----------------------+--------+----------+----------+
1 row in set (0.00 sec)
```

This table of information includes two very important columns, Msg_type and Msg_text. The Msg_type column will display the text status, error, info, or warning. The Msg_text column contains the rest of the message. As you can see in the example above, the Msg_type is a status message and the Msg_text says OK. This is good!

In the next example, the Msg_type is an error message, and the Msg_text is helpful enough; in an attempt to backup the fax table to a directory called /root, the action failed. The likely culprit is a lack of proper permissions to the /root directory.

```
mysql> BACKUP TABLE fax TO '/root;
+---------------+--------+----------+---------------------------+
| Table         | Op     | Msg_type | Msg_text                  |
+---------------+--------+----------+---------------------------+
| contactDB.fax | backup | error    | Failed copying .frm file  |
| contactDB.fax | backup | status   | Operation failed          |
+---------------+--------+----------+---------------------------+
2 rows in set (0.00 sec)
```

The RESTORE TABLE command works much the same way as BACKUP TABLE. After you move the two backup files to your other development machine (or if you just want to restore the files in a different MySQL database on the same system), the RESTORE TABLE syntax is

```
RESTORE TABLE table_name FROM '/path/to/backup/dir'
```

To restore the `master_name` table, assuming the files are in a temporary location such as `/tmp`, use:

```
mysql> RESTORE TABLE master_name FROM '/tmp';
+----------------------+---------+----------+----------+
| Table                | Op      | Msg_type | Msg_text |
+----------------------+---------+----------+----------+
| contactDB.master_name | restore | status   | OK       |
+----------------------+---------+----------+----------+
1 row in set (0.03 sec)
```

You're looking for a `Msg_text` value of `OK`, indicating that the restoration went smoothly. During the restoration, the index file is rebuilt, bringing the total number of files in the data directory to three per table, as usual.

Be aware that `RESTORE TABLE` will not overwrite existing tables! If you attempt to restore a table to a database in which one already exists, you will get this lovely response:

```
mysql> RESTORE TABLE master_name FROM '/tmp';
+-------------+---------+----------+-------------------------+
| Table       | Op      | Msg_type | Msg_text                |
+-------------+---------+----------+-------------------------+
| master_name | restore | error    | table exists, will not  |
|             |         |          | overwrite on restore    |
+-------------+---------+----------+-------------------------+
1 row in set (0.00 sec)
```

Using `myisamchk`

The `myisamchk` utility doesn't have anything directly to do with backing up or restoring tables. However, this utility is used to check and repair tables, which is especially important after restoring archived files, to make sure everything was put back together properly.

> You can use `myisamchk` anytime you want to, not necessarily after doing a backup. If you are just checking and repairing tables independent of a restoration, it's also a good idea to have a backup handy, in case the repairs don't work.

The `myisamchk` utility is run from the command line, using the following syntax, within the data directory for the database containing the table you wish to check:

```
myisamchk [options] table_name
```

21

The list of available options is quite long, but the common options are

- -c or --check—Checks the table for errors.
- -e or --extend-check—Thorough check for errors; this takes a very long time and is not usually necessary, as --medium-check takes care of most instances. Use sparingly!
- -m or --medium-check—Checks the table for errors and will catch 99.9% of them. Unless you're in dire straits and need --extend-check, use --medium-check.
- -i or --information—Print additional statistics about the table being checked.

To check the master_name table in the contactDB database, using the --medium-check option and printing additional information, run this command from the contactDB data directory:

```
#prompt> myisamchk --medium-check -i master_name
```

The following output shows a wealth of information, as well as what was fixed:

```
Checking MyISAM file: master_name
Data records:        9  Deleted blocks:        0
- check file-size
- check key delete-chain
- check record delete-chain
- check index reference
- check data record references index: 1
Key: 1: Keyblocks used:   5% Packed:    0% Max levels:  1
- check data record references index: 2
Key: 2: Keyblocks used:   7% Packed:   88% Max levels:  1
- check data record references index: 3
Key: 3: Keyblocks used:   6% Packed:   90% Max levels:  1
Total:    Keyblocks used:   6% Packed:   86%

- check record links
Records:              9  M.recordlength:   31  Packed:         79%
Recordspace used: 98%  Empty space:       1%  Blocks/Record: 1.00
Record blocks:        9  Delete blocks:     0
Record data:        280  Deleted data:      0
Lost space:           6  Linkdata:         34

User time 0.01, System time 0.07
Maximum resident set size 0, Integral resident set size 0
Non-physical pagefaults 57, Physical pagefaults 266, Swaps 0
Blocks in 0 out 0, Messages in 0 out 0, Signals 0
Voluntary context switches 0, Involuntary context switches 0
```

Without specifying the -i option, just the actions are displayed. The resulting output is adequate for most people:

```
Checking MyISAM file: master_name
Data records:        9   Deleted blocks:        0
- check file-size
- check key delete-chain
- check record delete-chain
- check index reference
- check data record references index: 1
- check data record references index: 2
- check data record references index: 3
- check record links
```

You can also specify the full path to the table if you are running `myisamchk` from outside the data directory:

#prompt> myisamchk /path/to/database/table_name.MYI

Or, to check all tables in a database, use

#prompt> myisamchk /path/to/database/*.MYI

Beyond simply checking the integrity of tables, `myisamchk` can repair tables as well, using the `-r` or `--recover` option:

```
#prompt> myisamchk -r master_name
- recovering (with sort) MyISAM-table 'master_name.MYI'
Data records: 9
- Fixing index 1
- Fixing index 2
- Fixing index 3
```

The `myisamchk` utility can be the best friend of a database administrator. There are numerous options for the utility, and to learn more about them please read the MySQL manual section on table maintenance at `http://www.mysql.com/doc/T/a/Table_maintenance.html`

Summary

Like all important files, a database should be backed up regularly. Usually, a database is backed up by dumping the structure and contents of the tables to a single file or by storing copies of the table data and structural files on removable media. This hour taught you to use of the `mysqlhotcopy` utility to create backup copies of the table data and structural files. This utility goes through a process of locking tables, flushing tables, copying files, and then releasing the locks, which ensures the integrity of the tables that you are backing up.

Additionally, the `BACKUP TABLE` and `RESTORE TABLE` SQL commands can be used from within the MySQL monitor to backup the relevant data and structural files of a table.

21

When invoked, the restoration process rebuilds the index file. The RESTORE TABLE command cannot be used to restore a table that already exists in a database but is used to recreate the table structure, data, and indexes in a different database.

The mysqlhotcopy and BACKUP TABLE/RESTORE TABLE methods require specific permissions, or they will fail. Users must at least have write access to the target locations for the backup files, and must have RELOAD and SELECT privileges for the database or single tables slated for backup.

After restoring tables, or any time when you want to check the integrity of your tables, the myismachk utility can be run from the command line. The many options for this utility, ranging from various levels of error checking to full-fledged table repairing, will allow the user to get an idea of what needs to be fixed and then fix it.

Workshop

The Workshop is designed to help you anticipate possible questions, review what you've learned, and begin learning how to put your knowledge into practice.

Quiz

1. Which MySQL privileges must a user have in order to run the mysqlhotcopy script?

2. What does BACKUP TABLE do with the index file for a table?

3. Which myisamchk option will catch 99.9% of all errors yet is much nicer on your system than the --extend-check option?

Answers

1. The user must have SELECT and RELOAD privileges for all tables in the database that is being backed up.

2. Nothing; the index file is re-created when the RESTORE TABLE SQL command is used to restore the table.

3. The --medium-check option.

Activities

1. If you have the proper file system and MySQL permissions, practice using mysqlhotcopy to backup the tables in the contactDB database.

2. If you have the proper permissions, practice using myisamchk to check the integrity of your tables, and repair them if necessary.

HOUR 22

Basic Administrative Commands

Left to its devices, a MySQL server will usually hum along smoothly. However, a good database administrator will keep a watchful eye on things, and the basic administrative commands in this hour will help you do just that.

In this hour, you will learn

- How to use the FLUSH command to clean up tables, caches, and log files
- How to use SHOW commands to retrieve information about databases, tables, and indexes
- How to use SHOW commands to find system status information

Using the FLUSH Command

Users with reload privileges for a specific database can use the FLUSH command to clean up the internal caches used by MySQL. Often, only the root-level user has the appropriate permissions to issue administrative commands such as FLUSH.

The FLUSH syntax is

FLUSH *flush_option*

The common options for the FLUSH command are

- PRIVILEGES
- TABLES
- HOSTS
- LOGS

You've used the FLUSH PRIVILEGES command before, after adding new users. This command simply reloads the grant tables in your MySQL database, allowing the changes to take effect without stopping and restarting MySQL. When you issue a FLUSH PRIVILEGES command, the Query OK response will assure you that the cleaning process occurred without a hitch.

```
mysql> FLUSH PRIVILEGES;
Query OK, 0 rows affected (0.10 sec)
```

The FLUSH TABLES command will close all tables currently open or in use and essentially give your MySQL server a millisecond of breathing room before starting back to work. When your caches are empty, MySQL can better utilize available memory. Again, you're looking for the Query OK response:

```
mysql> FLUSH TABLES;
Query OK, 0 rows affected (0.21 sec)
```

The FLUSH HOSTS command works specifically with the host cache tables. If you are unable to connect to your MySQL server, a common reason is that the maximum number of connections has been reached for a particular host, and it's throwing errors. When MySQL sees numerous errors on connection, it will assume something is amiss and simply block any additional connection attempts to that host. The FLUSH HOSTS command will reset this process and again allow connections to be made:

```
mysql> FLUSH HOSTS;
Query OK, 0 rows affected (0.00 sec)
```

The FLUSH LOGS command closes and re-opens all log files. If your log file is getting to be a burden and you want to start a new one, this command will create a new, empty log file. Weeding through a year's worth of log entries in one file looking for errors can be a chore, so try to flush your logs at least monthly.

```
mysql> FLUSH LOGS;
Query OK, 0 rows affected (0.04 sec)
```

You can also use the `mysqladmin` utility to issue the following FLUSH commands:

```
#prompt> mysqladmin -u root -p[password] flush-privileges
#prompt> mysqladmin -u root -p[password] flush-tables
#prompt> mysqladmin -u root -p[password] flush-hosts
#prompt> mysqladmin -u root -p[password] flush-logs
```

Using `reload` in place of `flush-privileges` accomplishes the same goal.

Using the SHOW Command

There are several different uses of the SHOW command, which will produce output displaying a great deal of useful information about your MySQL database, users, and tables. Depending on your access level, some of the SHOW commands will not be available to you or will provide only minimal information. The root-level user has the ability to use all of the SHOW commands, with the most comprehensive results.

The common uses of SHOW include the following, which you'll soon learn about in more detail:

```
SHOW GRANTS FOR user
SHOW DATABASES [LIKE something]
SHOW [OPEN] TABLES [FROM database_name] [LIKE something]
SHOW CREATE TABLE table_name
SHOW [FULL] COLUMNS FROM table_name [FROM database_name] [LIKE something]
SHOW INDEX FROM table_name [FROM database_name]
SHOW TABLE STATUS [FROM database_name] [LIKE something]
SHOW STATUS [LIKE something]
SHOW VARIABLES [LIKE something]
```

The SHOW_GRANTS command will display the privileges for a given user at a given host. This is an easy way to check up on the current status of a user, especially if you have a request to modify a user's privileges. With SHOW_GRANTS, you can check first to see that the user doesn't already have the requested privileges. For example, see the privileges available to the supercontact user:

```
mysql> SHOW GRANTS FOR supercontact@localhost;
+-------------------------------------------------------------------+
| Grants for supercontact@localhost                                 |
+-------------------------------------------------------------------+
| GRANT USAGE ON *.* TO 'supercontact'@'localhost'                  |
| IDENTIFIED BY PASSWORD '34f3a6996d856efd'                         |
| GRANT ALL PRIVILEGES ON contactDB.* TO 'supercontact'@'localhost' |
+-------------------------------------------------------------------+
2 rows in set (0.00 sec)
```

If you're not the root-level user or the `supercontact` user, you'll get an error. Unless you're the root-level user, you can see only the information relevant to your user. For example, the `supercontact` user isn't allowed to view information about the root-level user:

```
mysql> SHOW GRANTS FOR root@localhost;
ERROR 1044: Access denied for user:'supercontact@localhost' to database 'mysql'
```

Be aware of your privilege level throughout the remainder of this hour. If you are not the root-level user, some of these commands will not be available to you or will display only limited information.

Retrieving Information About Databases and Tables

You've used a few of the basic `SHOW` commands earlier in this book to view the list of databases and tables on your MySQL server. As a refresher, the `SHOW DATABASES` command does just that—it lists all the databases on the MySQL server:

```
mysql> SHOW DATABASES;
+---------------------+
| Database            |
+---------------------+
| contactDB           |
| mysql               |
+---------------------+
2 rows in set (0.00 sec)
```

You can also use the `LIKE` operator to weed down your result list, if you have a longer list of databases:

```
mysql> SHOW DATABASES LIKE 'con%';
+-----------------+
| Database (con%) |
+-----------------+
| contactDB       |
+-----------------+
1 row in set (0.00 sec)
```

Once you've selected a database to work with, you can also use `SHOW` to list the tables in the database. In this case, we're using `contactDB`:

```
mysql> SHOW TABLES;
+---------------------+
| Tables_in_contactDB |
+---------------------+
| address             |
| company             |
| email               |
| fax                 |
```

```
| job_function          |
| master_name           |
| myTest                |
| name_company_map      |
| personal_notes        |
| telephone             |
| testTable             |
+-----------------------+
11 rows in set (0.01 sec)
```

> You don't actually have to select the database before listing the tables in it. You can use SHOW TABLES FROM database_name to get the list of tables in database_name, no matter which database you're actually using—as long as your user has the proper permissions.

If you add OPEN to your SHOW TABLES command, you will get a list of all the tables in the table cache, showing how many times they're cached and in use:

mysql> SHOW OPEN TABLES;
```
+-------------------------+---------------------+
| Open_tables_in_contactDB | Comment            |
+-------------------------+---------------------+
| name_company_map        | cached=1, in_use=0 |
| email                   | cached=1, in_use=0 |
| testTable               | cached=1, in_use=0 |
| company                 | cached=1, in_use=0 |
| job_function            | cached=1, in_use=0 |
| master_name             | cached=1, in_use=0 |
| myTest                  | cached=1, in_use=0 |
| fax                     | cached=1, in_use=0 |
| telephone               | cached=1, in_use=0 |
| address                 | cached=1, in_use=0 |
| personal_notes          | cached=1, in_use=0 |
+-------------------------+---------------------+
11 rows in set (0.00 sec)
```

Using this information in conjunction with the FLUSH TABLES command you learned earlier in this hour will help keep your database running smoothly. If SHOW OPEN TABLES shows that tables are cached numerous times but aren't currently in use, go ahead and use FLUSH TABLES to free up that memory.

Retrieving Table Structure Information

A very helpful command is SHOW CREATE TABLE, which does what it sounds like—it shows you the SQL statement used to create a specified table:

```
mysql> SHOW CREATE TABLE master_name;
+-------------+------------------------------------------------------------+
| Table       | Create Table                                               |
+-------------+------------------------------------------------------------+
| master_name | CREATE TABLE `master_name` (                               |
|             |  `name_id` smallint(5) unsigned NOT NULL auto_increment,    |
|             |  `name_dateadded` datetime default '0000-00-00 00:00:00',   |
|             |  `name_datemodified` datetime default '0000-00-00 00:00:00',|
|             |  `firstname` varchar(75) default NULL,                      |
|             |  `lastname` varchar(75) default NULL,                       |
|             |  PRIMARY KEY  (`name_id`),                                  |
|             |  KEY `idx_fn` (`firstname`),                                |
|             |  KEY `idx_ln` (`lastname`)                                  |
|             |  ) TYPE=MyISAM                                              |
+-------------+------------------------------------------------------------+
1 row in set (0.00 sec)
```

This is essentially the same information you'd get if you dumped the table schema, but the SHOW CREATE TABLE command can be used quickly if you're just looking for a reminder or a simple reference to a particular table creation statement.

If you need to know the structure of the table but don't necessarily need the SQL command to create it, you can use the SHOW COLUMNS command:

```
mysql> SHOW COLUMNS FROM testTable;
+-----------+-------------+------+-----+---------+----------------+
| Field     | Type        | Null | Key | Default | Extra          |
+-----------+-------------+------+-----+---------+----------------+
| id        | int(11)     |      | PRI | NULL    | auto_increment |
| testField | varchar(75) | YES  |     | NULL    |                |
+-----------+-------------+------+-----+---------+----------------+
2 rows in set (0.00 sec)
```

> The SHOW FULL COLUMNS command returns the information from SHOW COLUMNS plus one more column called privileges. The privileges column shows the privileges you have for that table, such as SELECT, UPDATE, INSERT, and so on.

The SHOW INDEX command will display information about all the indexes present in a particular table. The syntax is

```
SHOW INDEX FROM table_name [FROM database_name]
```

This command produces a table full of information, ranging from the column name to cardinality of the index. This table is often so wide that it will wrap in your display, as shown in Figure 22.1.

FIGURE 22.1

Output of
SHOW INDEX
command.

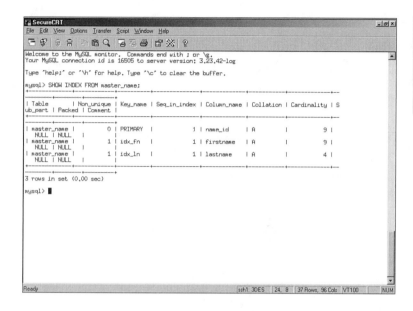

The columns returned from this command are described in Table 22.1.

TABLE 22.1 Columns in the SHOW INDEX Result

Column Name	Description
Table	The name of the table.
Non_unique	1 or 0.
	1 = index can contain duplicates.
	0 = index can't contain duplicates.
Key_name	The name of the index.
Seq_in_index	The column sequence number for the Index; starts at 1.
Column_name	The name of the column.
Collation	The sort order of the column, either A (ascending) or NULL (not sorted).
Cardinality	Number of unique values in the index.
Sub_part	On a partially-indexed column, this shows the number of indexed characters, or NULL if the entire key is indexed.
Packed	The size of numeric columns.
Comment	Any additional comments.

Another command that produces a wide table full of results is the SHOW TABLE STATUS command. The syntax of this command is

```
SHOW TABLE STATUS [FROM database_name] LIKE 'something'
```

This command produces a table full of information, ranging from the size and number of rows to the next value to be used in an auto_increment field, as shown in Figure 22.2.

FIGURE 22.2

Output of
SHOW TABLE STATUS
command for
one table.

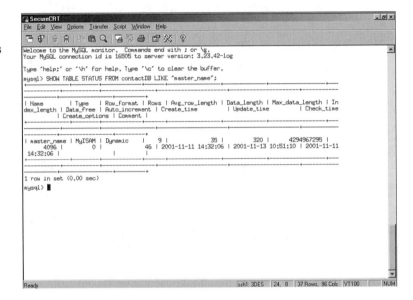

The columns returned from this command are described in Table 22.2.

TABLE 22.2   Columns in the SHOW TABLE STATUS Result

Column Name	Description
Name	The name of the table.
Type	The table type: MyISAM, BDB, InnoDB, or Gemini.
Row_format	The row storage format: fixed, dynamic, or compressed.
Rows	The number of rows.
Avg_row_length	The average row length.
Data_length	The length of the data file.
Max_data_length	The maximum length of the data file.
Index_length	The length of the index file.
Data_free	The number of bytes allocated but not used.

continues

TABLE 22.2 Continued

Auto_increment	The next value to be used in an auto_increment field.
Create_time	The date and time of when the table was created (in datetime format).
Update_time	The date and time of when the data file was last updated (in datetime format).
Check_time	The date and time of when the table was last checked (in datetime format).
Create_options	Any extra options used in the CREATE TABLE statement.
Comment	Any comments added when the table was created. Additionally, InnoDB tables will use this column to report the free space in the tablespace.

Retrieving System Status

The SHOW STATUS and SHOW VARIABLES commands will quickly provide important information about your database server. The syntax for these commands is simply SHOW STATUS or SHOW VARIABLES, nothing fancy.

You can also use the mysqladmin utility to issue commands that will produce the same results:

```
#prompt> mysqladmin -u root -p[password] extended-status
#prompt> mysqladmin -u root -p[password] variables
```

There are no less than 54 status variables as the output of SHOW STATUS, but the most useful are

- Aborted_connects—The number of failed attempts to connect to the MySQL server. Anytime you see an aborted connection, you should investigate the problem. It could be related to a bad username and password in a script, or your number of simultaneous connections could be set too low.

- Connections—The aggregate number of connection attempts to the MySQL server during the current period of uptime.

- Max_used_connections—The maximum number of connections that have been in use simultaneously during the current period of uptime.

- Slow_queries—The number of queries that have taken more than long_query_time, which defaults to 10 seconds. If you have more than one, it's time to investigate your SQL syntax!

- Uptime—Total number of seconds the server has been up during the current period of uptime.

You can find a comprehensive list of SHOW STATUS variables and an explanation of their values in the MySQL manual, located at http://www.mysql.com/doc/S/H/SHOW_STATUS.html.

The SHOW VARIABLES command produces even more results than SHOW STATUS— approximately 82! The variables reported from SHOW VARIABLES control the general operation of MySQL, and include the following useful tidbits:

- connect_timeout—Shows the number of seconds the MySQL server will wait during a connection attempt before it gives up.
- have_innodb—Will show YES if MySQL supports InnoDB tables.
- have_bdb—Will show YES if MySQL supports Berkeley DB tables.
- max_connections—The allowable number of simultaneous connections to MySQL before a connection is refused.
- port—The port on which MySQL is running.
- table_type—The default table type for MySQL, usually MyISAM.
- version—The MySQL version number.

You can find a comprehensive list of the variables returned by the SHOW VARIABLES results and an explanation of their values in the MySQL manual at http://www.mysql.com/doc/S/H/SHOW_VARIABLES.html. Once you know the values you have, you can change them in your MySQL configuration file or startup command.

Summary

Paying attention to your MySQL server will ensure that it continues to run smoothly. Basic administration commands, such as FLUSH and SHOW [something], will help you to recognize and quickly fix potential problems.

The FLUSH PRIVILEGES command reloads the grant tables, so you don't have to restart your MySQL server after adding or modifying users. FLUSH TABLES will close all open tables, whereas FLUSH HOSTS will clean out the host cache and FLUSH LOGS will start new log files. All of these commands are designed to give MySQL a millisecond of rest time and breathing room if it's under a heavy load.

Numerous SHOW commands will display structural information about databases, tables, and indexes, as well as how the system is performing. SHOW STATUS will give you a snapshot of the system performance, such as the uptime and maximum number of connections that have been made simultaneously. SHOW VARIABLES will produce results that remind you of your MySQL configuration values, such as the default table types in use, and much more.

Workshop

22

The Workshop is designed to help you anticipate possible questions, review what you've learned, and begin learning how to put your knowledge into practice.

Quiz

1. Which FLUSH command resets the MySQL log files?
2. To quickly determine whether MySQL has support for InnoDB tables, would you use SHOW STATUS or SHOW VARIABLES?
3. Write a SQL statement that will allow you to see the SQL statement used to create a table called myTable.

Answers

1. FLUSH LOGS
2. SHOW VARIABLES
3. SHOW CREATE TABLE myTable

Activity

Use the SHOW STATUS command to retrieve information about your MySQL server, and then issue FLUSH commands to clean up the server. After each command, use SHOW STATUS again to see which commands affect which results in the SHOW STATUS results display.

PART VIII

Interfacing with MySQL

Hour

HOUR 23

Using MySQL with Perl

With Perl, you can manipulate your MySQL database through shell scripts or CGI programs that are part of your Web site. The Perl DBI ("Database Interface") and MySQL DBD ("Database Definition") modules together form a simple interface for issuing SQL queries and retrieving results.

In this hour, you will learn

- How to connect to MySQL using Perl
- How to issue queries using Perl
- How to insert and select data through Perl scripts

Getting Access to Perl

If you host your Web site at an Internet Service Provider, it's likely that you have a "virtual hosting agreement" with this provider. As part of that agreement, you may have access to Perl as well as MySQL. If you have shell access to your account, you can test for the existence of Perl by using the following command:

```
prompt#> which perl
/usr/bin/perl
```

If Perl is not found on your system, talk to your Internet Service Provider to find specific instructions for accessing Perl on their servers. If you are the system administrator for your own Web server and would like to install Perl on your system, please visit the Perl documentation at `http://www.perl.com/pub/q/documentation/`.

Accessing the Perl DBI and MySQL DBD

Access to Perl is one thing, but the ability to use the database interface modules for MySQL is another. The Perl DBI and the MySQL DBD work together to allow Perl scripts to talk to the MySQL database server in order to issue commands and retrieve results.

If you use an Internet Service Provider, be sure to ask their technical support folks whether the Perl DBI and MySQL DBD are installed on their system. If you are the system administrator for your own server and wish to install the Perl DBI and MySQL DBD modules, please visit the Perl modules documentation area at `http://www.perl.com/CPANlocal/modules/index.html`.

If the Perl DBI and MySQL DBD are installed and accessible, you can use Perl to write scripts that interface directly with your MySQL database. Think of these scripts as another method to issue queries to your database instead of using the MySQL command-line interface. You can issue queries and then retrieve and display data through these scripts.

Quick Perl Test

Once you're sure that Perl is available to you, there's one good way to test your installation of Perl: the infamous "Hello World" script!

1. Type **which perl** to find the location of Perl if you don't remember from the previous test in this hour.

2. Open a text editor and type the following as the first line:

   ```
   #!/usr/bin/perl
   ```

> The /usr/bin/perl path should be replaced with the result of which perl if it's not /usr/bin/perl on your system. This line indicates the location of the Perl interpreter, which is crucial to running a Perl script.

3. Type the next line of the script, which simply tells Perl to print a little message:

   ```
   print "Hello World!\n";
   ```

As with most programming languages, the instruction terminator (the semi-colon) is necessary to tell the parsing engine that the instruction is over and that it needs to move on to the next one.

4. Save this file as `helloworld.pl`, and ensure executable permissions are used by typing the following at the prompt:

```
prompt#> chmod +x helloworld.pl
```

5. Now test your script by typing the following at the prompt:

```
prompt#> perl helloworld.pl
```

6. You should see the following result:

```
Hello World!
```

The remainder of this hour provides a very brief overview of writing simple scripts to access a MySQL database. You'll want to spend some time learning Perl through the Perl Web site at `http://www.perl.com/` and the numerous FAQs, mailing lists, and tutorials available to you.

Connecting to MySQL with Perl

To successfully use the Perl DBI/MySQL DBD functions for talking to MySQL, MySQL must be running somewhere to which your scripts can connect—not necessarily the same machine as your Web server. You also must have a user created (with a password), and you must know the database name to which you want to connect.

When you know all of these things, you're ready to make that first simple connection. In all sample scripts in this hour, the example database name is `contactDB`, the example user is `supercontact`, and the example password is `somepass`. Substitute your own information when you try this out if you don't want to connect to the example database created in previous hours.

A guide to the Perl DBI and MySQL DBD can be found at `http://mysql.turbolift.com/mysql/DBD_3.21.X.php3`.

23

Making the Initial Connection

The MySQL DBI is used in conjunction with the `DBD::mysql` module to provide access to a MySQL database. In your script, you have to first tell Perl that you want to use the DBI. These next few steps will create a simple script that logs on and logs off your MySQL database.

1. Create a text file starting with the path to Perl:

   ```
   #!/usr/bin/perl
   ```

2. Tell the Perl interpreter that you want to use the DBI:

   ```
   use DBI;
   ```

3. Make the initial connection:

   ```
   my $database_handler = DBI->connect("DBI:mysql:contactDB", "supercontact",
   "somepass");
   ```

   When the connection is made, values are placed in the object called `$database_handler`. You'll reference the `$database_handler` object throughout your script.

> If you need to specify a hostname in the connection, use:
> ```
> my $database_handler = DBI->connect("DBI:mysql:contactDB:
>             hostname","supercontact", "somepass");
> ```

4. Add some conditions to test the validity of the `$database_handler` object:

   ```
   if (!$database_handler) {
           die "Cannot connect to database!\n";
   } else {
           print "database_handler value is $database_handler\n";
   }
   ```

5. Save the file as `testdbi.pl` and make it executable.

6. At the prompt, type:

   prompt#> perl testdbi.pl

If the connection was successful, you should see something like this:

```
prompt#> perl testdbi.pl
database_handler value is DBI::db=HASH(0x81965c4)
```

If you attempt to connect to a database that doesn't exist, you will get a warning and a message, such as

```
DBI->connect(MyDB) failed: Access denied for user: 'supercontact@localhost'
to database 'MyDB' at testdbi.pl line 5
Cannot connect to database!
```

One thing is missing from the simple connection script: disconnecting! To explicitly close the connection at the end of the script, use the disconnect() function:

```
$database_handler -> disconnect();
```

Your new script, including the disconnect function, should look something like the following:

```perl
#!/usr/bin/perl

use DBI;

my $database_handler = DBI->connect("DBI:mysql:contactDB", "supercontact",
"somepass");

if (!$database_handler) {
        die "Cannot connect to database!\n";
} else {
        print "database_handler value is $database_handler\n";
}

$database_handler -> disconnect();
```

In the next section, you'll extend this simple script to query your MySQL database.

Executing Queries

There are three basic steps to executing a SQL statement after a connection is made: preparing the statement, executing the statement, and (optionally) retrieving the results. The first query you'll make is to create a little table for testing purposes. The table will be called myTest and will have two fields: id and sampletext.

First, create a new text file and insert the Perl code that opens a connection to your MySQL database, as shown previously:

```perl
#!/usr/bin/perl

use DBI;

my $database_handler = DBI->connect("DBI:mysql:contactDB", "supercontact",
"somepass");
```

Next, prepare the statement:

```perl
$statement_handler = $database_handler->prepare("CREATE TABLE myTest
        (id int not null primary key auto_increment, sampletext varchar (100))");
```

Test whether the statement handler is defined. If it's not defined, use the `errstr` function in DBI to print an error message:

```
if (!defined $statement_handler) {
        die "$DBI::errstr\n";
}
```

Now execute the statement:

```
else {
        $statement_handler->execute;
}
```

Your code so far should look like the following:

```
#!/usr/bin/perl
use DBI;

my $database_handler = DBI->connect("DBI:mysql:contactDB", "supercontact",
"somepass");

$statement_handler = $database_handler->prepare("CREATE TABLE myTest
        (id int not null primary key auto_increment, sampletext varchar (100))");

if (!defined $statement_handler) {
        die "$DBI::errstr\n";
} else {
        $statement_handler->execute;
}
```

Save this file as `testdbi_statement.pl`, and change its permissions to be executable. Run the script by typing

prompt#> perl testdbi_statement.pl

If the query was successful, you should see absolutely nothing as output because the script (as written) will output something only if an error occurs.

Try to run the script again. You should get an error because the `myTest` table should already exist if the first execution of the script was indeed successful.

```
DBD::mysql::st execute failed: Table 'myTest' already exists
at testdbi_statement.pl line 11.
```

Everything is working together as it should. Clean up the script a little bit before moving on; you should free the statement handler when you're through using it and also close the connection to the database. At the end of your script, add these two lines:

```
$statement_handler -> finish;
$database_handler -> disconnect;
```

So that your script now looks like this:

```perl
#!/usr/bin/perl
use DBI;

my $database_handler = DBI->connect("DBI:mysql:contactDB", "supercontact",
"somepass");

$statement_handler = $database_handler->prepare("CREATE TABLE myTest
        (id int not null primary key auto_increment, sampletext varchar (100))");

if (!defined $statement_handler) {
        die "$DBI::errstr\n";
} else {
        $statement_handler->execute;
}

$statement_handler -> finish;
$database_handler -> disconnect;
```

Now that you have a test table to work with, move on to the next section to insert some data.

Working with MySQL Data

Inserting, updating, deleting, and retrieving data all revolve around the use of the prepare() and execute() functions. For INSERT, UPDATE, and DELETE, no additional scripting is required after the query has been executed because you're not displaying any results (unless you want to). For SELECT, you have a few options for displaying the data retrieved by your query. Let's start with the basics and insert some data, so you have something to retrieve later on.

Inserting Data with Perl

The easiest method for inserting data is to simply hard code the INSERT statement. For example:

```perl
#!/usr/bin/perl
use DBI;

my $database_handler = DBI->connect("DBI:mysql:contactDB", "supercontact",
"somepass");

# create the SQL statement
$sql = "INSERT INTO myTest VALUES ('', 'fake text')";

#prepare the statement
$statement_handler = $database_handler->prepare($sql);
```

```
#test and execute the statement
if (!defined $statement_handler) {
        die "$DBI::errstr\n";
} else {
        $statement_handler->execute;
}

$statement_handler -> finish;
$database_handler -> disconnect;
```

Call this script testdbi_insert.pl, make it executable, and execute it. The result should be a row added to the myTest table and no error output to the screen. Add a few more rows so there's some data to work with as you continue this hour. You can verify the addition of data through the MySQL command line interface:

```
mysql> select * from myTest;
+----+-------------+
| id | sampletext  |
+----+-------------+
|  1 | fake text   |
|  2 | fake text 2 |
|  3 | fake text 3 |
+----+-------------+
3 rows in set (0.01 sec)
```

Retrieving Data with Perl

Since you have a few rows in your myTest table, you can write a little script to retrieve that data. The only addition we'll make to the previous script is the use of the fetchrow function in order to grab results.

```
#!/usr/bin/perl
use DBI;

my $database_handler = DBI->connect("DBI:mysql:contactDB", "supercontact",
"somepass");

# create the SQL statement
$sql = "SELECT id, sampletext FROM myTest";

#prepare the statement
$statement_handler = $database_handler->prepare($sql);

#test and execute the statement
if (!defined $statement_handler) {
        die "$DBI::errstr\n";
} else {
        $statement_handler->execute;
}
```

```
#fetch values and print that you did it
while ($statement_handler->fetchrow) {
        print "fetched something\n";
}
$statement_handler -> finish;
$database_handler -> disconnect;
```

Call this script testdbi_select.pl, make it executable, and execute it. The result should
be a message of "fetched something" for each row in your table. For example, with three
rows in the table, the resulting output is

```
prompt#> perl testdbi_select.pl
fetched something
fetched something
fetched something
```

Assuming you want to actually use the data that you fetched, next you will change the
"fetched something" message into the actual display of the values fetched. Modify
the while statement so that it names the slots fetched from your table, as in the following:

```
while (($id, $sampletext) = $statement_handler ->fetchrow()) {
```

Next, use the print statement to print a display that you'd like to see, then close the
while statement, as follows:

```
        print "ID: $id\tSample Text:$sampletext\n";
}
```

Your new code should look like this:

```
#!/usr/bin/perl
use DBI;

my $database_handler = DBI->connect("DBI:mysql:contactDB", "supercontact",
"somepass");

# create the SQL statement
$sql = "SELECT id, sampletext FROM myTest";

#prepare the statement
$statement_handler = $database_handler->prepare($sql);

#test and execute the statement
if (!defined $statement_handler) {
        die "$DBI::errstr\n";
} else {
        $statement_handler->execute;
}
#fetch values and print data
while (($id, $sampletext) = $statement_handler ->fetchrow()) {
        print "ID: $id\tSample Text:$sampletext\n";
```

```
}

$statement_handler -> finish;
$database_handler -> disconnect;
```

When you execute this new script, you should see the actual output from each row in your table. For example:

```
prompt# > perl testdbi_select.pl
ID: 1    Sample Text:fake text
ID: 2    Sample Text:fake text 2
ID: 3    Sample Text:fake text 3
```

That's all there is to it: the three very basic steps to working with DBI and MySQL. Now, considering that the man page for DBI is about 4100 lines, you can imagine that there are a lot more functions available to you than those described in this hour! Most of the DBI functions are alternate methods of retrieving data or are used to gather information about the table structure in question.

Connecting Perl and MySQL isn't all that difficult. Just remember that the DBI functions are there as a gateway to the MySQL command line interface. If there's something you want to do with the MySQL monitor, you can probably find a corresponding function for it in DBI.

Summary

Using the Perl DBI and MySQL DBD, your Perl scripts can connect to and issue queries to a MySQL database. These scripts act as a gateway to the database server; anything you'd enter using the MySQL command line interface, you can code into a Perl script.

To connect to MySQL with Perl using the DBI/DBD combination, you need to know your MySQL username, password, and database name. Using the DBI connect() function, you can connect to a database to use throughout the life of the script.

Once connected, all statements go through a two-step process of preparation and execution. The SQL statement is prepared using the DBI prepare() function and then executed using the DBI execute() function. Should an error occur, you can use the DBI errstr() function to produce an error message.

If you are retrieving data, one popular function for use in gathering results is the fetchrow() DBI function. This is just one method of many; the DBI man page is the place to look for comprehensive DBI information.

Q&A

Q **If my ISP doesn't provide the Perl DBI and MySQL DBD, can I install it myself?**

A Installing the Perl DBI and MySQL DBD requires root-level permissions. It is unlikely that you would be able to do this yourself in a virtual hosting environment.

Q **What changes must I make for the shell scripts to become CGI scripts?**

A A CGI script is essentially a shell script in the `cgi-bin` directory of a Web server. Place your scripts in that directory, and ensure that the permissions allow the script to be executed.

23

Workshop

The Workshop is designed to help you anticipate possible questions, review what you've learned, and begin learning how to put your knowledge into practice.

Quiz

1. What two modules work together to allow Perl and MySQL to talk to each other?

2. What two steps are required for a SQL statement to produce a result?

3. How would you disconnect from the MySQL database, given a database handler reference called `$dh`?

Answers

1. The Perl DBI (database interface) and MySQL DBD (database definition) modules work together.

2. SQL statements are prepared and then executed.

3. Use:

   ```
   $dh -> disconnect;
   ```

Activity

Create a Perl script that displays the contents of your `master_name` table in your content management database. Once it's working through the shell, make it a CGI script, and access the script through your Web browser. You will have to format the display results differently, using HTML instead of ASCII.

HOUR **24**

Using MySQL with PHP

PHP is a very popular and simple server-side scripting language. If you have access to a Web server with PHP installed, you can use this language to create Web-based interfaces to your MySQL database.

In this hour, you will learn

- The very basics of how PHP works
- How to connect to MySQL using PHP
- How to insert and select data through PHP scripts

Getting Access to PHP

If you host your Web site at an Internet Service Provider, it's likely that you have a "virtual hosting agreement" with this provider. As part of that agreement, it is quite possible that you have access to PHP as well as MySQL, and they should already be configured to play nicely with each other.

An easy way to tell if PHP and MySQL are installed and ready for your use is to open a text file and put the following line in it and nothing else:

```
<? phpinfo() ?>
```

Save this file as `test.php`, and place it on your Web server in the document root directory. Then, use your Web browser to access the file on your Web site. If your Web site URL is `www.mydomain.com`, access `http://www.mydomain.com/test.php`. If PHP is installed, accessing this script in this manner will produce a long page of information. The `phpinfo()` function automatically produces this page, showing you what sorts of things are installed, your environment, your settings, and so on.

> If running this script does not produce the desired output, talk to your Internet Service Provider to find specific instructions for accessing PHP on their servers.

If you are the system administrator for your own Web server and would like to install PHP on your system, please visit the PHP Web site at `http://www.php.net/`, and utilize the installation instructions found in the PHP Manual.

With PHP installed and accessible, you can jump right in and use PHP to write scripts that interface directly with your MySQL database. Think of these scripts as another method to issue queries to your database, instead of using the MySQL command-line interface. You can issue queries and then retrieve and display data in your own formatting, therefore making your Web site dynamic.

How PHP Works

PHP code is written in plain text, and PHP files sit on your Web server just waiting to jump into action when called upon. The sequence goes something like this, assuming you're working with files with the extension of `.php`:

1. A user's Web browser requests a document with a `.php` extension.
2. The Web server realizes that it's a PHP file and sends the request on to the PHP parser.
3. The PHP parser finds the requested file and scans it for PHP code.
4. When the PHP parser finds PHP code, it executes that code and places the resulting output into the place in the file formerly occupied by the code.
5. This new output file is sent back to the Web server.
6. The Web server sends it along to the Web browser.
7. The Web browser displays the output.

Now, to combine PHP code with HTML, the PHP code must be set apart from the HTML. This is done using PHP start and end tags. The PHP parser will attempt to execute anything between these tags, which usually look like this: `<?php` and `?>` or this: `<?` and `?>`

Using this basic "Hello World" script as an example, you see a file that is primarily HTML but has a section of PHP stuck in the middle:

```
<HTML>
<HEAD>
<TITLE>"Hello World" Script</TITLE>
</HEAD>
<BODY>
<? echo "<P>Hello World!</p>"; ?>
</BODY>
</HTML>
```

If you run this script from a PHP-enabled Web server, you would see the following output in your Web browser:

```
Hello World!
```

When you view the HTML source in your Web browser, you'll see that it contains only HTML code. That's because the following block of PHP was executed and produced the HTML output:

```
<? echo "<P>Hello World!</p>"; ?>
```

The `echo` function is used to output information; in this case, it is used to print the HTML output:

```
<P>Hello World!</P>
```

> As with most programming languages, the instruction terminator (the semi-colon) is necessary to tell the parsing engine that the instruction is over and that it should move on to the next one. One of the most common errors in PHP programming is simply forgetting to use the instruction terminator.

The remainder of this hour provides a very brief overview of the PHP language and how to write simple scripts to access a MySQL database. For a comprehensive guide to PHP, please read the PHP Manual at `http://www.php.net/manual/`.

Variables and Types in PHP

Variables in PHP are not much different than variables in any other programming language.

- They cannot begin with a numeric character.
- They can contain numbers or the underscore character (_).
- They are case-sensitive.

Variable types in PHP include the following (as well as a few others not explained here, such as objects):

- Arrays
- Integers and Floating-Point Numbers
- Strings
- Variables from HTML Forms
- Variables from Cookies
- Environment Variables

More information on these and other types can be found in the PHP Manual, at
`http://www.php.net/manual/en/language.types.php`

Operators in PHP

You have already used operators in MySQL, and PHP operators are not much different; if you're familiar with any programming language, you've got the bases covered.

- Arithmetic Operators bear a striking resemblance to simple math and include the addition (+), subtraction (–), multiplication (*), division (/), and modulus (%) operators.
- Assignment Operators include the basic assignment operator (=), but other assignment operators include binary arithmetic and string operators, such as +=, –=, and .=, which are quite useful.
- Comparison Operators compare two values and return true or false. You have equal to (==), not equal to (!=), greater than (>), less than (<), greater than or equal to (>=), and less than or equal to (<=).
- Increment/Decrement Operators add or subtract from a variable. For example, ++$a increments $a by 1 and returns $a, whereas $a++ returns $a and then increments $a by 1. Use --$a and $a-- to decrement $a.

- Logical Operators determine the status of conditions and, in the context of control structures, such as `if` or `while` statements, execute certain code based on which conditions are true and which are false. The logical operators are not (`!`), and (`&&`), and or (`||`).

More information about operators can be found in the PHP Manual at `http://www.php.net/manual/en/language.operators.php`.

Control Structures in PHP

PHP scripts are built as a series of statements, and control structures determine how those statements are executed. Control structures usually surround a series of conditions, such as "If it is raining, carry an umbrella." Curly braces (`{` and `}`) are used to separate the groups of statements from the remainder of the program, like so

```
if (it is raining) {
        carry an umbrella
}
```

Just like operators and variable types, there's nothing new in PHP if you're familiar with programming languages in general; control structures include

- `if...else if...else`
- `while`
- `for`
- `switch`
- `foreach`

More information about control structures can be found in the PHP Manual at `http://www.php.net/manual/en/control-structures.php`

Connecting to MySQL with PHP

To successfully use the PHP functions for talking to MySQL, MySQL must be running somewhere to which your Web server can connect—not necessarily the same machine as your Web server. You also must have a user created (with a password), and you must know the database name to which you want to connect.

When you know all of these things, you're ready to make that first simple connection. Connections will stay alive for as long as a PHP script executes then will be automatically shut down.

In all sample scripts in this hour, the example database name is contactDB, the example user is supercontact, and the example password is somepass. Substitute your own information when you try this out if you don't want to connect to the example database created in previous hours.

> The PHP Manual section for all MySQL-related functions can be found at http://www.php.net/manual/en/ref.mysql.php. Use it!

Using mysql_connect()

The mysql_connect() function is the first function you must call when utilizing a PHP script to connect to MySQL because, without an open connection to MySQL, you won't get very far! The basic syntax for the connection is

```
mysql_connect("hostname", "username", "password");
```

Using actual sample values, the connection function would look like this

```
mysql_connect("localhost", "supercontact", "somepass");
```

This function returns a connection index upon a successful connection or returns false if the connection fails. A working example of a connection script follows, assigning the value of the connection index to a variable called $conn, then printing the value of $conn as proof of a connection:

```
<?
$conn = mysql_connect("localhost", "supercontact", "somepass");
echo "$conn";
?>
```

Save this script as mysqlconnect.php, and place it in the document area of your Web server. Access the script with your Web browser and, if successful, you will see something like the following in your Web browser:

Resource id #1

Connecting to MySQL using the mysql_connect() function is pretty straightforward. The connection closes when the script finishes its execution, but if you would like to explicitly close the connection, simply add the mysql_close() function at the end of the script, as follows:

```
<?
$conn = mysql_connect("localhost", "supercontact", "somepass");
echo "$conn";
mysql_close($conn);
?>
```

That's all there is to it. The next section will cover the query execution functions, which are far more interesting than simply opening a connection and letting it sit there!

Executing Queries

Since you're reading Hour 24 of a book on MySQL, you should know how to write a valid SQL statement, and that's half the battle of executing MySQL queries using PHP. The `mysql_query()` function in PHP is used to send your SQL query to MySQL. If successful, a result index is returned. If a failure occurs, the function returns false.

Before you use the `mysql_query()` function, you'll notice one piece of the puzzle is missing: picking the database to use. When you connect to MySQL through the command line interface, the database is specified in the connection string. With PHP, it's a separate function called `mysql_select_db()` with the following syntax:

```
mysql_select_db(database name, connection index);
```

So, to connect to the `contactDB` database, first use `mysql_connect()`, and then use `mysql_select_db()`, as follows:

```
<?
$conn = mysql_connect("localhost", "supercontact", "somepass");
mysql_select_db("contactDB",$conn);
?>
```

You now have two important pieces of information: the connection index (`$conn`) and the knowledge that PHP knows to use `contactDB` as the database throughout the life of this particular script. The connection index is used in `mysql_query()` syntax:

```
mysql_query(query, connection index);
```

In your script, first make the connection, and then execute a query. The following script creates a simple table called `testTable`:

```
<?
// open the connection
$conn = mysql_connect("localhost", "supercontact", "somepass");

// pick the database to use
mysql_select_db("contactDB",$conn);

// create the SQL statement
$sql = "CREATE TABLE testTable (id int not null primary key auto_increment,
        testField varchar (75))";

// execute the SQL statement
$result = mysql_query($sql, $conn);

// echo the result identifier
echo $result;
?>
```

24

When issuing queries using mysql_query(), the semi-colon at the end of the SQL statement is not required. The only semi-colon in that line should be at the end of the PHP command.

Since only a true or false result is returned by the mysql_query() function, the boring output of this script is:

1

The "1" equals true, meaning the query was successfully executed. A "0" would have indicated a failure. Access MySQL through the command line interface to verify the creation of the testTable table:

```
mysql> describe testTable;
+------------+-------------+------+-----+---------+----------------+
| Field      | Type        | Null | Key | Default | Extra          |
+------------+-------------+------+-----+---------+----------------+
| id         | int(11)     |      | PRI | NULL    | auto_increment |
| testField  | varchar(75) | YES  |     | NULL    |                |
+------------+-------------+------+-----+---------+----------------+
2 rows in set (0.00 sec)
```

Congratulations—you have successfully created a table in your MySQL database using PHP!

Retrieving Error Messages

Take a moment to learn the usage of the mysql_error() function, as it will become your friend. When used in conjunction with the die() function, mysql_error() will return a helpful error when you make a mistake.

For example, now that you have created a table called testTable, you won't be able to execute that script again without an error. So, let's make it do just that, but modify it first to utilize the mysql_error()function:

```
<?
// open the connection
$conn = mysql_connect("localhost", "supercontact", "somepass");

// pick the database to use
mysql_select_db("contactDB",$conn);

// create the SQL statement
$sql = "CREATE TABLE testTable (id int not null primary key auto_increment,
        testField varchar (75))";
```

```
// execute the SQL statement
$result = mysql_query($sql, $conn) or die(mysql_error());

// echo the result identifier
echo $result;
?>
```

You should now see something like the following in your Web browser:

Table 'testTable' already exists

How exciting! Move on the next section to start inserting data into your table, and soon you'll be retrieving and formatting it via PHP.

Working with MySQL Data

Inserting, updating, deleting, and retrieving data all revolve around the use of the mysql_query() function to execute the basic SQL queries. For INSERT, UPDATE, and DELETE, no additional scripting is required after the query has been executed because you're not displaying any results (unless you want to). For SELECT, you have a few options for displaying the data retrieved by your query. Let's start with the basics and insert some data, so you have something to retrieve later on.

Inserting Data with PHP

The easiest method for inserting data is to simply hard code the INSERT statement. For example:

```
<?
// open the connection
$conn = mysql_connect("localhost", "supercontact", "somepass");

// pick the database to use
mysql_select_db("contactDB",$conn);

// create the SQL statement
$sql = "INSERT INTO testTable values ('', 'some value')";

// execute the SQL statement
$result = mysql_query($sql, $conn) or die(mysql_error());

// echo the result identifier
echo $result;
?>
```

You may wonder why you need to echo the result identifier if you're just inserting data? Well, you don't have to; it's just there for kicks. You can clean this script up a bit by replacing the query execution line so that it simply executes and prints a relevant statement if successful:

```
<?
// open the connection
$conn = mysql_connect("localhost", "supercontact", "somepass");

// pick the database to use
mysql_select_db("contactDB",$conn);

// create the SQL statement
$sql = "INSERT INTO testTable values ('', 'some value')";

// execute the SQL statement
if (mysql_query($sql, $conn)) {
        echo "record added!";
} else {
        echo "something went wrong";
}
?>
```

Running this script will result in a row being added to the testTable table. To enter more records than just the one shown in the script, you can either make a long list of hard-coded SQL statements and use mysql_query() multiple times to execute these statements, or you can create a form-based interface to the record addition script.

To create the form for this script, you really only need one field because the id field can automatically increment. The action of the form will be the name of the record-addition script; let's call it insert.php. So, your HTML form might look something like the following:

```
<HTML>
<HEAD>
<TITLE>Insert Form</TITLE>
</HEAD>
<BODY>
<FORM ACTION="insert.php" METHOD=POST>
<P>Text to add:<br>
<input type=text name="testField" size=30>
<p><input type=submit name="submit" value="Insert Record"></p>
</FORM>
</BODY>
</HTML>
```

Save this file as `insert_form.html`, and put it in the document root of your Web server. Next, create the `insert.php` script; the value entered in the form will replace the hard-coded values in the SQL query with a variable called `$testField`.

```
<?
// open the connection
$conn = mysql_connect("localhost", "supercontact", "somepass");

// pick the database to use
mysql_select_db("contactDB",$conn);

// create the SQL statement
$sql = "INSERT INTO testTable values ('', '$testField')";

// execute the SQL statement
if (mysql_query($sql, $conn)) {
        echo "record added!";
} else {
        echo "something went wrong";
}
?>
```

24

Save the script as `insert.php`, and put it in the document root of your Web server. In your Web browser, access the HTML form that you created. It should appear something like Figure 24.1.

FIGURE 24.1
HTML form for adding a record.

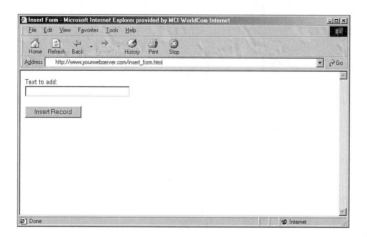

Enter a string in the "Text to add" field, as shown in Figure 24.2.

FIGURE 24.2

*Text typed in
form field.*

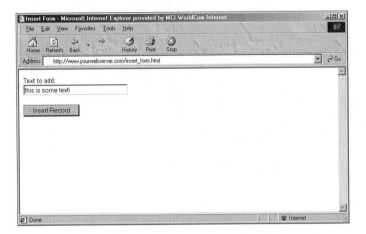

Finally, press the Insert Record button to execute the insert.php script and insert the
record. If successful, you will see results similar to Figure 24.3.

FIGURE 24.3

*Record
successfully
added.*

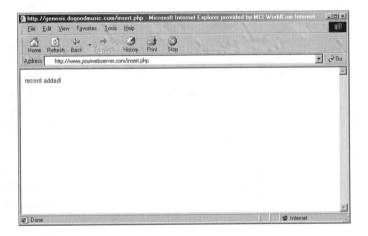

To verify your work, you can use the MySQL command line interface to view the
records in the table:

```
mysql> select * from testTable;
+----+--------------------+
| id | testField          |
+----+--------------------+
|  1 | some value         |
|  2 | this is some text! |
+----+--------------------+
2 rows in set (0.00 sec)
```

Next you'll learn how to retrieve and format results with PHP.

Retrieving Data with PHP

Since you have a few rows in your testTable table, you can write a PHP script to retrieve that data. Starting with the basics, write a script that issues a SELECT query but doesn't overwhelm you with result data; let's just get the number of rows. To do this, use the mysql_numrows() function. This function requires a result, so when you execute the query, put the result index in $result.

```
<?
// open the connection
$conn = mysql_connect("localhost", "supercontact", "somepass");

// pick the database to use
mysql_select_db("contactDB",$conn);

// create the SQL statement
$sql = "SELECT * FROM testTable";

// execute the SQL statement
$result = mysql_query($sql, $conn);

//get the number of rows in the result set
$number_of_rows = mysql_numrows($result);
echo "The number of rows is $number_of_rows";
?>
```

Save this script as count.php, place it in your Web server document directory, and access it through your Web browser. You should see a message such as:

The number of rows is 2

The number should be equal to the number of records you recall inserting during testing. Now that you know there are some records in the table, you can get fancy and fetch the actual contents of those records. You can do this a few ways, but the easiest method is to retrieve each row as an array.

What you'll be doing is using a while statement to go through each record in the result set, place the values of each field into a specific variable, then display the results on screen. The syntax of mysql_fetch_array() is

```
$newArray = mysql_fetch_array($result);
```

Follow along using this sample script:

```
<?
// open the connection
$conn = mysql_connect("localhost", "supercontact", "somepass");
```

24

```
// pick the database to use
mysql_select_db("contactDB",$conn);

// create the SQL statement
$sql = "SELECT * FROM testTable";

// execute the SQL statement
$result = mysql_query($sql, $conn);

//go through each row in the result set and display data
while ($newArray = mysql_fetch_array($result)) {
        // give a name to the fields
        $id  = $newArray['id'];
        $testField = $newArray['testField'];

        //echo the results on screen
        echo "The ID is $id and the text is $testField <br>";
}
?>
```

Save this script as select.php, place it in your Web server document directory, and access it through your Web browser. You should see a message for each record entered into testTable, as in Figure 24.4.

FIGURE 24.4
Selecting records from MySQL.

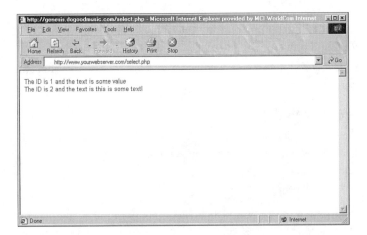

Essentially, you can create an entire database-driven application using just four or five MySQL functions. This hour barely scratched the surface of using PHP with MySQL; there are many more MySQL functions in PHP, as you'll learn in the next section!

Additional MySQL Functions in PHP

There are approximately 40 MySQL-specific functions in PHP. Most of these functions are simply alternate methods of retrieving data or are used to gather information about the table structure in question.

For a complete list of functions, with practical examples, visit the MySQL section of the PHP Manual at `http://www.php.net/manual/en/ref.mysql.php`.

Summary

Using PHP and MySQL to create dynamic, database-driven Web sites is a breeze. Just remember that the PHP functions are essentially a gateway to the database server; anything you'd enter using the MySQL command line interface, you can use with `mysql_query()`!

To connect to MySQL with PHP, you need to know your MySQL username, password, and database name. Using `mysql_connect()` and `mysql_select_db()`, you can connect to and select a database to use throughout the life of the script.

Once connected, you issue standard SQL commands with the `mysql_query()` function. If you have issued a `SELECT` command, you can use `mysql_numrows()` to count the records returned in the result set. If you want to display the data found, you can use `mysql_fetch_array()` to get all the results during a loop and display them on screen.

Q&A

Q If my ISP doesn't offer PHP, can I install it myself?

A Installing PHP requires root-level permissions and the ability to modify the Web server configuration files. It is unlikely that you would be able to do this yourself in a virtual hosting environment. However, PHP is a cross-platform scripting language that works with virtually every Web server imaginable, so you could install PHP and a Web server on your own personal machine for testing purposes.

24

Workshop

The Workshop is designed to help you anticipate possible questions, review what you've learned, and begin learning how to put your knowledge into practice.

Quiz

1. What is the primary function used to make the connection between PHP and MySQL, and what information is necessary?
2. Which PHP function retrieves a MySQL error message?
3. Which PHP function is used to count the number of records in a result set?

Answers

1. The `mysql_connect()` function creates a connection to MySQL and requires the host name, user name, and password.
2. The `mysql_error()` function returns a MySQL error message.
3. The `mysql_numrows()` function counts the number of records in a result set.

Activity

Create a PHP script that displays the contents of your `master_name` table in your content management database.

PART IX

Appendices

Appendix

APPENDIX A

Installing MySQL

Regardless of whether you are the administrator of your own database server or you want to install MySQL in a development environment for testing purposes, you have several options to choose from when installing MySQL. These options range in price from free to a few hundred dollars, depending on the distribution and the company whose product you choose.

How to Get MySQL

The method of obtaining MySQL depends on which distribution you want to use. These methods range from downloading a large file (or several large files) to buying an off-the-shelf product. The following list details the most common distribution methods for MySQL:

- MySQL AB distributes the Open Source version of MySQL at http://www.mysql.com/. There is no shrink-wrapped product; what you get is simply what you download from the Web site, which includes binary distributions for Windows and Linux/Unix as well as RPMs and source distributions.

- NuSphere Corporation sells a product called Enhanced MySQL, which is based on the Open Source version of MySQL but with additions and enhancements, such as the Gemini table type. NuSphere's products are available for purchase as a shrink-wrapped products from its Web site, `http://www.nusphere.com/`.

- AbriaSoft distributes MySQL as part of its Merlin Server (a Web development plat-form), which is available for download and purchase at its Web site, `http://www.abriasoft.com/`.

- Linux distribution CDs usually contain some version or other of the Open Source MySQL distribution, although they're usually a bit out of date.

Installing MySQL 3.23 or 4.0 on Windows

The MySQL installation process on Windows is quite simple—the developers from MySQL AB have packaged up everything you need in one ZIP file with a setup program! Once you download the ZIP file, extract its contents into a temporary directory and run the `setup.exe` application. After the `setup.exe` application installs the MySQL server and client programs, you're ready to start the MySQL server.

The following steps detail the installation of MySQL 4.0 from MySQL AB on Windows, and they show you what you might expect if you install MySQL in a Windows 95/98/NT/2000/XP environment for testing and development (many users install MySQL on personal Windows machines to get a feel for working with the database before deploying MySQL in a production environment):

1. Visit the MySQL 4.0 download page at `http://www.mysql.com/downloads/mysql-4.0.html` and find the Windows section on the page. You want to download the Installation files (Zip) rather than Cygwin downloads (`tar.bz2`).

If you have the tools and skills to compile your own Windows binary files, select the Cygwin source download and follow the instructions contained in the source distribution.

2. Clicking the Download link will take you to a page of mirror sites. Select the mirror site closest to you and then download the file. It is currently around 17.5MB, so you may be waiting awhile, depending on your connection speed.

3. Once the Zip file is on your hard drive, extract its contents to a temporary directory.

4. From the temporary directory, find the setup.exe file and double-click it to start the installation. You will see the first screen of the installation wizard, as shown in Figure A.1. Click Next to continue.

FIGURE A.1

Step 1 of the MySQL Installation Wizard.

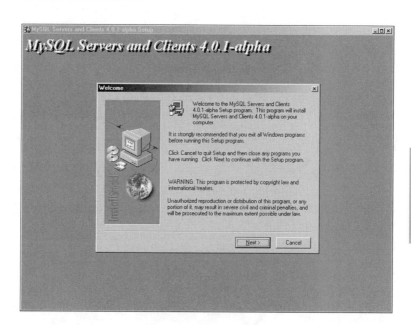

5. The second screen in the installation process, shown in Figure A.2, contains valuable information regarding the installation location. The default installation location is C:\mysql, but if you plan to install MySQL in a different location, this screen shows you a few changes you will have to make on your own. The information on this screen is also important for Windows NT users who wish to start MySQL as a service. Read the information and note anything relevant to your situation; then click Next to continue.

Figure A.2

Step 2 of the MySQL Installation Wizard. Note any relevant information before continuing.

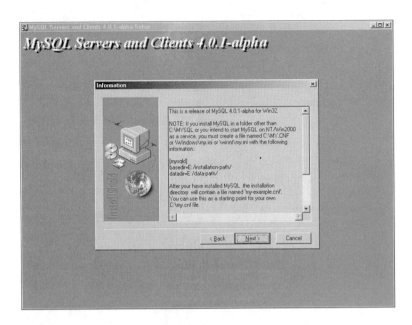

6. The third screen in the installation process, shown in Figure A.3, has you select the installation location. If you want to install MySQL in the default location, click Next to continue. Otherwise, click Browse and navigate to the location of your choice; then click Next to continue.

Figure A.3

Step 3 of the MySQL Installation Wizard, in which you select an installation location.

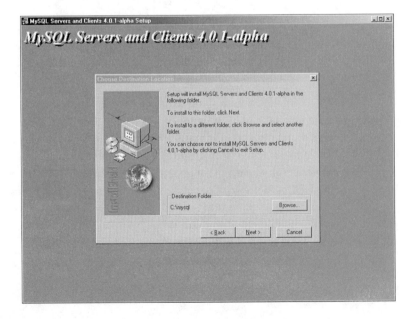

7. The fourth screen, shown in Figure A.4, has you select the installation method—either Typical, Compact, or Custom. Select Typical and click Next to continue.

FIGURE A.4

Step 4 of the MySQL Installation Wizard, in which you select an installation type.

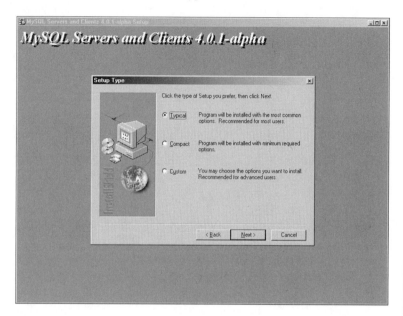

8. The installation process will now take over and install files in their proper locations. When the process is finished, you will see a confirmation of completion, as shown in Figure A.5. Click Finish to complete the setup process.

FIGURE A.5

MySQL has been installed.

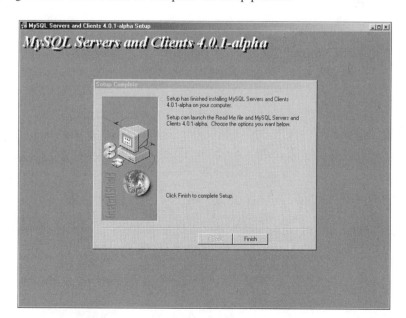

A

There are no fancy shortcuts installed in your Windows Start menu after an installation of MySQL from MySQL AB, so now you must start the process yourself. If you navigate to the `C:\mysql\bin` directory, you will find numerous applications ready for action, shown in Figure A.6.

FIGURE A.6

Directory listing of MySQL applications.

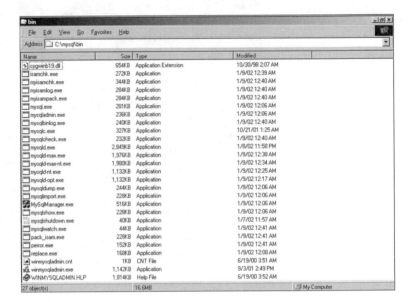

The `winmysqladmin.exe` application, shown in Figure A.7, is a great friend to Windows users who are just getting started with MySQL. If you double-click this file, it will start the MySQL server and place a "stoplight" icon in your taskbar. If you right-click this icon, you can launch a graphical user interface for maintaining and monitoring your new server.

WinMySQLAdmin will automatically interpret environment information, such as IP address, machine name, and so on. The tabs across the top allow you to view system information and also edit MySQL configuration options.

For example, if you select the "my.ini Setup" tab, you will see the MySQL configuration file and also be able to edit information from that screen, as shown in Figure A.8.

FIGURE A.7

WinMySQLAdmin started and ready for action.

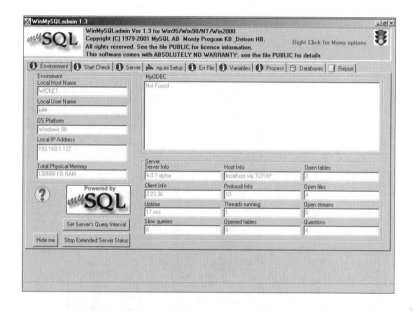

FIGURE A.8

Editing my.ini with WinMySQLAdmin.

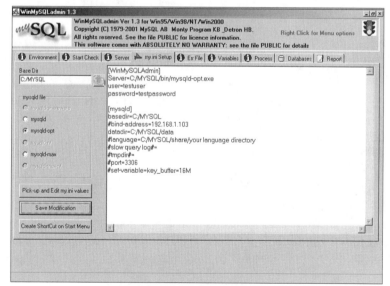

You can also view server configuration information by selecting the Variables tab, as shown in Figure A.9. This information is similar to the output of the SHOW VARIABLES command.

FIGURE A.9
Server configuration information.

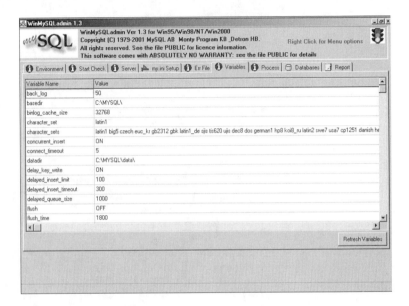

To shut down the MySQL server and/or the WinMySQLAdmin tool, right-click again on the stoplight icon in your taskbar and select the appropriate choice. As long as the MySQL server is running, you can run additional applications through a console window, such as the MySQL monitor.

Installing MySQL 3.23 or 4.0 on Linux/Unix

Installation of MySQL 3.23 or 4.0 on Linux/Unix is also straightforward, especially if you use the recommended installation method—using RPMs. Several RPMs make up a full distribution, but for a minimal installation you need the following:

- MySQL-VERSION.i386.rpm—The MySQL server
- MySQL-client-VERSION.i386.rpm—The standard MySQL client programs

To perform the minimal installation, type the following at your prompt:

```
#prompt> rpm -i MySQL-VERSION.i386.rpm MySQL-client-VERSION.i386.rpm
```

You can also install MySQL from a binary distribution, which requires `gunzip` and `tar` to uncompress and unpack the distribution and also requires the ability to create groups and users on the system. The first series of commands in the binary distribution installation process has you adding a group and a user and unpacking the distribution, as follows:

```
#prompt > groupadd mysql
#prompt > useradd -g mysql mysql
#prompt > cd /usr/local
#prompt > gunzip < /path/to/mysql-VERSION-OS.tar.gz | tar xvf -
```

Next, the instructions tell you to create a link with a shorter name:

```
#prompt > ln -s mysql-VERSION-OS mysql
#prompt > cd mysql
```

Once unpacked, the README and INSTALL files will walk you through the remainder of the installation process for the version of MySQL you've chosen. In general, the next series of commands will be used:

```
#prompt > scripts/mysql_install_db
#prompt > chown -R root  /usr/local/mysql
#prompt > chown -R mysql /usr/local/mysql/data
#prompt > chgrp -R mysql /usr/local/mysql
#prompt > chown -R root /usr/local/mysql/bin
```

You're now ready to start the MySQL server.

Troubleshooting Your Installation

If you have any problems during the installation of MySQL, the first place you should look is the "Problems and Common Errors" chapter of the MySQL manual, which is located at `http://www.mysql.com/doc/P/r/Problems.html`.

Highlights of common problems include the following:

- Incorrect permissions do not allow you to start the MySQL daemon. If this is the case, be sure you have changed owners and groups to match those indicated in the installation instructions.

- If you see the message "Access denied" when connecting to MySQL, be sure you are using the correct username and password.

- If you see the message "Can't connect to server," make sure the MySQL daemon is running.

- When defining tables, if you specify a length for a field whose type does not require a length, the table will not be created. For example, you should not specify a length when defining a field as TEXT (as opposed to CHAR or VARCHAR).

If you're still having trouble after reading the manual, sending an e-mail to the MySQL mailing list (see `http://www.mysql.com/documentation/lists.html` for more information) will likely produce results. You can also purchase support contracts from MySQL AB for a very low fee.

If you have purchased a version of MySQL other than the one distributed by MySQL AB, you should turn to the documentation and support options for that product. These companies also usually have additional support contracts that can be purchased.

APPENDIX B

Using MyODBC

MyODBC is a driver used to make a connection between ODBC-aware applications and a MySQL database. MyODBC can be installed on Windows 95/98/NT/2000 as well as on most Unix platforms. Freely available from MySQL AB, you can download the latest version of MyODBC from `http://www.mysql.com/downloads/api-myodbc.html`.

MyODBC is often used to connect an application to a remote MySQL database, specifically to use the data stored in that database. For example, you can connect to MySQL from Microsoft Access through MyODBC and use data stored in a MySQL database to populate a Microsoft Access database or a Microsoft Excel spreadsheet, and vice versa.

MyODBC is not limited to connecting MySQL with desktop applications. It is also used as a gateway for programming languages such as ColdFusion and Microsoft Active Server Pages to connect directly to your MySQL database.

When you're exporting data from an application such as Microsoft Access to MySQL, using MyODBC can be a much more efficient process than dumping data and using a tool such as `mysqlimport` to populate your tables. This is especially true in an environment where the administrator is a novice database user—or if the administrator only knows the Microsoft way of doing things.

Creating a Microsoft Excel spreadsheet using data from MySQL is another use for MyODBC. By importing data directly into your application, you can use the remote data to create reports, charts, and graphs without having to re-key in all the data stored in your fancy MySQL database.

Yet another use for MyODBC is to link remote MySQL tables to tables with the same structure in a local database system, such as Microsoft Access. This way, administrators (or regular office workers) can use a graphical user interface that they're comfortable with, in Microsoft Access, to update the remote database. These users never have to look at a command line, and your remote database is updated in real time, without the lag time of regularly scheduled import and export procedures.

Installing MyODBC on Windows

MySQL AB maintains and distributes the MyODBC application. The following instructions outline the installation and configuration of MyODBC 3.51 on a Windows machine.

> You may also install MyODBC on other platforms such as Linux. For source files or installation binaries, visit the MyODBC downloads area of the MySQL Web site and find the appropriate files for your platform. Follow the installation instructions contained in the distribution you selected.

1. Visit the MySQL 3.51 download page, at `http://www.mysql.com/downloads/ api-myodbc.html`, and find the Windows section on the page. You want to download the Installation files (EXE) driver installer.

If you have the tools and skills to compile your own Windows binary files, select the Windows source packages and follow the instructions contained in the source distribution.

2. Clicking the Download link will take you to a page of mirror sites. Select the mirror site closest to you and then download the file. Unlike the 17.5MB MySQL installation file, the MyODBC file is only about 600KB, so the download should be speedy.

3. Once the executable file is on your hard drive, double-click it to start the installation. You will see the first screen of the MyODBC Installation Wizard, as shown in Figure B.1. Click Next to continue.

FIGURE B.1

Step 1 of the MyODBC Installation Wizard.

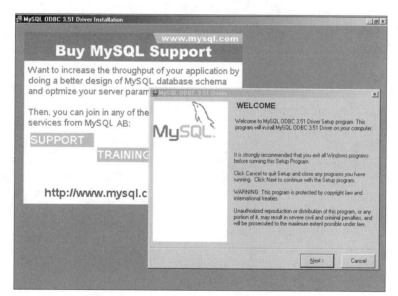

4. The second screen of the MyODBC Installation Wizard, shown in Figure B.2, contains a Readme file. Read through the information regarding licensing and use; then click Next to continue.

FIGURE B.2

Step 2 of the MyODBC Installation Wizard.

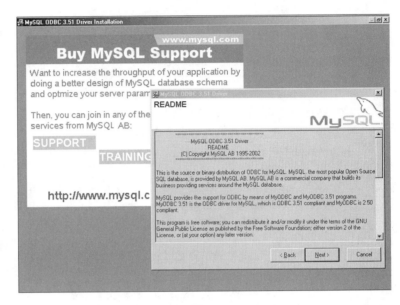

5. The third screen of the MyODBC Installation Wizard, shown in Figure B.3, handles the entire installation, after you click Next to continue.

FIGURE B.3

Step 3 of the MyODBC Installation Wizard.

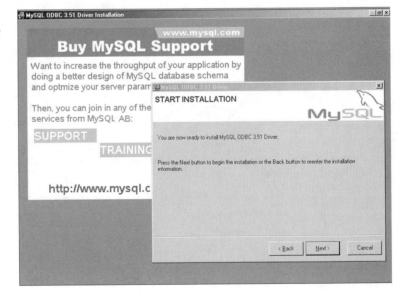

6. When the installation is finished, the confirmation screen will appear, as shown in Figure B.4. Click Finish to exit the installer.

FIGURE B.4

Confirmation that the MyODBC Installation Wizard has finished its process.

Now that MyODBC is installed, you need to configure your system(s) to utilize this application in order to talk to MySQL. The next section outlines this process.

Configuring MyODBC

After downloading and installing MyODBC on your Windows machine, you must create an ODBC DSN to facilitate the connection between an application and your MySQL server.

To set up a DSN on your Windows machine, follow these steps:

1. From your Windows Start menu, select Settings, Control Panel. If you are using Windows 2000, double-click Administrative Tools.

2. Double-click the icon for ODBC Data Sources (32 bit). If you are using Windows 2000, double-click Data Sources (ODBC). You should now see the ODBC Data Source Administrator, as shown in Figure B.5.

FIGURE B.5

The ODBC Data Source Administrator, used to create a DSN.

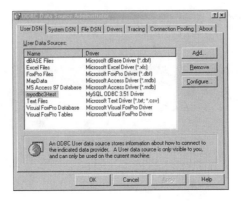

3. In the ODBC Data Source Administrator, make sure the User DSN tab is selected and then click the Add button. The Create New Data Source dialog box will appear, as shown in Figure B.6.

FIGURE B.6

The Create a New Data Source dialog box.

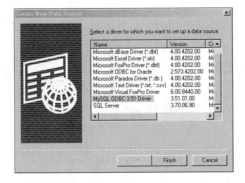

If you are adding a data source for use with a Web-based application such as ColdFusion, create a system DSN instead of a user DSN.

4. Select MySQL ODBC 3.51 Driver from the list and then click Finish. The DSN Configuration dialog box will appear, as shown in Figure B.7.

FIGURE B.7

Fill out the information in this dialog box to complete the configuration of your MySQL data source.

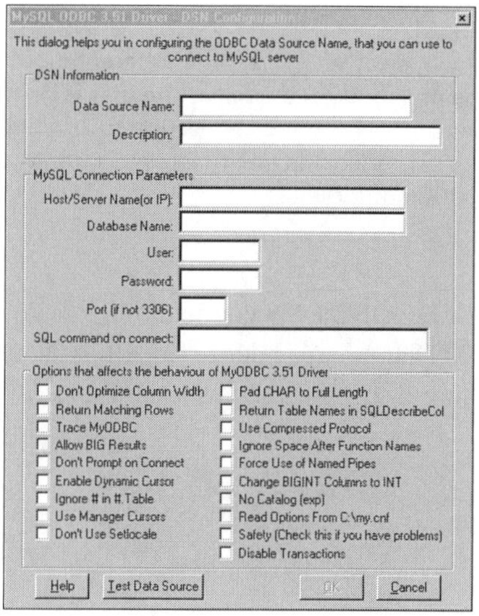

5. Complete the DSN Information section by giving it a name and a description. Then, complete the information in the MySQL Connection Parameters section, based on the information you should already know after installing MySQL on your own machine. Figure B.8 shows an example of a completed configuration.

FIGURE B.8

Sample configuration of a MyODBC DSN.

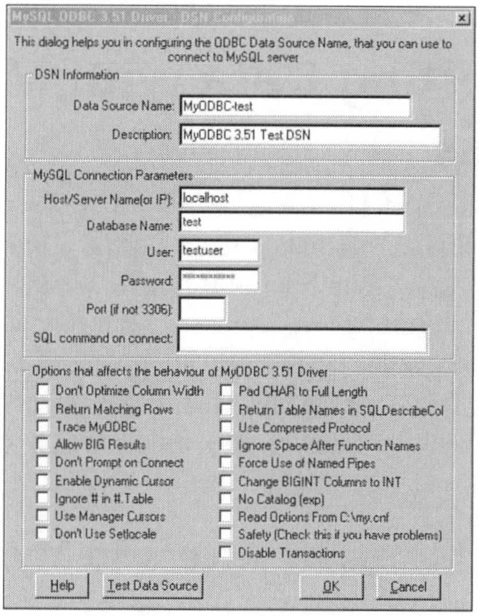

B

> If you wish to connect to MySQL on a different machine, enter the appropriate hostname or IP address as well as the username and password used to connect. Remember, if you are connecting to a remote machine, your MySQL grant tables must reflect the ability to connect to MySQL from a remote machine (that is, not localhost).

6. After completing the MyODBC DSN configuration, make sure MySQL is running and then click the Test Data Source button. Hopefully, you will see a response like the one shown in Figure B.9, indicating a successful test.

FIGURE B.9

Successful connection test using the new MyODBC DSN.

For information on the check box options in the configuration dialog box, see the "Connection Parameters" section in the MyODBC manual, at
`http://www.mysql.com/products/myodbc/manual.html#Connection_parameters`.

When the configuration is complete, you're ready to start your local, ODBC-aware application and specify the DSN you created through the ODBC administrator.

Importing/Exporting Data with MySQL and Microsoft Access

One of the more common uses of MyODBC is to act as the intermediary between Microsoft Access and MySQL. Often, this action comes at a time when a company wants to move to MySQL, away from Microsoft Access, but has an incredible amount of information in existing Microsoft Access databases. Manually entering Microsoft Access data into a new MySQL database is never a primary option, nor is scrapping all the data and starting from scratch. This is where MyODBC comes in quite handy, because it facilitates the connection between the two applications. In this section, you'll learn the simple steps for importing and exporting data between these two applications.

Exporting from Microsoft Access to MySQL

Assume you have a table in a Microsoft Access database that contains basic contact information, such as name, address, telephone number, and e-mail address. If you create a matching table structure in MySQL, you can export the existing Microsoft Access data in just a few clicks. Figure B.10 shows the data in Microsoft Access.

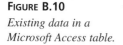

FIGURE B.10

Existing data in a Microsoft Access table.

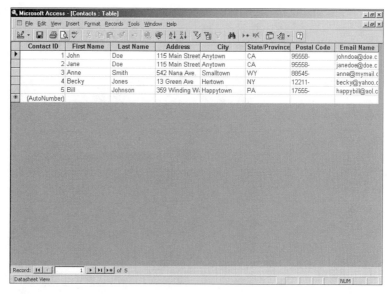

Here are the steps to follow:

1. Select Save As from the File menu. The Save As dialog box will appear. Select To an External File or Database, as shown in Figure B.11, and click OK to continue.

FIGURE B.11

Selecting the export option.

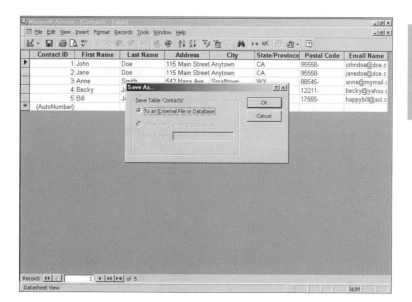

B

2. In the Save As Type dialog box, select ODBC Databases () and click OK. The Export dialog box will appear, as shown in Figure B.12. Accept the default name or change it to something else; then click OK to continue.

FIGURE B.12
Providing the appropriate export name.

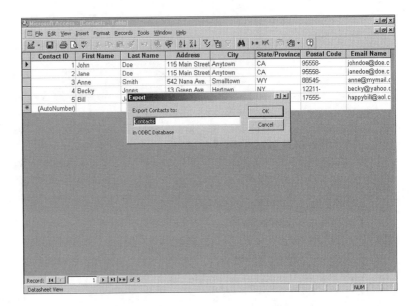

3. From the Select Data Source dialog box, select the Machine Data Source tab and highlight the MyODBC database, as shown in Figure B.13. Click OK to continue.

FIGURE B.13
Select the MyODBC data source.

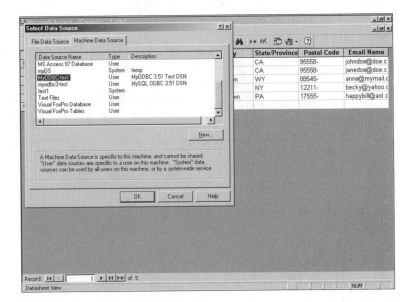

4. The tables will now be linked together and the information from Microsoft Access will populate the MySQL table called Contacts. You can verify the export by connecting to MySQL and selecting data from the table, as shown in Figure B.14.

FIGURE B.14

Verifying the data export to MySQL.

Importing into Microsoft Access from MySQL

Importing data from an existing MySQL table to an existing Microsoft Access table can also be achieved with a few mouse clicks—and the process looks quite similar:

1. With a blank Microsoft Access database ready and waiting, select Get External Data, Import from the File menu.

2. In the Files of Type dialog box, select ODBC Databases () and click OK.

3. From the Data Source dialog box, select the MyODBC DSN and click OK.

4. Select the tables you wish to import and then click OK. Your data will be imported to Microsoft Access from the MySQL table.

B

APPENDIX C

Reserved Words

"Reserved Words" are words that have special meaning to MySQL. These words may already be the names of SQL commands or data types, or they may be other words that have meaning within the nuts and bolts of MySQL. You cannot use any of the following reserved words as names for tables or fields within your database.

TABLE C.1 Reserved Words

ADD	ALL	ALTER
ANALYZE	AND	AS
ASC	BETWEEN	BIGINT
BINARY	BLOB	BOTH
BY	CASCADE	CASE
CHANGE	CHARACTER	COLUMN
CONSTRAINT	CREATE	CROSS
CURRENT_DATE	CURRENT_TIME	CURRENT_TIMESTAMP
DATABASE	DATABASES	DAY_HOUR

continues

TABLE C.1 Continued

DAY_MINUTE	DAY_SECOND	DECIMAL
DEFAULT	DELAYED	DELETE
DESC	DISTINCTROW	DOUBLE
DROP	ELSE	ENCLOSED
ESCAPED	EXISTS	EXPLAIN
FIELDS	FLOAT	FOR
FOREIGN	FROM	FULLTEXT
GRANT	GROUP	HAVING
HIGH_PRIORITY	HOUR_MINUTE	HOUR_SECOND
IF	IGNORE	IN
INDEX	INFILE	INNER
INSERT	INSERT_ID	INTEGER
INTERVAL	INTO	IS
JOIN	KEY	KEYS
KILL	LAST_INSERT_ID	LEADING
LEFT	LIKE	LIMIT
LINES	LOAD	LOCK
LONG	LONGBLOB	LONGTEXT
LOW_PRIORITY	MASTER_LOG_SEQ	MASTER_SERVER_ID
MATCH	MEDIUMBLOB	MEDIUMTEXT
MIDDLEINT	MINUTE_SECOND	NATURAL
NOT	NULL	NUMERIC
ON	OPTIMIZE	OPTION
OPTIONALLY	OR	ORDER
OUTER	OUTFILE	PARTIAL
PRECISION	PRIMARY	PRIVILEGES
PROCEDURE	PURGE	READ
REAL	REFERENCES	RENAME
REPLACE	REQUIRE	RESTRICT
RETURNS	REVOKE	RIGHT
RLIKE	SELECT	SET
SHOW	SMALLINT	SONAME
SQL_AUTO_IS_NULL	SQL_BIG_RESULT	SQL_BIG_SELECTS

continues

TABLE C.1   Continued

SQL_BIG_TABLES	SQL_BUFFER_RESULT	SQL_CALC_FOUND_ROWS
SQL_LOG_BIN	SQL_LOG_OFF	SQL_LOG_UPDATE
SQL_LOW_PRIORITY_UPDATES	SQL_SAFE_UPDATES	SQL_SELECT_LIMIT
SQL_SLAVE_SKIP_COUNTER	SQL_SMALL_RESULT	SQL_WARNINGS
SSL	STARTING	STRAIGHT_JOIN
TABLE	TABLES	TERMINATED
THEN	TINYBLOB	TINYINT
TINYTEXT	TO	TRAILING
UNION	UNIQUE	UNLOCK
UNSIGNED	UPDATE	USAGE
USE	USING	VALUES
VARBINARY	VARCHAR	VARYING
WHEN	WHERE	WITH
WRITE	YEAR_MONTH	ZEROFILL

If you try to create a table using one of the reserved words as the table name, the following error will occur:

```
mysql> CREATE TABLE unsigned (id int);
ERROR 1064: You have an error in your SQL syntax near
'unsigned (id int)' at line 1
```

Similarly, if you create a table using a reserved word as the name of any field in the table, the following error will occur:

```
mysql> CREATE TABLE test (id int, cross varchar(10));
ERROR 1064: You have an error in your SQL syntax near
'cross varchar(10))' at line 1
```

There are also a few reserved words from ANSI SQL92 that are allowed as table and field names in MySQL: ACTION, BIT, DATE, ENUM, NO, TEXT, TIME, and TIMESTAMP. If you use any of these in your MySQL database and then at some point need to convert your MySQL database to another system, such as Oracle or Microsoft SQL Server, you will have to eliminate the usage of these nonstandard words.

C

APPENDIX **D**

Practical MySQL/PHP Examples

In Hour 24, "Using MySQL with PHP," you learned the very basics of inserting and retrieving data from MySQL using the PHP scripting language. This appendix provides a few more useful examples for integrating MySQL and PHP within your Web site.

The elements you have learned throughout the book, in addition to the examples in this appendix, are enough to get you well on your way to building your own projects. Essentially, dynamic Web sites and applications are nothing more than many INSERT, UPDATE, and DELETE statements placed in the proper logical order. Remember that, and you won't overcomplicate your scripts.

Creating Access Logs and Reports

You are limited to the types of information you can automatically log on a Web site without user intervention. All Web servers keep a basic access log, with entries such as the following:

```
64.186.175.18 - - [01/Mar/2002:00:21:49 -0800] "GET /extra/showall.php HTTP/1.1"
200 15821 "http://www.thickbook.com/extra/index.html" "Mozilla/4.0 (compatible;
MSIE 5.5; Windows 98; MCIWORLDV2)"
```

This entry shows the IP address and time of the access, the file requested, the status of
the request and the number of bytes sent back, the referring page, and, finally, the Web
browser used. If you just want to know how many hits are made on your home page,
using one of the many log analysis packages to parse your server's access log might be a
bit of overkill for such simple tasks.

The examples in this section include a simple hit counter on a page and a synopsis report
of accesses to numerous pages.

The Basic Hit Counter

A basic hit counter simply captures the number of hits to a specific page and displays
them to the user. Because you don't have to track the date or time a person accessed the
page or any other fancy information (you just to track the hit itself), your table can be
simple. The following CREATE TABLE statement creates a table with three fields (id,
page_name, and hits):

```
mysql> CREATE TABLE test_track (id INT NOT NULL PRIMARY KEY AUTO_INCREMENT,
    -> page_name VARCHAR (50), hits INT);
Query OK, 0 rows affected (0.00 sec)
```

The id and page_name fields exist so you can hold hit counts for multiple pages in one
table. Each page will only have the one row, because you will use an UPDATE statement to
increment the hits field. Seed the test_track table with a record for the test script:

```
mysql> INSERT INTO test_track VALUES (1, 'test1', 0);
Query OK, 1 row affected (0.00 sec)
```

Now it's time to create the script. Open a text editor and create the following script,
called hitcount.php. First, open a PHP block and assign a value for $page_name:

```
<?php
$page_name = "test1";
```

Next, use the mysql_connect() and mysql_select_db() functions to connect to MySQL
and use the proper database. Substitute your own information for the placeholder information used here:

```
$db = @mysql_connect("localhost", "youruser", "yourpass");
@mysql_select_db("yourDB", $db);
```

Create the SQL statement that updates the hits field for the record with the corresponding
page_name value; then issue the query with the mysql_query() function and close the
PHP block:

```
$sql = "UPDATE test_track SET hits = hits + 1 WHERE page_name = '$page_name'";
@mysql_query($sql);
?>
```

Display whatever you wish to the user using HTML. Here's an example:

```
<HTML>
<HEAD>
<TITLE>Test Hit Count Page</TITLE>
</HEAD>
<BODY>
<H1 align=center>You have been counted!</H1>
</BODY>
</HTML>
```

Place the file in the document root of your Web server and access it with a Web browser. You should see something like what's shown in Figure D.1.

FIGURE D.1

Accessing the hitcount.php *script.*

If you view the data in the test_track table, you will see that the value of hits has been incremented for this page:

```
mysql> SELECT * FROM test_track;
+----+-----------+------+
| id | page_name | hits |
+----+-----------+------+
|  1 | test1     |    1 |
+----+-----------+------+
1 row in set (0.00 sec)
```

D

Of course, one of the most important aspects of a hit counter is to actually display the number of accesses on the particular page. To do that, you simply issue another MySQL query to retrieve the value of the hits field. Be sure you do so after incrementing the count!

Add these lines before the close of the PHP block in the original script:

```
$sql2 = "SELECT hits FROM test_track WHERE page_name = '$page_name'";
$res = @mysql_query($sql2);
$hits = @mysql_result($res,0,'hits');
```

The first line creates another SQL statement, retrieving the number of hits in the test_track table for the given script. The second line issues the query and places the result in a result set. The third line retrieves the result from the result set so that it is usable to print.

After the heading in the HTML, add the following line, which uses the retrieved result to display the number of hits to the user:

```
<P align=center>The current number is <?php echo "$hits"; ?>.</p>
```

The code should now look like this:

```
<?php
$page_name = "test1";

$db = @mysql_connect("localhost", "youruser", "yourpass");
@mysql_select_db("yourDB", $db);

$sql = "UPDATE test_track SET hits = hits + 1 WHERE page_name = '$page_name'";
@mysql_query($sql);

$sql2 = "SELECT hits FROM test_track WHERE page_name = '$page_name'";
$res = @mysql_query($sql2);
$hits = @mysql_result($res,0,'hits');

?>
<HTML>
<HEAD>
<TITLE>Test Hit Count Page</TITLE>
</HEAD>
<BODY>
<H1 align=center>You have been counted!</H1>
<P align=center>The current number is <?php echo "$hits"; ?>.</p>
</BODY>
</HTML>
```

If you access the script with your Web browser, you will see the message as well as the count, as in Figure D.2.

Figure D.2

Accessing the hitcount.php *script and seeing the number of hits.*

Souped-up Hit Counter and Report

By taking the simple hit counter one step further, you can log many of the same items as in the Web server access logs. Unlike in the simple hit counter, where each page has its hits stored in one incrementing field, the souped-up hit counter stores one record for each hit.

You will have an id field and a page_name field, as in the test_track table, but the similarities end there. Three additional fields are user_agent, IP_address and date_added, and the generic hits field goes away. The table creation statement is shown here:

```
mysql> CREATE TABLE super_track (id INT NOT NULL PRIMARY KEY AUTO_INCREMENT,
    -> page_name VARCHAR(50), user_agent TEXT, IP_address VARCHAR (20),
    -> date_added DATETIME);
Query OK, 0 rows affected (0.00 sec)
```

In your PHP script, you will use environment variables to fill the user_agent and IP_address fields, using the getenv() PHP function:

```
$user_agent = getenv("HTTP_USER_AGENT");
$IP_address = getenv("REMOTE_ADDR");
```

D

The remainder of the script is similar to the basic hit counter, with a few minor adjustments. First, replace the UPDATE command with an INSERT command, because you need to add a distinct record for each access to the page. Also, when retrieving the hit count for later display, you must use the COUNT() function to count the distinct records rather than simply retrieving the number of hits. The new script might look something like the following, if you also decide to display the user agent and IP address for kicks:

```php
<?php
$page_name = "test1";
$user_agent = getenv("HTTP_USER_AGENT");
$IP_address = getenv("REMOTE_ADDR");

$db = @mysql_connect("localhost", "youruser", "yourpass");
@mysql_select_db("yourDB", $db);

$sql = "INSERT INTO super_track VALUES
        ('', '$page_name', '$user_agent', '$IP_address', now())";
@mysql_query($sql);

$sql2 = "SELECT COUNT(*) FROM super_track WHERE page_name = '$page_name'";
$res = @mysql_query($sql2);
$hits = @mysql_result($res,0,'COUNT(*)');

?>
<HTML>
<HEAD>
<TITLE>Test Hit Count Page</TITLE>
</HEAD>
<BODY>
<H1 align=center>You have been counted!</H1>
<P align=center><strong>User Agent:</strong> <?php echo "$user_agent"; ?></p>
<P align=center><strong>IP Address:</strong> <?php echo "$IP_address"; ?></p>
<P align=center>The current number is <?php echo "$hits"; ?>.</p>
</BODY>
</HTML>
```

Call this script super_count1.php and place it in the document root of your Web server. If you access the script with your Web browser, you will see something like what's shown in Figure D.3. Of course, your values will be different for $user_agent and $IP_address.

FIGURE D.3

Accessing the
`super_count1.php`
script and seeing the
number of hits plus
additional information.

Make a few copies of this script, changing the value of $page_name in each. Then access the scripts a few times to make some entries in the super_track table. These will make your access reports, which you'll create in a moment, much more interesting.

This report script (call it `report.php`) will evolve through a few steps. First, just create a simple count of the total hits to the tracked pages:

```php
<?php
$db = @mysql_connect("localhost", "youruser", "yourpass");
@mysql_select_db("yourDB", $db);

//total count
$count_sql = "SELECT COUNT(*) AS total_count FROM super_track";
$count_res = @mysql_query($count_sql);
$total_count = @mysql_result($count_res, 0, "total_count");
?>
<HTML>
<HEAD>
<TITLE>My Access Report</TITLE>
</HEAD>
<BODY>
<h1>My Access Report</h1>
<P><strong>Total Accesses For All Pages:</strong>
<?php echo "$total_count"; ?></p>
</BODY>
</HTML>
```

D

When you view the page through your Web browser, you will see something like
Figure D.4.

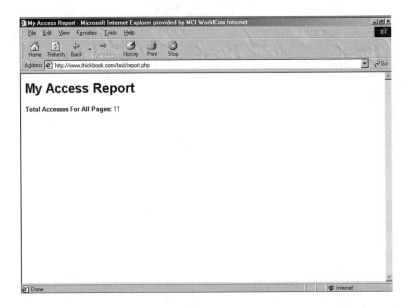

Now that is some kind of boring! Let's count the distinct user agents and IP addresses
that made the accesses to your pages and then display them with their counts:

```php
<?php
$db = @mysql_connect("localhost", "youruser", "yourpass");
@mysql_select_db("yourDB", $db);

//total count
$count_sql = "SELECT COUNT(*) AS total_count FROM super_track";
$count_res = @mysql_query($count_sql);
$total_count = @mysql_result($count_res, 0, "total_count");

//user agent counts
$user_agent_sql = "SELECT DISTINCT user_agent, COUNT(user_agent) AS ua_count
FROM super_track GROUP BY user_agent ORDER BY ua_count DESC";
$user_agent_res = @mysql_query($user_agent_sql);

$user_agent_block = "<ul>";
while ($row_ua = @mysql_fetch_array($user_agent_res)) {
    $user_agent = $row_ua['user_agent'];
    $user_agent_count = $row_ua['ua_count'];
```

```
    $user_agent_block .= "<li>$user_agent
    <ul>
    <li><em>accesses per browser: $user_agent_count</em>
    </ul>
    ";
}
$user_agent_block .= "</ul>";

//IP address counts
$IP_sql = "SELECT DISTINCT IP_address, COUNT(IP_address) AS IP_count
FROM super_track GROUP BY IP_address ORDER BY IP_count DESC";
$IP_res = @mysql_query($IP_sql);

$IP_block = "<ul>";
while ($row_IP = @mysql_fetch_array($IP_res)) {
    $IP_address = $row_IP['IP_address'];
    $IP_count = $row_IP['IP_count'];
    $IP_block .= "<li>$IP_address
    <ul>
    <li><em>accesses per IP address: $IP_count</em>
    </ul>
    ";
}
$IP_block .= "</ul>";
?>
<HTML>
<HEAD>
<TITLE>My Access Report</TITLE>
</HEAD>
<BODY>
<h1>My Access Report</h1>

<P><strong>Total Accesses For All Pages:</strong>
<?php echo "$total_count"; ?></p>

<P><strong>Web Browsers Used:</strong>
<?php echo "$user_agent_block"; ?>

<P><strong>IP Addresses:</strong>
<?php echo "$IP_block"; ?>

</BODY>
</HTML>
```

When you view this new script through your Web browser, you will see something like Figure D.5.

D

FIGURE D.5

Report showing total access count, plus breakdown of user agents and IP addresses.

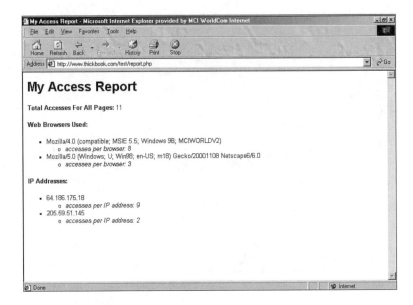

This is a much more interesting report! The final modification to make is to show specific page-access breakdowns. As you've probably guessed by now, this follows the same select-and-loop pattern as the retrieval of the user agent and IP information.

Add the following block of PHP to your script:

```
//page counts
$page_name_sql = "SELECT DISTINCT page_name, COUNT(page_name) AS page_count
FROM super_track GROUP BY page_name ORDER BY page_count DESC";
$page_name_res = @mysql_query($page_name_sql);

$page_name_block = "<ul>";
while ($row_pn = @mysql_fetch_array($page_name_res)) {
    $page_name = $row_pn['page_name'];
    $page_count = $row_pn['page_count'];

    $page_name_block .= "<li>$page_name
    <ul>
    <li><em>accesses per page: $page_count</em>
    </ul>
    ";
}
$page_name_block .= "</ul>";
```

In the HTML section, add the following:

```
<P><strong>Individual Pages:</strong>
<?php echo "$page_name_block"; ?>
```

Save the file, then view it through your Web browser. You will see something like Figure D.6.

FIGURE D.6

*The final report, show-
ing total access count,
plus a breakdown of
user agents, IP
addresses, and pages.*

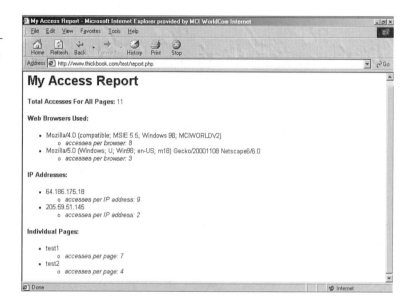

Creating a simple report such as this is a lot easier than wading through your Web server's access logs. However, I wouldn't recommend completely replacing your access logs with a database-driven system because of the system overhead involved. Instead, target your page tracking to something particularly important to you or your company.

Creating an Online Poll

Online polls, although easy to create, can be as simple or as complex as you want to make them. The complexity arises from determining how often a person can vote and when to display the poll form versus the poll results. These are both decisions you can figure out on your own, and you can adjust your script accordingly. In this section, you'll simply create the poll tables, the form for voting, and the script to display the results.

This example uses three tables for the poll information. The first table is a master table, which holds the text for the poll question as well as an ID that will be used in the other poll tables:

```
mysql> CREATE TABLE poll_master (id INT NOT NULL PRIMARY KEY AUTO_INCREMENT,
    -> poll_question VARCHAR (255));
Query OK, 0 rows affected (0.03 sec)
```

D

The second table holds the possible answers to the poll question. Included in this table is a poll_id field, which corresponds to an entry in the poll_master table:

```
mysql> CREATE TABLE poll_answers (id INT NOT NULL PRIMARY KEY AUTO_INCREMENT,
    -> poll_id INT, answer VARCHAR (50));
Query OK, 0 rows affected (0.00 sec)
```

The third and final table holds the votes. It includes a poll_id field, corresponding to an entry in the poll_master table, and an answer_id field, corresponding to an entry in the poll_answers table:

```
mysql> CREATE TABLE poll_votes (id INT NOT NULL PRIMARY KEY AUTO_INCREMENT,
    -> poll_id INT, answer_id INT, vote CHAR(1) DEFAULT 1);
Query OK, 0 rows affected (0.00 sec)
```

The sample poll question will be "Do you like MySQL?" Therefore, add this to the poll_master table:

```
mysql> INSERT INTO poll_master VALUES ('', 'Do you like MySQL?');
Query OK, 1 row affected (0.00 sec)
```

Next, add the possible answers to the poll_answers table. The possible answers are Yes, No, and Undecided:

```
mysql> INSERT INTO poll_answers VALUES ('', 1, 'Yes');
Query OK, 1 row affected (0.00 sec)
mysql> INSERT INTO poll_answers VALUES ('', 1, 'No');
Query OK, 1 row affected (0.00 sec)
mysql> INSERT INTO poll_answers VALUES ('', 1, 'Undecided');
Query OK, 1 row affected (0.00 sec)
```

The poll_votes table will be populated through a voting form, so open your favorite text editor and create a script called poll_vote.php. This script will handle both the submission form and the display of the results. The following script will create and display the voting form (the process includes retrieving the poll question and then retrieving the poll answers, all the while building a voting form):

```
<?php

$db = @mysql_connect("localhost", "youruser", "yourpass");
@mysql_select_db("yourDB", $db);

//get the poll question for display
$getQ = "select poll_question, id from poll_master";

$getQ_res = @mysql_query($getQ);

$poll_question = @mysql_result($getQ_res,0,'poll_question');
$poll_id = @mysql_result($getQ_res,0,'id');
```

```
//start creating the display block
$display_block = "
<P><strong>The question is:</strong><br>
$poll_question</p>";

if ($op != "vote") {
    //haven't voted, so show form

    //get the poll question and answers
    $getQ = "select poll_question, id from poll_master";

    $getQ_res = @mysql_query($getQ);

    $poll_question = @mysql_result($getQ_res,0,'poll_question');
    $poll_id = @mysql_result($getQ_res,0,'id');

    //start creating the display block
    $display_block = "
    <P><strong>The question is:</strong><br>
    $poll_question</p>
    <form method=post action=\"$PHP_SELF\">
    <input type=\"hidden\" name=\"poll_id\" value=\"$poll_id\">
    <input type=\"hidden\" name=\"op\" value=\"vote\">
    ";

    //retrieve the possible answers
    $getAnswers = "SELECT id, answer FROM poll_answers
    WHERE poll_id = $poll_id";

    $getAnswers_res = @mysql_query($getAnswers);

    while ($answers = @mysql_fetch_array($getAnswers_res)) {
        $answer = $answers['answer'];
        $answer_id = $answers['id'];

        $display_block .= "
        $answer <input type=radio name=\"answer_id\"
        value=\"$answer_id\"><br>";
    }

    $display_block .= "
    <P><input type=submit name=\"submit\" value=\"vote!\">
    </form>";
}
?>
<HTML>
<HEAD>
<TITLE>Poll Page</TITLE>
</HEAD>
<BODY>
<H1>Poll</H1>
```

D

```
<?php echo "$display_block"; ?>
</BODY>
</HTML>
```

When viewed in your Web browser, you will see a form like the one shown in Figure D.7.

The voting form.

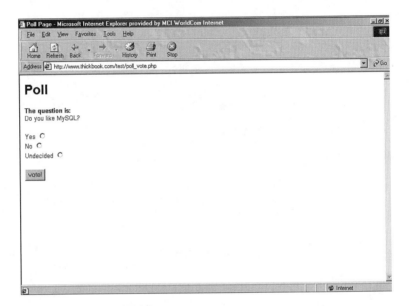

You must now finish the script by adding the "else" condition, which will add the vote and then display the up-to-date results. Here's the code for this condition:

```
//add vote
$addVote = "INSERT INTO poll_votes VALUES ('', $poll_id, $answer_id, 1)";

@mysql_query($addVote);

//get the total number of votes, for a percentage
$getTotal = "SELECT SUM(vote) AS total_answers FROM poll_votes
WHERE poll_id = $poll_id";

$getTotal_res = @mysql_query($getTotal);

$total_answers = @mysql_result($getTotal_res,0,'total_answers');

//get the answers, and total number of votes for each
$getAnswers = "select poll_answers.id, poll_answers.answer,
SUM(poll_votes.vote) AS sum_vote
FROM poll_answers, poll_votes
```

```
WHERE poll_answers.poll_id = $poll_id AND
poll_votes.answer_id = poll_answers.id
GROUP BY poll_answers.id";

$getAnswers_res = @mysql_query($getAnswers);

while ($answers = @mysql_fetch_array($getAnswers_res)) {
    $answer = $answers['answer'];
    $sum_vote = $answers['sum_vote'];

    //get the percentage of votes
    $pct = 100 * (round($sum_vote / $total_answers, 2))."%";

    //create the display of votes and results
    $display_block .= "
    $answer $sum_vote ($pct)<br>";
}
```

So, if you add this block of code to the original `poll_vote.php` script, you should come up with the following:

```
<?php

$db = @mysql_connect("localhost", "youruser", "yourpass");
@mysql_select_db("yourDB", $db);

//get the poll question for display
$getQ = "select poll_question, id from poll_master";

$getQ_res = @mysql_query($getQ);

$poll_question = @mysql_result($getQ_res,0,'poll_question');
$poll_id = @mysql_result($getQ_res,0,'id');

//start creating the display block
$display_block = "
<P><strong>The question is:</strong><br>
$poll_question</p>";

if ($op != "vote") {
    //haven't voted, so show form

    //get the poll question and answers
    $getQ = "select poll_question, id from poll_master";

    $getQ_res = @mysql_query($getQ);

    $poll_question = @mysql_result($getQ_res,0,'poll_question');
    $poll_id = @mysql_result($getQ_res,0,'id');

    //start creating the display block
    $display_block = "
```

D

```
<P><strong>The question is:</strong><br>
$poll_question</p>
<form method=post action=\"$PHP_SELF\">
<input type=\"hidden\" name=\"poll_id\" value=\"$poll_id\">
<input type=\"hidden\" name=\"op\" value=\"vote\">
";

//retrieve the possible answers
$getAnswers = "SELECT id, answer FROM poll_answers
WHERE poll_id = $poll_id";

$getAnswers_res = @mysql_query($getAnswers);

while ($answers = @mysql_fetch_array($getAnswers_res)) {
    $answer = $answers['answer'];
    $answer_id = $answers['id'];

    $display_block .= "
    $answer <input type=radio name=\"answer_id\"
    value=\"$answer_id\"><br>";
}

    $display_block .= "
    <P><input type=submit name=\"submit\" value=\"vote!\">
    </form>";

} else {

    //add vote
    $addVote = "INSERT INTO poll_votes VALUES ('', $poll_id, $answer_id, 1)";

    @mysql_query($addVote);

    //get the total number of votes, for a percentage
    $getTotal = "SELECT SUM(vote) AS total_answers FROM poll_votes
    WHERE poll_id = $poll_id";

    $getTotal_res = @mysql_query($getTotal);

    $total_answers = @mysql_result($getTotal_res,0,'total_answers');

    //get the answers, and total number of votes for each
    $getAnswers = "select poll_answers.id, poll_answers.answer,
    SUM(poll_votes.vote) AS sum_vote
    FROM poll_answers, poll_votes
    WHERE poll_answers.poll_id = $poll_id AND
    poll_votes.answer_id = poll_answers.id
    GROUP BY poll_answers.id";

    $getAnswers_res = @mysql_query($getAnswers);

    while ($answers = @mysql_fetch_array($getAnswers_res)) {
```

```
        $answer = $answers['answer'];
        $sum_vote = $answers['sum_vote'];

    //get the percentage of votes
    $pct = 100 * (round($sum_vote / $total_answers, 2))."%";

    //create the display of votes and results
    $display_block .= "
    $answer $sum_vote ($pct)<br>";
    }
}
?>
<HTML>
<HEAD>
<TITLE>Poll Page</TITLE>
</HEAD>
<BODY>
<H1>Poll</H1>
<?php echo "$display_block"; ?>
</BODY>
</HTML>
```

If you select the Yes radio button and click the Vote! button, the page will reload, count
the vote, and produce a display such as the one shown in Figure D.8.

FIGURE D.8

Successful vote.

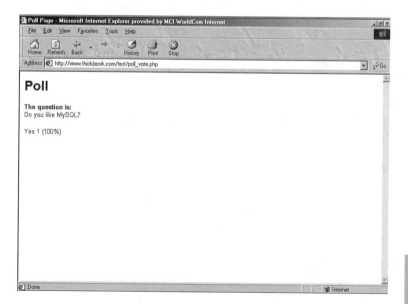

As you can see, the Yes answer now has one vote and 100 percent of the votes. However, this script did not originally take into account that some answers may not receive votes. It's still a good idea to show them, so you can modify the retrieval block so that it appears as follows:

```
//get the answers
$getPossAnswers = "select id, answer FROM poll_answers
WHERE poll_id = $poll_id ";

$getPossAnswers_res = @mysql_query($getPossAnswers);

while ($answers = @mysql_fetch_array($getPossAnswers_res)) {
    $answer = $answers['answer'];
    $answer_id = $answers['id'];

    //get votes for this answer
    $getAnswers = "select SUM(vote) AS sum_vote FROM poll_votes
WHERE poll_id = $poll_id AND answer_id = $answer_id";

    $getAnswers_res = @mysql_query($getAnswers);

    $sum_vote = @mysql_result($getAnswers_res,0,'sum_vote');

    if ($sum_vote == "") {
        $sum_vote = 0;
    }

    //get the percentage of votes
    $pct = 100 * (round($sum_vote / $total_answers, 2))."%";

    //create the display of votes and results
    $display_block .= "
    $answer $sum_vote ($pct)<br>";
}
```

Now, when you vote, you will see all the vote counts, even if the vote count is zero, as shown in Figure D.9.

With a little cleanup to the HTML, so that the form fields align nicely, and some validation to dissuade users from simply reloading the page in order to vote again, you can use this script as a perfectly fine polling mechanism.

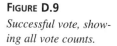

FIGURE D.9

Successful vote, showing all vote counts.

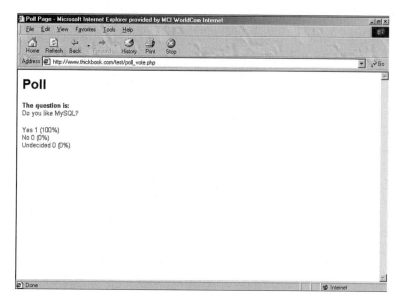

Storing Uploaded Files in Your Database

You may have the need to store binary files in your MySQL database, and in this instance the BLOB data type will be used. Usually, you are only storing alphanumeric text in your database and therefore never need to use a BLOB field. The name BLOB comes from the term *binary large object*, and it's the perfect choice for storing the data that makes up an image or other type of file.

Before creating your database table, remember that some databases have a limit on table sizes. MySQL has a 4GB limit on table size, which is a heck of a lot of 50KB image files, but it's only a few digitized movie trailers. In this example, we'll be using small image files. In the database table my_images, you will define an ID field, a field to hold the binary data, and three fields related to file name, size, and type:

```
mysql> CREATE TABLE my_images (id INT NOT NULL PRIMARY KEY AUTO_INCREMENT,
    -> binary_data BLOB, filename VARCHAR (50), filesize INT,
    -> filetype VARCHAR (50));
Query OK, 0 rows affected (0.00 sec)
```

D

With the table defined, you can now create the file upload form and accompanying script to handle the upload. The process of uploading a file via an HTML form should go something like this:

1. The user accesses the upload form and sees a text field and the Browse button in her browser.

2. The user browses her hard drive for the file she wants to upload, and when the selection is made, the file path and name appears in the text field.

3. User clicks the Submit button, and the file data is sent to the Web server.

4. The script checks whether a file was sent and then takes that file and does something with it. In this case, it inserts the data into the database.

5. The PHP script returns a message to the user indicating that the action was successful.

When a file is uploaded, several variables are created from the input field. If your image field is called img1, you now have access to the following items:

- $img1—The actual binary data.
- $img1_name—This is the file name of the file that was uploaded.
- $img1_size—The size of the uploaded file, in bytes.
- $img1_type—The MIME type of the uploaded file. This is set by the browser, so it might not be available, depending on the browser.

In the database table, you've defined fields for the binary data, the file name, the file size, and the file type. You only need one input field in your form, so the HTML is pretty simple:

```
<HTML>
<HEAD>
<TITLE>Send Binary Data to Your Database</TITLE>
</HEAD>
<BODY>
<H1>Upload a File:</H1>

<FORM enctype="multipart/form-data" method="post" action="insert_data.php">
<INPUT type="file" name="img1" size="30">
<br><br>
<INPUT type="submit" name="submit" value="Send this File">

</FORM>
</BODY>
</HTML>
```

Next, create the upload form. Call it `insert_data.php`, because that's what it says in the form action! The first thing to do is to connect to the database:

```php
<?php

$db = @mysql_connect("localhost", "youruser", "yourpass");
@mysql_select_db("yourDB", $db);
```

The next step opens the temporary file that's been uploaded, for reading only. Then, it reads all the data into a variable called `$binary_data`. After all that, the `addslashes()` function is used to escape any special characters:

```php
$binary_data = addslashes(fread(fopen($img1, "r"), filesize($img1)));
```

Next, you simply insert the record into the database:

```php
$insert_data = "INSERT INTO my_images VALUES
('', '$binary_data', '$img1_name', '$img1_size',  '$img1_type')";

@mysql_query($insert_data);
```

Then, close the PHP block and return a message to the user:

```php
?>
<HTML>
<HEAD>
<TITLE>Successful File Insertion!</TITLE>
<BODY>

<H1>Success!</H1>

<P>You have inserted the following into your database:<br>
<?php echo "$img1_name"; ?>, a <?php echo "$img1_size"; ?>  byte file with a
mime type of <?php echo "$img1_type"; ?>.</P>

</BODY>
</HTML>
```

Go back to your script and upload a file. When you click the form submission button, you will see something like what's shown in Figure D.10.

D

FIGURE D.10

Successful file upload.

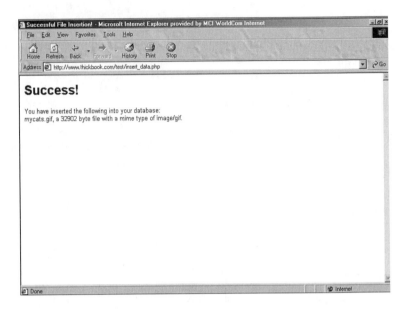

Retrieving Images Files from Your Database

The script for retrieving and viewing image files stored in your database is a remarkably simple one. When dealing with image files, you have two options for storing the data in your database: You can call a script that will display the data, or you can use the script as the source in an <IMG> tag. Same script, different execution method.

Now build the script that selects the data and the file type from the database, using a hard-coded ID number. First, start the PHP block and connect to the database:

```
<?php

$db = @mysql_connect("localhost", "youruser", "yourpass");
@mysql_select_db("yourDB", $db);
```

Create and execute the SQL statement and get the values from the result set:

```
$get_image = "select binary_data, filetype from my_images where id = 1";
$get_image_result = @mysql_query($get_image);

$binary_data= @mysql_result($get_image_result,0,"binary_data");
$filetype = @mysql_result($get_image_result,0,"filetype");
```

Because you'll be displaying something other than text or HTML to the user, you need to send a header that says just what type of content you're sending. This is where the value of $filetype comes into play:

```
header("Content-type: $filetype");
```

Then, simply return the binary data to the browser. Because you have specified the file type, your browser will display it properly. Close the PHP block when you are finished and then save the file as show_image.php:

```
echo "$binary_data";
?>
```

When you access the script, you should see the file you uploaded. Figure D.11 shows the file I uploaded.

FIGURE D.11

Display of uploaded file.

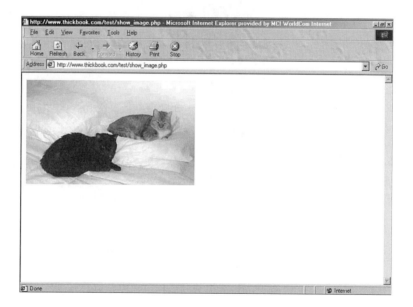

The other way to display this image is to use the script as the value of the SRC attribute in the <IMG> tag, like so:

```
<HTML>
<HEAD>
<TITLE>My Image</TITLE>
</HEAD>
<BODY>
<H1>Look at this:</H1>
<IMG SRC="show_image.php">
</BODY>
</HTML>
```

D

Call this file `show_image.html` and view it with your Web browser. You should still see the original graphic previously uploaded, with the added text string "Look at this:" because it's now surrounded by normal HTML (see Figure D.12).

FIGURE D.12

Display of uploaded file, surrounded by HTML.

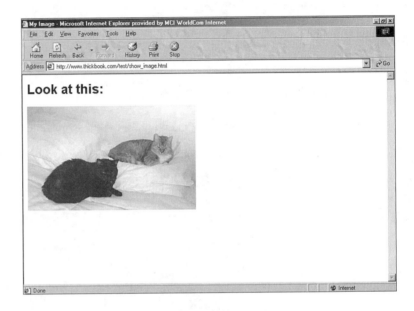

INDEX

SAMS
Teach Yourself
in 24 Hours

When you only have time for the answers™

Sams Teach Yourself in 24 Hours *gets you the results you want—fast! Work through 24 proven 1-hour lessons and learn everything you need to know to get up to speed quickly. It has the answers you need at the price you can afford.*

Sams Teach Yourself PHP in 24 Hours

Matt Zandstra
ISBN: 0-672-32311-7
$24.99 US/$37.95 CAN

Other Sams Teach Yourself in 24 Hours Titles

TCL/TK
Venkat Sastry
ISBN: 0-672-31749-4
$24.99 US/$37.95 CAN

Java 2
Rogers Cadenhead
ISBN: 0-672-32036-3
$24.99 US/$37.95 CAN

C++
Jesse Liberty
ISBN: 0-672-31516-5
$19.99 US/$29.95 CAN

Linux
Craig & Coletta Witherspoon
ISBN: 0-672-31993-4
$24.99 US/$37.95 CAN

HTML & XHTML
Dick Oliver
ISBN: 0-672-32076-2
$24.99 US/$37.95 CAN

CGI
Rafe Colburn
ISBN: 0-672-31880-6
$24.99 US/$37.95 CAN

JavaScript
Michael Moncur
ISBN: 0-672-32025-8
$24.99 US/$37.95 CAN

Perl
Clinton Pierce
ISBN: 0-672-32276-5
$29.99 US/$44.95 CAN

All prices are subject to change.

SAMS

www.samspublishing.com